VIDEO GAME HISTORY

GAME ON!

FROM PONG AND PAC-MAN TO MARIO, MINECRAFT, AND MORE

DUSTIN HANSEN

FEIWEL AND FRIENDS

SQUARE FISH

NEW YORK

SQUARE
FISH

An imprint of Macmillan Publishing Group, LLC
175 Fifth Avenue, New York, NY 10010
fiercereads.com

Our books may be purchased in bulk for promotional, educational, or business
use. Please contact your local bookseller or the Macmillan Corporate
and Premium Sales Department at (800) 221-7945 ext. 5442 or by email
at MacmillanSpecialMarkets@macmillan.com.

Game screenshots captured by Dillon West

Image of Pong Cabinet p. 3 © Rob Boudon; Image of Atari E.T. Dig p. 47 ©
taylorhatmaker; Image of Zelda Cartridge p. 61 © David B. Fant; Image of melted
Gameboy display p. 83 © Lordcolus; Image of LAN Party p. 129 © Toffelginkgo;
Image of Dance Dance Revolution Extreme machine p. 181 © True Tech Talk Time;
Image of Guitar Hero Controller p. 242 © Masem; Image of iPhone p. 280 ©
Daniel Zanetti

Images of Magnavox Odyssey p. 5, Commodore 64 p. 28, Atari 2600 p. 40,
Nintendo Entertainment System p. 54, Nintendo Famicom p. 58, Nintendo Game
Boy p. 78, SEGA Genesis p. 91, Super NES p. 112, Sony PlayStation p. 138,
Dual Shock Controller p. 149, Nintendo 64 p. 153, SEGA Saturn p. 155, Microsoft
Xbox p. 231, Nintendo Wii p. 247, Sony PlayStation 3 p. 267 © Evan Amos

This book is an independent history of video games, and is not endorsed,
sponsored, or authorized by any video game companies.

Library of Congress Cataloging-in-Publication Data

Names: Hansen, Dustin, author.
Title: Game on! : video game history from Pong and Pac-man to Mario,
  Minecraft, and more / Dustin Hansen.
Description: New York : Feiwel & Friends, 2016. | Audience: Age 9 to 18.
Identifiers: LCCN 2016027564 (print) | LCCN 2016050547 (ebook) |
  ISBN 978-1-250-29445-6 (paperback) | ISBN 978-1-250-08096-7 (ebook)
Subjects: LCSH: Video games—History—Juvenile literature. | BISAC: JUVENILE
  NONFICTION / Games & Activities / Video & Electronic Games. | JUVENILE
  NONFICTION / Computers / Entertainment & Games.
Classification: LCC GV1469.3 .H357 2016 (print) | LCC GV1469.3 (ebook) |
  DDC 794.8—dc23
LC record available at https://lccn.loc.gov/2016027564

Originally published in the United States by Feiwel and Friends
First Square Fish edition, 2019
Book designed by Raphael Geroni
Square Fish logo designed by Filomena Tuosto

1 3 5 7 9 10 8 6 4 2

To the most talented men and women I've ever worked with, the (2004) NFL Street Development Team. I could still whoop you all today. Well, except Barney. That guy is a legend. And maybe Snagy. And Burnside. Okay, and probably Vandy. But the rest of you would be mine.

CONTENTS

A LIVING HISTORY: TO THOSE THAT CAME BEFORE vi

PONG 1972: GAME, SET, MATCH x

INSERT: *Hot Tubs, Pool Tables, and Soda Machines* 6

SPACE INVADERS 1978: A FIRST INVASION 8

INSERT: *The Amazing Input/Output Machine* 14

PAC-MAN 1980: THANK YOU, PIZZA 16

INSERT: *Just One Byte* 22

ZORK 1980: YOU ARE LIKELY TO BE EATEN BY A GRUE 26

DONKEY KONG 1981: IT'S ON LIKE DONKEY KONG! 34

INSERT: *Can I Take It Home?* 39

E.T. THE EXTRA-TERRESTRIAL 1982: DON'T PHONE HOME 42

SUPER MARIO BROS. 1985: THE PLAN, THE PEOPLE, AND THE PLUMBER 50

THE LEGEND OF ZELDA 1986: IT'S DANGEROUS TO GO ALONE! TAKE THIS. 56

INSERT: *Lefties Unite!* 64

JOHN MADDEN FOOTBALL 1988: IT'S IN THE GAME 66

INSERT: *The Madden Curse* 74

TETRIS 1989: LINE 'EM ALL UP 76

INSERT: *Games for Brains* 84

SONIC THE HEDGEHOG 1991: SO FAST, YOU'LL NEED A BARF BAG 86

INSERT: *Every Hero Needs a Villain* 93

STREET FIGHTER II 1991: HADOUKEN! 96

MORTAL KOMBAT 1992: FATALITY!: VIOLENCE AND THE ESRB 102

INSERT: *ESRB Breakdown* 108

SUPER MARIO KART 1992: AN ALL-STAR CAST 110

INSERT: *What Is an IP?* 116

MYST 1993: GET LOST IN A BOOK. LITERALLY. 118

DOOM 1993: A PLANET FULL OF GUNS 124

INSERT: *Art Meets Math* 131

TOMB RAIDER 1996: A NEW FACE, A NEW SYSTEM, A NEW ERA 134

INSERT: *All I Need Is a Hero* 142

GRAN TURISMO 1997: GENTLEMEN, START YOUR ENGINES 146

INSERT: *The Battle Royale!* 152

FINAL FANTASY VII 1997: NOT AS FINAL AS YOU THOUGHT 156

INSERT: *I Can't Remember Why I Came Here* 162

HALF-LIFE 1998: WELCOME TO BLACK MESA 166

INSERT: *Gabe Newell: Let Off Some Steam* 174

DANCE DANCE REVOLUTION 1999: STEP IN A NEW DIRECTION 178

INSERT: *Let's Get Physical* 184

POKÉMON YELLOW 1999: GOTTA CATCH 'EM ALL 188

THE SIMS 2000: PLENTY OF ROOM TO EXPAND 196

INSERT: *The Killer App* 204

GRAND THEFT AUTO III 2001: HIJACKED! 206

INSERT: *We're All a Bunch of Cheaters* 212

WORLD OF WARCRAFT 2004: WOWZERS! 218

INSERT: *Create-a-Player* 225

HALO 2 2004: ONE DOWN, FIFTY BILLION TO GO 228

INSERT: *Prepare to Be Sorted* 235

GUITAR HERO 2005: BRING ON THE PLASTIC! 238

WII SPORTS 2006: TIGHTEN YOUR SHOELACES AND YOUR WRIST STRAP 244

PORTAL 2007: THE CAKE IS A LIE 252

INSERT: *Come On, Just One More Try* 259

LITTLE BIG PLANET 2008: I'LL PLAY YOURS, YOU PLAY MINE 262

FARMVILLE 2009: E-I-E-I-OOOO 270

INSERT: *Making It Mobile* 276

ANGRY BIRDS 2009: WHO YOU CALLIN' ANGRY? 278

INSERT: *All Kinds and Sizes* 285

MINECRAFT 2009: KICK IT UP ANOTHER NOTCH! 288

INSERT: *Major Achievement Unlocked* 296

UNCHARTED 2 2009: ARMOR? I DON'T NEED NO STINKIN' ARMOR! 298

LEAGUE OF LEGENDS 2009: TEN MILLION AND COUNTING 306

INSERT: *Can You See Me Now?* 315

SKYLANDERS 2011: GREETINGS, PORTAL MASTER! 318

THE WALKING DEAD 2011: TELL ME A STORY? 326

INSERT: *Blowing Against the Wind* 333

OVERWATCH 2016: ON THE SHOULDERS OF HEROES 336

THE FUTURE: TOMORROW AND BEYOND 346

One of the most interesting things about writing a book about the history of video games is that when it comes to history in general, video games are super young.

I mean, how many other history books can you think of where the original people involved with the topic are still alive? Not to mention, most of them are still innovating and doing new things in the game industry today.

It's cool, when you think about it. Everything is really new. Even Pong is still new enough that if you looked around, you could find a copy, in some format, and check it out today. The game industry is alive and growing, and that is very exciting.

I remember my grandpa John telling me that he loved his career because he was always learning. He was a veterinarian, and new advancements in medicine happened all the time. He had to study to keep up on things. When I was lucky enough to enter the game industry, I discovered the same joy my grandfather had known. Minus the puppies but with way more Left 4 Dead office LAN party breaks, of course.

NFL Legends Football 98 © Accolade

I started making games in 1997, painting digital football players for a game by Accolade Software called Legends Football 98. I had to paint each frame of the animation by hand, because 3D graphics weren't advanced enough at that point to be of any help. It was pretty cutting-edge stuff at the time, but a short six years later I was making complex 3D digital sculptures of those same football players for Electric Arts' NFL Street. Three years later I was messing around with controllerless systems like the Xbox Kinect, and creating 3D graphics for games on the Nintendo 3DS that actually displayed things in 3D without needing fancy glasses.

NFL Street © Electronic Arts, Inc.

And now I'm working with a group of crazy smart innovators at a company called The Void, where we are marrying VR (virtual reality) with real-world locations. The best way I can describe it is that we are building a digital theme park where you not only play a game, you get to be *in* the game. It's mind-blowingly cool if I do say so myself, and something I never dreamed about when I was touching up 2D sprites of Jerry Rice on my 386 PC in 1997.

The video game industry goes through big changes every year, but even the most advanced, high-tech, innovative ideas stand on the shoulders of games that have come before.

There'd be no Madden NFL if Pong hadn't put the first sports game on a gaming console.

Would we have Grand Theft Auto V without The Legend of Zelda showing us what an open world looked like back in 1986 on the Nintendo Entertainment System?

And Forza Motorsport 6 owes a lot to the racing games of the past. In fact, they paid homage in their promotional commercial in 2015, where they showed their realistic-looking Ford GT zipping through pixelated versions of older games like Gran Trak 10, R.C. Pro-Am, Pole Position, and Ridge Racer, just to name a few. A tagline on the Forza Motorsport website claimed, "Every pixel and line of code ever written has been leading up to this moment."

Xbox's Forza Motorsport 6 TV commercial © Microsoft Corporation

I couldn't have said it better myself.

The games we play today, as well as the games we will fall in love with tomorrow, promise us hours of enjoyment. Days, weeks, years of fun lie just around the corner, but it is important to take a look back from time to time, to get a better understanding of those that came before.

So, gamer, put on the old time-traveling helmet. Crank the dial back on the Wayback Machine to a time before the Internet. To a time before cell phones and color TVs. Way back to a time before controllers, handheld gaming devices, social media, and even microwave pizza.

Let's go back to the beginning. After all, these are not just the games that influenced the game designers of today and tomorrow. These are the games that shaped us all.

PONG

1972

GAME, SET, MATCH

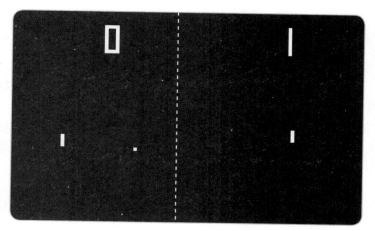

Pong © Atari Interactive, Inc.

It wasn't the first game. Not by a long shot.

In fact, Pong wasn't even the first digital *tennis* game. Some say it wasn't even the most complicated or most advanced, or even the most innovative game of its day.

So why do so many people consider Pong the godfather of video games?

It might be because Pong is just a fun word to say. Go ahead. Say it out loud. You know you want to. I'll wait. Heck, I'll even join you.

Pong. POOOOONG! Pingity-Pong Pongity-Pong.

See, it's fun! And in the end, the game was just as simple as rattling off a bunch of pong nonsense, and *that* is what made Pong so great. It was easy. The games before Pong were interesting, and innovative, and difficult, and usually could only be played by other computer and software engineers. But Pong didn't need instructions, only cost a quarter to play, and instead of sitting inside a computer lab, the first Pong machine stood in a busy tavern. But I'm getting ahead of myself.

For now, let's rewind a bit and see how Pong came to life.

In the early days of computer games, there was a ton of confusion about who created what first. Part of the problem was that creating games at that time required hardware that cost mountains of cash, and part of it was

Before Atari decided on the name Pong, the game was code-named Darlene, after one of the early Atari employees. While Darlene is a perfectly fine name, it isn't nearly as fun to say as . . . go ahead. I know you can't stop now. POOOONG!

Pong has been featured in many popular TV shows like *That '70s Show, King of the Hill,* and *Saturday Night Live.*

that people didn't really understand what games were back then.

Although there were a lot of inventions that could make a pretty good claim to being the first video game, there's no doubt who made the first successful game. It was video game pioneer Nolan Bushnell.

While attending the University of Utah in 1962, Bushnell spent most of his time studying in the computer engineering lab. While he was there, he got the chance to play a game called Spacewar! and he was hooked. The game was played on a living room–sized computer called a PDP-10, and it was complex, challenging, and most of all, addicting.

Up until that point, the closest thing people had ever seen to a video game was probably pinball. If you haven't seen a pinball machine, you really should try to find one. Basically, you shoot a one-inch metal ball up through a slot and it bounces around, knocking over "pins" and bouncing off lights and rubber-coated bumpers. Sounds like fun, right? Well, it was, and still is, a popular form of gaming, but what Bushnell saw on the PDP-10 changed everything.

Attending college was expensive back then—still is, actually—and to pay for school Nolan worked in the arcade of a local amusement park called Lagoon.

The arcades in the 1960s didn't look at all like the arcades of today. They were filled with pinball machines, photo booths, and mechanical fortune-tellers. While Nolan Bushnell loved the arcade's shiny lights and loud sounds, he could see an even brighter future just out of reach. Bushnell had a vision of people dropping quarter after quarter into digital machines to play games like Spacewar! But the technology needed to make that happen didn't quite match Bushnell's vision. It took nearly a decade to put his dream into motion, but in 1972, the planets aligned and Bushnell started Atari.

Nolan Bushnell was a pretty good engineer himself, but he was also smart enough to hire Al Alcorn, who Nolan recognized at once to be a better engineer than he ever dreamed of becoming. Under Bushnell's direction and with

The problem with Spacewar! was that it was so difficult you needed to be an actual astronaut to pilot the game's digital ship.

In 1960 it cost twenty-five cents to play a game of pinball. Sounds about right, doesn't it? I mean, it still costs a quarter to play most arcade games today. Well, do you know what else cost twenty-five cents in 1960? A GALLON of gas. If arcade prices jumped up as fast as gas prices, it would cost around three dollars to play a single game!

Alcorn's impressive engineering abilities, Atari was ready to test their invention in a few short months.

On November 29, 1972, the modern video game industry was born when Bushnell installed his Pong arcade machine in a local bar, crossed his fingers, and hoped that the game would be a hit. Word traveled fast in Sunnyvale, California, and people flocked to Andy Capp's Tavern for a chance to give Bushnell's electronic tennis game a try.

Al Alcorn had no experience in computer games, so Nolan Bushnell assigned him the job of creating Pong as a warm-up exercise. Talk about making a good first impression on your boss!

Pong arcade cabinet © Rob Boudon

Between the time Bushnell played Spacewar! in 1960 and the launch of Atari in 1972, the world had changed a lot. Russians sent the first human to space in 1961, the computer mouse was invented in 1964, the first portable calculator was invented in 1967, and the first man walked on the moon in 1969. Oh, and the US used the Internet for the first time in 1969.

Why?
Well, because:

1. It was cheap. Only twenty-five cents.

2. You played it against your friends, and what's more fun than humiliating your friends in a game of digital Ping-Pong?

3. *Pong* was just plain fun to say. PONG! PONG! PONGITY-PONGITY-PING-PONG! PONNNNG!

4. Pong was EASY. All you had to do was hit the ball back to your opponent, and the game took care of the rest. Even the score! Told you we'd get back to Pong being EASY.

Back and forth, back and forth, until someone earns eleven points. Drop in another quarter and play again. And again.

AND AGAIN!

The *play again* pattern happened so many times that first night at Andy Capp's Tavern, that by the next day Al Alcorn received a call telling him Pong was busted. Frustrated and a little worried, Alcorn rushed over with a bag of tools. Turns out it didn't take an engineer to see what was wrong.

Inside the homebuilt cabinet, Alcorn had rigged a milk carton to catch quarters. There were so many quarters jammed inside that Pong had stopped working. Alcorn emptied the quarters into his tool bag, turned Pong back on, and walked out with a huge grin on his face.

Everybody loved Pong, and soon people were lining up at Andy Capp's Tavern before it even opened, waiting outside to ambush Pong and give it another go.

Bushnell had struck gold, and he did everything he could to grow Atari as fast as possible. He leased out a huge abandoned roller-skating rink and started production of Pong arcade cabinets right away. There were obstacles in the way, the first being that he had to hire

Pong was shown in the 2008 Disney film *WALL-E*. The two main characters, WALL-E and EVE, are shown in front of the game, and later on, WALL-E plays the game by himself in one of his many attempts to awaken EVE from her sleep mode.

people who had no knowledge of how to build an arcade game, but the setbacks did little to slow Bushnell's vision. His dream of a video arcade was on the horizon, and he was determined to make it a reality.

Magnavox Odyssey © Evan Amos

Pong wasn't the first digital tennis game, a fact that would later cost Bushnell and Atari a lot of money as they settled a court case with Magnavox for patent infringement (basically, copycatting). In April of 1972, Bushnell got a sneak peek at a new video game system called the Magnavox Odyssey, an invention by computer science engineer Ralph Baer. The Odyssey was battery-operated, hooked directly to your TV, and featured a digital tennis game very similar to Pong. The system launched in August of that year, three short months before Pong found its way to Andy Capp's Tavern.

A free-to-play version of Pong was conceptualized by Nolan Bushnell to entertain children in a doctor's office, initially titled Snoopy Pong after the popular *Peanuts* character Snoopy. Bushnell also designed an arcade cabinet similar to Snoopy's doghouse, but opted to rename the game *Puppy Pong* to avoid legal action. Probably a good idea considering his case with Magnavox.

HOT TUBS, POOL TABLES, AND SODA MACHINES

• • • • • • • • • • • • • • • •

Another thing that Atari pioneered was the idea that in order to make creative games, you needed a creative space to work in. Back in the early days of Atari, the company was housed inside an old warehouse. There were very few walls, "Bohemian Rhapsody" was blasting from boom boxes spread around the office, and the place was rife with hippie culture, man.

Atari employees were encouraged to celebrate victories by partying at the office. The hours were long, but why go home when there is a hot tub in the office, drinks of all kinds in the fridge, music jamming in the air, and everywhere you looked there was a nerd just like you, giving up their personal time to make great games? I can't help but imagine them as the modern-day Robin Hood's Merry Men, but with fewer green tights and more flip-flops and cutoff Levi's shorts.

It was a creative place and a creative time, and it worked. It led to what would come to be known as the golden age of video games. And in the video game biz, when someone finds that something works, others follow.

Creative and crazy offices are still part of the appeal of working in the game industry. EA in Redwood Shores, California, boasts its own Starbucks, multiple arcades, a theater, a soccer field, a sand volleyball court, a full gym complete with a full-sized hardwood basketball court, a day care for parents who work and want to be close to their young children, an amazing restaurant that serves everything from sushi to hamburgers, and that's just the beginning.

Video game companies around the world love to let their creativity inspire their offices, and their offices inspire their creativity. It's actually really helpful, and if you don't believe me, you can try it out yourself. Try hanging a couple of cool posters in your room, put a handful of amiibos posing on a shelf, stack a few books from your favorite author on your bookshelf (hint, hint).

If you do, I'll bet you'll start to imagine new and cool creative ideas. But do me a favor. When you get a good idea, write it down! Because I'm telling you from experience, if you don't write them down, they will float right out your door and move on to the next guy or gal.

Ideas are funny like that.

SPACE INVADERS

1978

A FIRST INVASION

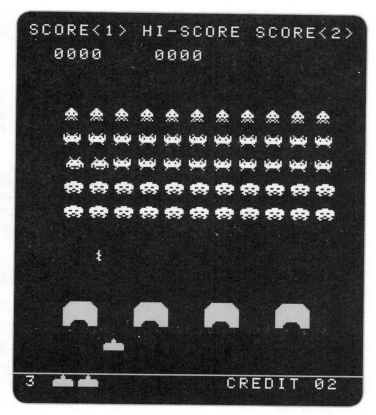

Space Invaders © Taito Corporation (Japan), Midway Games, Inc. (North America)

At first it was all about beating your friends in digital tennis. Head-to-head battles that usually involved lots of shouting and bragging. And probably a bit of crying, too.

But it wasn't long before the single-player craze hit the arcades.

It started with thirty-six invaders, three defensive bunkers, and a laser-firing tank with enough gusto to defend planet Earth.

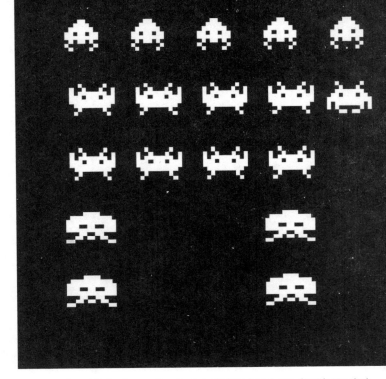

Space Invaders © Taito Corporation (Japan), Midway Games, Inc. (North America)

The game was built to impress. The refrigerator-sized arcade machine was covered top to bottom in artwork to set the mood, and it featured two white buttons, one to move left AND one to move right! Next to the twin direction buttons, you'd find a superslick firing button the color of danger itself, red. But what you couldn't see was the massive speaker hidden inside the beast, which pumped out a sound track some say inspired *Jaws* when it hit the big screen five years later.

For only one quarter you got three lives, and with a little practice—okay, with a LOT of practice—you could last for hours.

It was the summer of 1978, the game was called Space Invaders, and it invaded the allowance of every kid tall

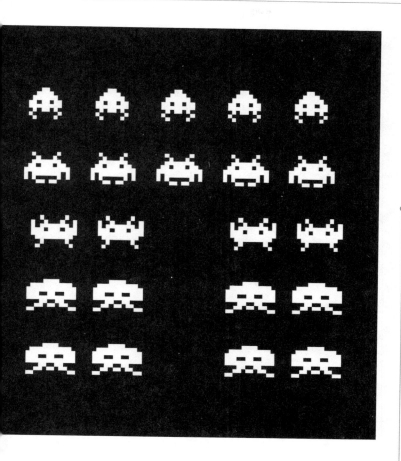

Midway Games started in 1958 as a manufacturer of amusement park games, and in 1973 they became the first big player in the American arcade game scene. In the 1970s they formed a tight alliance with Japanese arcade giant Taito. The two companies worked well together, importing each other's games and sharing ideas for many years to come.

enough to see the screen. Not to mention their older brothers and sisters and half their fathers.

Space Invaders went on to set record after record after it invaded the planet. More than four hundred thousand arcade cabinets were made, and the game pulled in more than 3.8 billion dollars by 1982. If you factor in inflation, that would be THIRTEEN BILLION DOLLARS today, making it one of the highest-grossing video games of all time.

Yeah. Billion. With a *B*!

That was just the beginning. The 3.8 billion dollars doesn't include the twelve spin-offs that rolled out over the next thirteen years. This house-sized wad of cash also doesn't include the merchandising: everything from candy to T-shirts, which are just as cool now as they were back

Nishikado admitted that while he loves video games, he is actually quite horrible at playing them. He kept the secret for more than thirty years, but in a recent interview he admitted that he struggles to complete even the first level of his Space Invaders game.

On October 7, 2011, New Jersey native Richie Knucklez blasted his way into the record books by doubling the previous high score recorded in *The Guinness Book of World Records*. Knucklez kept firing away until his score read an unbelievable 110,510 points.

in the 1980s. And today there are almost as many Space Invaders clones on the Internet as there are dancing cats in sombreros.

Looking back, one of the most amazing things about Space Invaders is that it was created by one man, Tomohiro Nishikado. Not only did Nishikado create the art and game design for Space Invaders, he spent a year developing the necessary hardware for the game to run, putting together a computer from scratch.

Nishikado was a one-man wrecking crew. He was as comfortable sketching spaceships and aliens on graph paper as he was soldering circuits on a breadboard.

But wait, there's more! Nishikado's desire to innovate led him to a long list of firsts. Firsts that are part of every gamer's vocabulary today.

1. Space Invaders made the concept of "high score" popular. Can you imagine a game without a high score nowadays?

2. Space Invaders was the first game to actually save the player's score. Before this, you'd have to convince your friends about the amazing game you had while they were outside playing baseball. Now you could just drag them back to the arcade and show them you were the Space Invaders king right there on the screen. That is, unless some bully like Charley Schultzwazer unplugged the machine just after you typed in your initials. Yeah, I'm still bitter about that one, Schultzy.

3. Nishikado introduced the never-ending horde. There was no way to actually win Space Invaders—the game just got faster and more difficult the longer you played.

4. Before Nishikado's masterpiece, players never had to dodge a bullet. Nishikado changed all

of this by allowing the player to avoid lasers and hide behind barriers. In other words, Space Invaders was the first shooter game—Halo's great-great-great-grandfather.

And last but not least . . .

5. Perhaps the most overlooked and underrated invention that Nishikado shared with us was his concept of a continuous background sound track. If you've played the game (and if you haven't, you really owe it to yourself to check it out), you'll recall the four descending bass notes repeating in a loop. This on its own would have been a step up from the rest of the pack, but Nishikado wasn't happy with "good enough." He wanted awesome, and he got it by changing the speed of the music as the game got harder. It was awesome! It made your heart pound and hands sweat as you gripped the joystick tighter with every move. Add in a layer of sound effects, a technique that had also never been used before, and any kid with a quarter in his pocket would come running like a rat to the Pied Piper.

If I were picking teams for anything from antigravity combat karaoke to underwater car repair, I'd pick Tomohiro Nishikado first. Seriously, this guy does it all.

Simply put, Space Invaders was, and perhaps always will be, the champ.

THE AMAZING INPUT/OUTPUT MACHINE

So, here's a question for you, gamer. Why do we call these wacky things that eat up all our spare time *VIDEO games*?

Sure, we call them things like *computer games*, or *electronic games*, but let's face it—we all still think of them as *VIDEO games*.

And it doesn't really make a lot of sense when you think about it. It's not like you're watching a video. You watch videos on YouTube or TV. And back in the day, when video games were just starting out, people watched videos on a VCR, which stands for *VIDEO cassette recorder*. Even that makes more sense.

But video games are totally different. You don't just sit there and watch a video game—you PLAY a video game. And they have computers inside them, and controllers plugged into them, and all that other good stuff.

Well, the explanation is actually quite simple, and it has to do with what a gaming console does.

A console, like the Atari 2600 or the PS4, is really just a fancy translator.

The games are written in specific language that is stored onto a cartridge, or disk, or a hard drive. If you try to jam an Atari 2600 cartridge into your TV, it won't do anything except scratch your new TV screen.

And the consoles also have controllers like joysticks, or motion controllers like on the Wii U, or maybe even a bright red plastic guitar. These controllers speak their own language, too.

Luckily for us, consoles not only speak the language of the video game cartridge and the controller (inputs), but they also speak fluent TV or *VIDEO* (output) language.

It takes information, or data that is stored on a cartridge or a disk, or, heck, even streamed over the Internet, and it translates that data to a *VIDEO* signal that you could play games on. Ya know—VIDEO games.

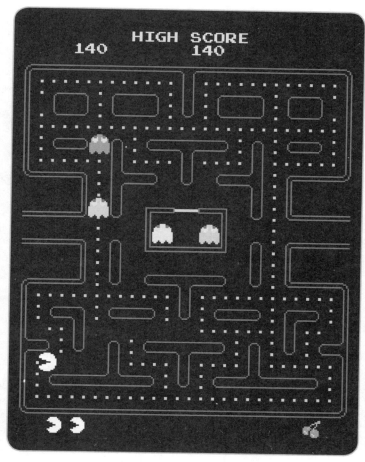

Pac-Man © Bandai Namco Games, Inc.

Blinky, Pinky, Inky, and ... Orangey? Stinky? No. Of course not. It needs to be something random, like Clyde.

Why random, you ask? Well, we'll get to that in a minute. I promise. You can count on me, because I am as predictable as Blinky.

Of course, this chomping ball of fun needs no introduction, but just to be safe, meet Pac-Man.

After the Pizza Hut app was launched on the Xbox 360, gamers gobbled up over one million dollars of pizza in the first four months!

1980 was quite a year for feathered hair and light blue polyester suits, but that wasn't all it was known for. Ronald Reagan was on his way to the White House. The fax machine was invented in Japan, and *Star Wars Episode V: The Empire Strikes Back* was the number one movie in the world. And, Luke, he's still your father.

The story of this hungry video game character begins in 1979, when an exhausted twenty-seven-year-old Namco employee, Toru Iwatani, was daydreaming while staring at one of the most important things in a video gamer's life. Pizza. No joke.

The legendary pie was missing two slices, which resembled a mouth, and Iwatani imagined the jaws opening and closing as it gobbled up everything in sight. What resulted from Iwatani's vision was Pakkuman, the first spark of what would become the Pac-Man we all know and love.

Actually, this might be a good time to point out something really important. We often think that new ideas, like video games or characters, come out of thin air. We might even think the video game idea fairies whisper into some lucky game designer's ear while she's sleeping, then—BLAMMO—out pops a shiny new stroke of genius. But in reality, more times than not, great ideas are inspired by the things that surround us. Like Iwatani's pizza, or his other reference, Popeye, whom he has quoted as an early inspiration for Pac-Man's habit of eating food to gain power. It's a cool thought that new ideas come from paying attention to what is around us, but it does make you wonder if Miyamoto, the famous Nintendo designer, hangs out with girlfriend-stealing, spiked-shelled turtles and mustached plumbers.

Anyway, back to 1980, a year after Iwatani and his famous pizza. Up until this point, video games were really geared toward boys. Especially in Japan, where arcades were overflowing with young men lining up with quarters to play Space Invaders and Asteroids. Iwatani knew that arcades would be more popular if he could attract girls as well as boys. So, he created the first video game mascot, added a maze component, and pumped it full of all the colors found in a bag of gummy bears. The name of the game was changed from Pakkuman to Puck-Man, and do you know what? It worked!

In October 1980, the game made its way to America, where a few more changes were made. The difficulty and speed were ramped up and all-new art was added to the cabinet. Smartly, the name was changed again to Pac-Man, in fear that the previous name might be "altered" into some pretty foul language.

Another big difference after the shift from Japan to America was Pac-Man's reception. In Japan, the game started off slow, but in America it was an overnight success. So successful, in fact, that it surpassed Space Invaders, the current king of the arcade hill, by earning over a billion dollars in quarters in its first year alone. By the early 1990s, the always-hungry Pac-Man had brought in over 2.5 billion dollars just in quarters. That is 125,000 pounds of quarters!

Possibly the biggest addition Pac-Man brought to the party was character and story. Before Pac-Man hit the arcades, games were mostly concerned with skill and action. Blasting incoming asteroids, playing a quick game of digital table tennis, or breaking through a brick wall were all experiences that proved to be addictive and fun, but gamers fell in love with Pac-Man in a whole new way.

For the first time, gamers were shown story by way of cut scenes between game levels. These cut scenes played like small movies, and involved memorable music, humor, and, of course, our hero, Pac-Man, always looking good in the end. Pac-Man was quickly becoming a pop icon, and he found his way to lunch boxes, shirts, and posters, and eventually made his way to TV, when *Pac-Man* became a hit in 1982.

Screenshot from "A Bad Case of the Chomps," Episode 1.12 of the *Pac-Man* TV show (*originally aired Dec. 11, 1982*)

While gamers were trying to play Pac-Man as long as they could on a single quarter, another toy craze was happening, only this time it was all about SPEED. The Rubik's Cube became popular in 1980, and immediately competitions started up to see who could solve it the fastest. I could solve it in about two minutes, but only if I was allowed to pull off the stickers and put them back in the right order. That's how you do it, right?

The Guinness Book of World Records named Pac-Man the most recognizable video game character of all time. Ninety-four percent of people asked recognized the little yellow guy. This means that if you have 100 Facebook friends, six of them still don't recognize Pac-Man. It's probably your grandparents.

Although Buckner & Garcia's "Pac-Man Fever" was a breakout hit, it wasn't the only song inspired by Pac-Man. "Weird Al" Yankovic, Lil' Flip, Bloodhound Gang, and many more have paid tribute to the dot-eating critter.

Shortly before Hanna-Barbera released the TV show, a rock duo by the name of Buckner & Garcia recorded "Pac-Man Fever." It soared to the top of the charts to become a top-ten single in 1981. The album containing the song became a gold record in 1982, by selling over one million copies, and to date it has sold over 2.8 million copies.

Before long, Pac-Man was a social juggernaut. Everyone knew the song, everyone watched the show, and of course, everyone played the game. We all had a bad case of Pac-Man fever, and the only cure was more quarters.

Like his predecessor, Tomohiro Nishikado of Space Invaders fame, Iwatani had his list of firsts, too.

1. **Pac-Man became the first video game mascot.**

2. **Iwatani and his team created the very first power-up. You know, those big pills that make all the ghosts turn royal blue and run away from Pac-Man. This little gem of an idea has found its way into just about every game launched since.**

3. **Pac-Man was the first game aimed at a female audience.**

4. **Nobody can forget that Pac-Man introduced us to cut scenes, fully animated cartoon-style movie shorts to entertain players between levels—not to mention give them a few seconds to crack their knuckles and massage their tired wrists.**

Add this up, add that it was also the first maze game to boot, and there is no doubt that Iwatani created a legend. Oh yeah. I almost forgot. The random naming of Clyde.

5. **Coming in at 5: Iwatani designed the first character AI, or "artificial intelligence," in a video game. But he didn't just create one**

smart ghost, he created four. Each ghost had its own personality. Blinky (red) and Pinky (pink) are the predictable ghosts, as they chase Pac-Man in the most direct way. Inky (blue) implements ambush attacks by focusing on a point thirty pixels behind Pac-Man, while Clyde (orange) is the most dangerous ghost of all, because his behavior is completely random.

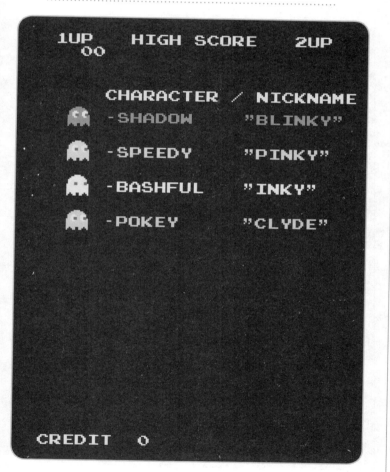

Pac-Man © Bandai Namco Games, Inc.

Turns out, a game inspired by three-fourths of a pizza is a whole lot more than simply munching dots.

It is possible to get a perfect score in Pac-Man, because it has a finite number of dots, ghosts, and fruit to chomp. This superhuman challenge is included in Ernest Cline's book *Ready Player One*, where his main character sets out to play a perfect game. Just in case you want to try, the score is 3,333,360. Good luck!

JUST ONE BYTE

Pac-Man might have started the hungry video game character craze, but it didn't end there. In fact, food has played a big part in video game history. Not only has it been a reward, like the fruit in Pac-Man, but it has become the universal symbol of health in games. If you're hungry or running low on energy, just chomp down on some dog meat in Fallout, or maybe some pumpkin pie in Minecraft, and you'll be good to go.

Check out my list of the top ten tempting video game snacks. But be warned, it may cause you to reach for a bag of Cheesy Poofs.

10. Mooshroom Stew—Minecraft

Ever milked a mooshroom by the pale moonlight? No? Well, don't worry, because that's not the only way to make a bowl of Minecraft mooshroom stew. You can craft a bowl of the hearty stuff with ease. All you need is a bowl, one red mushroom, and one green mushroom. After you've created your stew, it will pop a solid three drumsticks of food into your hunger bar.

9. Ramen Noodles—Cooking Mama

It's really hard to pick a food winner in this game. Everything you help Cooking Mama make looks wonderful, but the noodles are especially fun and yummy.

8. Burger Layers—Burger Time

Imagine a burger so large that it could take up an entire floor of an apartment building! Yeah. I know. I want one, too! Well, in the classic arcade hit Burger Time, each floor of the rickety building the chef runs through contains a different part of a hamburger: the bun on top, then a slice of cheese, some lettuce, the beef, and finally another bun. Running across the burger parts drops them to the layer below. Drop them all and you'll build a burger—the burger of your dreams. But beware, you're being chased by angry hot dogs and bitter pickle slices. Totally normal, right?

7. Pretzel—Ms. Pac-Man

With all the treats in Ms. Pac-Man, why would this one get a special place on this list? Well, because it's the only goodie in the game that isn't a piece of fruit. Nothing against fruit—I like a good banana as much as the next guy, but nothing beats a toasty, warm, salt-covered pretzel.

6. Moogle Pie—Final Fantasy XI

One look at this delicious braided loaf of syrupy apple goodness and you'll want to lick the screen. (Don't.) This treat packs quite a punch. It boosts every single attribute for your character by at least one point, and gives you a pile of health points and magic points. But perhaps my favorite part of the moogle pie is the description when you first find it.

This apple pie is made by (not of) moogles. Although slightly burnt, a magical spell placed upon it by the baker makes it seem more delicious than it really is.

5. Love Potion—The Sims

In order to make the love potion in The Sims, you need to have a chemistry set—the Concoctanation Station—and an enemy of the opposite gender. Yeah. An enemy. This fun little potion will make the person who hates you most in the game fall instantly in love with you. Beware, there will be kisses involved.

4. The Cake—Portal

In Portal, you are guided by the soothing yet robotic voice of GLaDOS. She's an artificial intelligence computer that "helps" you navigate the unpredictable Aperture Science. And she knows how to get what she wants. Early on, she promises you a cake if you help her out. But, well, I won't spoil it. I'm just saying, not everything in Portal is what it seems.

3. Lava Cookie—Pokémon

This crummy-looking snack isn't just tasty, it can cure any status effect from a hurt Pokémon. Poisoned? Eat a lava cookie. Burnt? Paralyzed? Confused? No problem. Just give your favorite Pokémon a lava cookie and she'll be back to normal.

2. The 1UP Mushroom—Super Mario Bros.

The green mushroom in the Mario franchise has become

an icon in video game lore. Just one look at it and you know you have to have it. Of course, they are usually hidden inside blocks or in hard-to-reach places, but they are totally worth it. Gobble one of these tasty treats and you'll get one extra life!

1. Elixir Soup—The Legend of Zelda: The Wind Waker

What's better than soup? Special magic soup made by your grandmother, of course. This isn't easy to find, but it's an important item that will restore all of your life energy and give you a magic power. Your attack power doubles until the first time you take damage. Man, grandmothers really are the best.

You just can't have a chapter on digital goodies and not mention two of the all-time great video game munchers, Yoshi and Kirby. These two Nintendo all-stars gobble up everything in their path, and use the energy-mojo-strength-whatnot they absorb through eating to do everything from transform into the item they devoured, to spit it out as a nice slobbery weapon. They have both munched their way into many gamers' hearts, including mine.

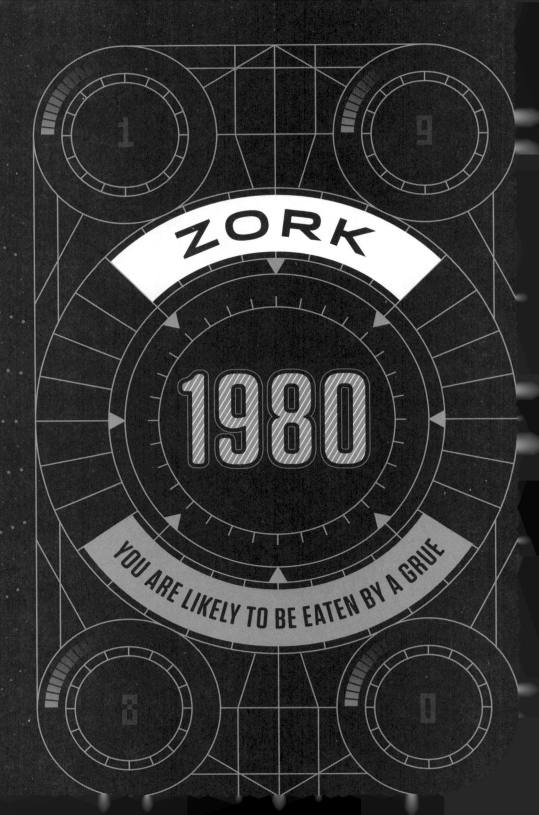

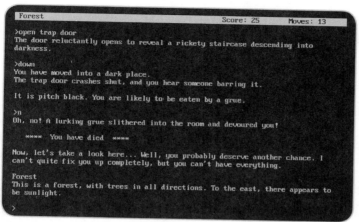

Zork © Infocom

I realize this might be hard to believe, but there was a time when computers were rare.

I know, I know. Today they are everywhere. School libraries are filled with computers. The checkout stand at the grocery store has one, or maybe two. The dentist's office? The movie theater? The water park? Heck, you can find them at the zoo, and even the animals are starting to get them.

But back in the 1970s this wasn't the case. Sure, arcades were popping up all over the place, but it wasn't like you could walk into your friend's house and find a Centipede arcade cabinet blipping away in the kitchen next to the dining room table.

Part of this was because computers in the 1970s were actually bigger than a dining room table. In fact, the PDP-11 was one of the most common computers at the time, and it was the size of the entire kitchen!

But everything was about to change with the invention of the personal computer. It started in office buildings, but it didn't take long for the "home computer" to make its way into every kid's bedroom.

The ape house in the Lincoln Park Zoo has given the chimpanzees access to touch-screen computers. Scientists are learning quite a bit about how apes understand their environment, and the apes are learning that nobody can beat level 151 of Candy Crush Saga without buying a lollipop or two. Or three.

Moms loved Zork! Okay, maybe not all moms, but there was no doubt that it was easier to get a mom to buy a game that forced kids to read than it was to ask her for a handful of quarters to run down to the arcade to zap aliens. Infocom took notice and started selling their games in bookstores, not just in the electronic stores like other games. Not a bad idea.

The computers were pretty basic and mostly used for paying bills and writing book reports. But it was Zork that had everyone fighting for the keyboard.

Commodore 64 © Evan Amos

And for Zork, a keyboard was all you needed. You didn't need a joystick because there were no graphics. You didn't need speakers, either, because there was no sound. Just words. Clever, entertaining, DANGEROUS words.

Yup. Words. You didn't just PLAY Zork, you READ Zork. But it totally worked because the story was just that good.

So, here's how Zork worked. You'd get a small snippet from the story, then it was your turn to decide what to do next. It went something (okay, exactly) like this.

West of House
You are standing in an open field west of a
white house, with a boarded front door.
There is a small mailbox here.
>_

And then it's your turn. What do you do? Do you go to the house? Do you look in the mailbox? Go on. It's your choice. Really, just shout it out. Oh, you want to "Look inside the mailbox." Good idea.

Opening the mailbox reveals:
A leaflet.
>_

You take the leaflet, by simply typing "Take the leaflet." You can read the leaflet, of course, but that is obvious, so there's a good chance you might try a couple other options first. Like . . .

"Eat the leaflet"
I don't think that the small leaflet would
agree with you.

>_

"Kill the leaflet"

What do you want to kill the small leaflet with?

>_

"Kill leaflet with sword"

You don't have that!

"Kill leaflet with bazooka"

You can't see any such thing.

Bummer, if only you had a bazooka.

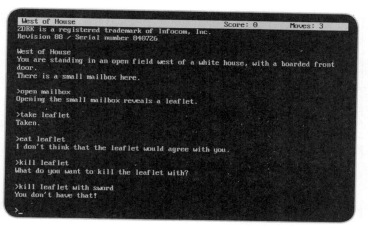

Zork © Infocom

Zork was written between 1977 and 1979 by MIT students Tim Anderson, Bruce Daniels, Dave Lebling, and Marc Blank. The young adventurers got the idea for Zork from playing the first-ever text adventure game, Advent, also called Colossal Cave Adventure. Advent was such a hit with Anderson, Daniels, Lebling, and Blank that they set to writing Zork right away. They had no idea that Zork would end up being one of the most important and well-respected games of all time.

As you can tell from this little sample, there are about a bazillion ways to explore (and goof around in) Zork, and all we've done so far is open a mailbox and try to eat/bazookafy a leaflet.

And the game gets better once you step inside the house and you get some real clues: an ancient oil lamp, an empty trophy case, and an intricately engraved sword. (Man, where was this sword when we were dealing with that leaflet?)

You look around and find a trapdoor that leads below the house, and the adventure begins. Getting in through the trapdoor is simple, but the real trick is getting back out.

The goal of the interactive fiction game was to return from the Great Underground Empire alive with the twenty treasures of Zork. Along the way you ran into grues, zork-mids, and all kinds of confusing and twisting corridors. Oh, and a character cleverly named "The Thief," who loves to pick your pocket, lie to you, and pick up anything you might have left behind to help you find your way.

And the enemies—oh, the enemies!—were terrifying! Okay, I know what you're thinking. You can't imagine being scared just reading about a troll that you can't even see, but there was something about *NOT* seeing the troll that made it even worse. And the trolls were deadly, but they were nothing compared to the grue.

What's a grue, you ask? Well, nobody really knows because nobody has ever seen one and lived to tell about it. They lurk in the pitch-dark, and they get closer to you with every move. Every decision. Every thought—until—GULP. "Oh no. You have walked into the slavering fangs of a lurking grue. You have died."

That simple eleven-word sentence haunted the nightmares of Zork players everywhere, and it is easy to see why. It's the monster hiding beneath your bed. It's the unseen spook in the dark closet. Man, I'm starting to give myself the willies. Words are powerful things, right?

Part of Zork's success was that the writers of the game had a real sense of humor. There was lots of techy nerd stuff in there, too—some of which has gone on to be part of the gamer vocabulary today, but it was the funny stuff that really kept players playing. For example, if you ever play Zork, and you should, say hello to the troll. If that isn't enough, try "smell the troll." Believe me, it's worth it, and it will be a gaming moment you will never forget.

The launch of Zork was pretty slow. In fact, in 1980, when the game was ready to go out on the TRS-80 home computer, the game was copied to a floppy disk by the developer, then they used a photocopier to make a copy of the instructions. They stuck the disk and the instructions in a plastic zip-top sandwich bag and sent it to the first buyer in the mail.

Not exactly like going to the big chain superstore and asking a guy in a blue vest if he'll unlock a massive glass case of video games for you so you can get the newest copy of Mario Kart, now, is it?

Zork started off pretty darn small, but the game's popularity exploded. Soon everyone at school was talking about how to get past the tricky parts, sharing maps they'd drawn on graph paper, and swapping ideas of funny things to try. And part of the reason people were swapping ideas is that Zork was HARD. Super hard.

Some gamers thought the game was intentionally trying to trick them. For example, there are twenty-eight unique ways to die in Zork. Twenty-eight! How many ways can you die in Pac-Man? Yeah, that's right. One.

But Infocom was there to help. Before Zork II hit the shelves, Zork's publisher, Infocom, started a newsletter that players could have mailed right to their own "small mailbox" called the *New Zork Times*. It had hints about how to get through tricky areas, interesting fake articles about the world of Zork, and funny parody articles advertising goods from the city of Frobozz. The newsletter was a cool addition to the game, and it led to something even bigger. After the Zork series (Zork I, Zork II, and Zork III) had shipped, Infocom released a whole new version of the game in a brand-new box. No cheap sandwich bags here. This new box was called the "gray box" series, and not only did it come with the game and instructions, it came with a bunch of cool stuff they called *feelies*. Feelies were maps, coins, illustrations, and other items from the land of Zork, and many players purchased the entire collection again just to have the feelies.

Just about everyone who owned a computer in the 1980s had a copy of Zork in one version or another. The game truly was a phenomenon and it smoothed the way for the story games we still play today. Games like The Legend of Zelda, Uncharted, Final Fantasy, and certainly The Walking Dead, Tales from the Borderlands, and The Wolf Among Us all owe a bit of who they are to Zork.

Even the name Zork had meaning to early computer nerds. The word is a nonsense word that hackers once used to define an unfinished program until it was ready to be installed on the system.

Later, Infocom sold hint books called InvisiClues. The books were printed with invisible ink that could only be revealed with a special marker, so players could get clues as needed without spoiling anything later in the game. Some critics claimed that Infocom made their games intentionally difficult to help push the sales of their InvisiClues books. Those critics were eaten by a grue.

But it's not just games that drew inspiration from Zork. Rapper MC Frontalot's song "It Is Pitch Dark" is all about facing the grue and the awesomeness that is Zork. In the hit spy TV series *Chuck*, the game is mentioned as one of Chuck's favorite childhood games, and Zork commands were used by CIA operatives as secret code in the show. And in megahit sitcom *The Big Bang Theory*, the character Sheldon Cooper loves Zork, and likes to play it on "Chinese and vintage video game night"—his quote, not mine. Zork comes up multiple times in *The Big Bang Theory*, and in one episode Sheldon delivers a line that is super-Zork-ish: "Hit troll with ax."

Infocom's interactive fiction game was more than a hit, it was a movement. And while Zork wasn't first, it was the one that really gave the story-driven games category its start. Interactive fiction games covered every reading taste out there, from mysteries, to science fiction, to pirates, and they owe it all to Zork.

I think you can boil down why Zork was such an important game into five innovative points.

1. **Zork was funny. That might not sound all that original now, but that is how innovation works. Someone does it first, then a lot of other people follow along.**

2. **Zork was smart. Not only was the writing funny, Zork was filled with inside jokes that only the geekiest of computer geeks understood. Heck, it even had a few MATH jokes. In fact, it could be said that Zork helped spawn the "it's cool to be a geek in the know" movement that is so huge today. And yes, it is cool to be a geek. Very cool.**

3. **Zork lived on outside the computer. The feelies, the *New Zork Times*, the InvisiClue books. These were all ways for players to stay involved with Zork when they were away from the computer. Remember, this was almost thirty-five years before the iPhone, and even if you could get a battery big enough to power the thing, lugging your Commodore 64 around to play Zork at recess was not advised. It was much easier to slip a zorkmid coin in your pocket.**

4. **Zork spoke your language. I mentioned earlier that Zork wasn't the first interactive fiction game. Many point to Advent as holding that honor. But the engineers who built Zork wrote a state-of-the-art tool called a**

language parser. It allowed players to write commands in plain English, which was a HUGE step up for the genre. For example, in Zork you could type, "Put sword, ax, torch, and map in chest," while in Advent you might be held to two- or three-word commands like "Ax in chest." Which, as you can see, could be taken in the wrong way. Ouch!

5. Zork had the first video game cliff-hanger. So, I hate to spoil the ending, but I'm gonna anyway. After you've collected the last trophy and placed it in the trophy case back in the white house, you are awarded the rank of Master Adventurer, and an ancient map with further instructions that send you to a "stone barrow." It turns out the entrance to the stone barrow is the end of Zork I and the beginning of Zork II. Zork fanatics had to wait for months for a chance to continue the story, but it was worth it.

Zork went on to ship another thirteen games in the series in one form or another. That doesn't even count all the games Zork inspired along the way. To this day there is a dedicated group of players that both write and play interactive fiction, and take it from this old game designer, it's a great way to learn how to design games. Oh, and to learn how to write fun and entertaining fiction.

You should give it a shot sometime. I promise, it's not as dangerous as lurking in a dark cave being hunted by a grue.

In 1984, Infocom published a game version of Douglas Adams's famous sci-fi novel, *The Hitchhiker's Guide to the Galaxy*. The game had a reputation for being particularly difficult—especially one instance where the player had to get a Babel fish out of a dispenser hold on a Vogon ship. It was so difficult, in fact, that Infocom celebrated their deviousness by selling shirts that read "I Got the Babel Fish"—a great inside joke for those who were lucky enough to proceed.

In Call of Duty: Black Ops, you can earn the achievement "Eaten by a Grue" by sneaking around until you find an antique computer terminal and playing Zork. The entire game is included, and most gamers nowadays find finishing Zork more challenging than finishing single-player campaign mode in COD: Black Ops.

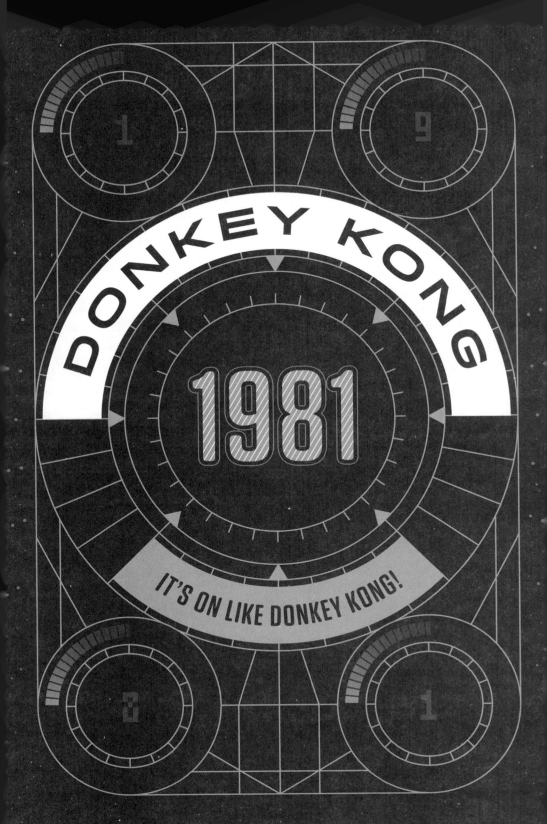

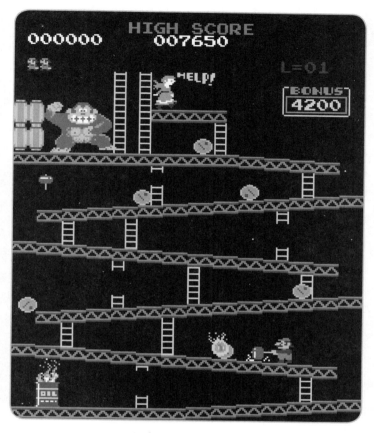

Donkey Kong © Nintendo

Hey, gamer, let me ask you a question. What do you think about Radar Scope?

Wait. You've never heard of Radar Scope?

Don't worry. It was a trick question. Nobody's heard of Radar Scope. Not because the game stunk—it was actually a pretty good space shooter. Nobody knows about this game because a few months after Nintendo shipped three thousand Radar Scope arcade cabinets to America, they decided to pull the plug on it. Literally. Nintendo had high hopes for Radar Scope, but nobody was playing it, so they decided to fix the game.

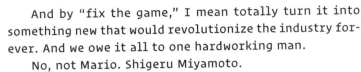

There are a lot of stories about where the name Donkey Kong actually came from—everything from a bad fax that made the Nintendo of America team misread *Monkey Kong*, thinking the *M* was a *D*, to its being named after King Kong. But in the end, Miyamoto said it was simpler than that. They wanted an English name because they knew the game would be a hit in America. The word *donkey* was used to imply something silly, or dumb, and in Japan, *kong* is a slang word used for an ape. Basically, Miyamoto and crew were naming the game Silly Ape, but they felt Donkey Kong was, well, just more fun to say.

And by "fix the game," I mean totally turn it into something new that would revolutionize the industry forever. And we owe it all to one hardworking man.

No, not Mario. Shigeru Miyamoto.

So, here's the story. It was 1980. Arcades were popping up in every mall across the globe, Luke Skywalker had just found out that Darth Vader was his father, and kids were getting kicked out of class for chewing grape Hubba Bubba (still the best bubble gum of all time). Disco was dead, and pop music was all the rage. Things were changing, and changing fast, and to be honest, arcade gamers were looking for something new. It seemed like every game out there that wasn't Pac-Man was a space shooter, and Radar Scope was lost in the mix of awesome that was 1980.

So the president of Nintendo at the time, Hiroshi Yamauchi, tapped on the shoulder of a young graphic artist, Shigeru Miyamoto, and asked him to see what he could do to make Radar Scope stand out. And, boy, did he deliver.

While Miyamoto was a great artist, he was a FANTAS-TIC storyteller, and he knew right away that the best way to make a game stand out in the arcades was to add a story. So he turned to one of his favorite cartoons for inspiration: Popeye. You know, the old pipe-smoking sailor guy your parents used to use as an example to get you to eat your spinach. Popeye had everything a young game designer needed: a hardworking hero, a supercute princess, and a big bully. But Miyamoto wasn't satisfied with good enough; he wanted GREAT. So he turned those elements into a carpenter that could bounce over anything in his path (Jump Man), a pretty princess in a pink dress (Lady), and a girlfriend-stealing ape named Donkey Kong.

While the story for Donkey Kong was a huge hit, there was one thing that gamers had never seen before that really made the game a winner. The jump button. Yeah, no joke. Before Donkey Kong, nobody had ever jumped in a video game. Sure, they had dodged back and forth and shot lasers and had even eaten dots, but it took until 1981 for a video game character to JUMP. And you know what, that little jump button changed gaming forever, and started a whole new gaming category: the platformer.

And to this day, the best way to define a platformer is to describe the game play in Donkey Kong. So, here goes. Jump Man starts in one point in the game screen (the bottom left corner), and he needs to use all of his skills to travel to another location (toward the princess at the top). Along the way he has to defeat or crush enemies (barrels with hammers), jump over obstacles (bouncing and flaming barrels), climb ladders, and avoid pits—oh, and jump from PLATFORM to PLATFORM. At any time if you mess up, miss the timing, or don't jump far enough, you're through. You must start over on the level that konged you, until you reach the top.

Another thing that you can't ignore when it comes to Donkey Kong is the music and the sound. You might not even realize that you recognize the music, but I know you do. Look it up—it's everywhere. And not only was the music great, the sound effects timed with the music made it even better. As soon as you dropped your quarter in the machine and hit the "Player 1" button, you saw Donkey Kong climbing a ladder with Lady under his arm. Dark and scary theme music creeps along. *Dum, da-doo-da, dooooooooo-dum.* At this time, Donkey Kong climbs to the top of the screen and stomps his feet six times on the dark red platform inside an abandoned building.

BOMP!

BOMP-BOMP-BOMP-BOMP-BOMP!

Then he grins at you, tempting you to even *try* to climb up after him.

Finally, the game asks you a very important question: How high can you get? When Jump Man's theme music (which is a lot more playful than Donkey Kong's) plays, you're ready to start.

Really, if you haven't played the game, you should give it a shot. There are fully playable versions on the interwebs, but even if you don't, you MUST check out the intro sequence on YouTube or something. The music is SO great, and you will totally recognize it.

By the time the game was ready to stand tall in arcades

Not only did gamers love Donkey Kong, but musicians did as well. Buckner & Garcia recorded a song called "Do the Donkey Kong," based on the game. And artists DJ Jazzy Jeff & The Fresh Prince rapped about it in their hit "Human Video Game." The song is awesome, nerdy, and shows that even back then, it was cool to be a GAMER!

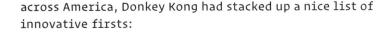

across America, Donkey Kong had stacked up a nice list of innovative firsts:

- **THE FIRST PLATFORMER.** For decades after Donkey Kong, Nintendo turned platformers into their bread and butter. But games like Sonic the Hedgehog, Ratchet & Clank, Mega Man, Little Big Planet, Banjo-Kazooie, and many more also followed in Jump Man's footsteps.

- **THE FIRST JUMP BUTTON.** Before Jump Man jumped on the scene, characters had to rely on running to get out of trouble. Thank you, Donkey Kong, for letting gamers around the world test their hops.

- **THE FIRST GAME SOLELY DESIGNED BY VIDEO GAME LEGEND SHIGERU MIYAMOTO.** While he'd worked on other games before, Donkey Kong was Miyamoto's first breakout title, and we all know it wasn't his last.

- And let's not forget this important tidbit: **DONKEY KONG INTRODUCED THE WORLD TO MARIO.**

Have you ever felt like you have wanted something your entire life, but you didn't realize you wanted it until you SAW it? That's kind of what Donkey Kong did for arcade junkies. It was a refreshing new take on arcade games, and the bright colors, sing-along sound track, and new jumping action branded it on the hearts of gamers everywhere.

But the biggest thing to come out of Donkey Kong was actually pretty little. It was a suspender-wearing everyday hero with a mustache. That's right, Jump Man, the star of Donkey Kong was none other than Mario. And, boy, was he ready to JUMP into video game history.

One might wonder why the president of Nintendo chose Shigeru Miyamoto to build Donkey Kong over the top of Radar Scope, thus wiping it from history. It's because Miyamoto was part of the Radar Scope team in 1980, so he was familiar with the hardware.

CAN I TAKE IT HOME?

Games expanded pretty fast the first few years or so of the gaming world. Just for argument's sake, let's say that Pong was the first big hit. Well, we already did, so let's say it again.

Pong was the first big hit.

And that first big hit led to every arcade in the world filling up with gamers and quarters.

While the arcade boom was going strong in 1975, the next natural thing to do was to bring the arcade craze into the front room of every home in America. Or at least, that's what Nolan Bushnell, the founder of Atari and cocreator of Pong, thought. So when department store giant Sears approached him and offered to help him put Pong in their stores, Bushnell jumped at the opportunity. Or Ponged. That's a verb, right? Ponged?

So Bushnell and Atari went into the home video game console business, and in a few short months a new craze was starting: home video gaming.

Pong on your own black-and-white TV was cool, but gamers wanted MORE. And two years later, Bushnell and Atari had just what they were looking for.

The Atari 2600!

It was AWESOME! It had fake wood paneling, six aluminum levers you could switch to change game modes, a slot for jamming in new game cartridges, super cool one-button joysticks, and it was in COLOR! One hundred twenty-eight colors on-screen at one time, to be exact.

Atari 2600 © Evan Amos

Now the games you played in the arcade could continue to drive you crazy at home.

There were nine games at launch, covering almost every genre we know and love today: Combat (a shooter), Blackjack (a casino game), Indy 500 (a racing game), Video Olympics (a sports game), and even Basic Math . . . which was basically math.

The original Atari 2600 came with the console, two joysticks, two paddle controllers, and a two-player game with twenty-seven variations called Combat. All this for $229!

But the big hits for Atari really started the following year in 1978, when a game programmed by a very famous duo of Steves arrived on shelves just in time for the holidays. It was called Breakout, and it was programmed by Steve Jobs and Steve Wozniak.

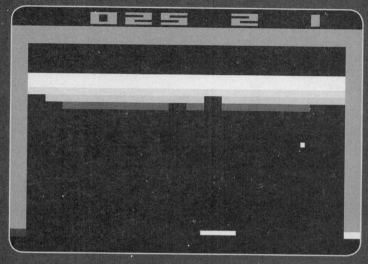

Breakout © Atari Interactive, Inc.

Yeah, *that* Steve Jobs. Before they gave us the Apple computers and the iPhone, Steve Jobs and Steve Wozniak were Atari employees.

Things kept on cruising for Atari, and it seemed like every game they made was plated in gold. That is, until Nolan Bushnell left Atari to start up something new, and things started going a little wonky.

The company Nolan Bushnell left Atari to develop was called Pizza Time Theatre. The company was a cool idea, but it didn't become popular until he changed the name to Chuck E. Cheese. Say what you will about Nolan Bushnell, but the guy knows how to keep us entertained.

Some say it was because they grew too fast. Some say it was because of the hot tubs in the office. But most people blame it on a little alien with a big heart and a glowing finger.

E.T. THE EXTRA-TERRESTRIAL

1982

DON'T PHONE HOME

1

9

8

2

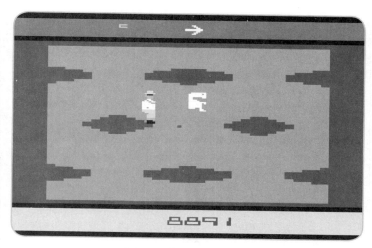

E.T. © Atari Interactive, Inc.

I'll bet you a warm handful of Reese's Pieces that you've heard Atari's E.T. game is the worst game in video game history. It's legendary, for all the wrong reasons.

But do you know how it happened? Or what actually makes the game so horrible that millions of copies were buried in a dump in New Mexico?

No? Well, you've come to the right place, 'cause I've got the scoop.

All right, let's get a few things out of the way first. Yes. It is true. E.T. the Extra-Terrestrial was a bad game. Maybe not the worst game ever made, but it was really bad. The game, if you didn't know, was based on the huge hit movie *E.T.*, directed by Steven Spielberg. It was a story about a kid who finds an alien, whom they name E.T., and the boy and his siblings have to find a way for E.T. to contact his family in outer space to get home before he grows too weak. It is an amazing story about being a hero and helping a friend. It's full of laughs and adventure. Oh, and Reese's Pieces.

The game was about . . . well, I'm not really sure, and neither was anyone else.

E.T., with his elevator neck and glowing finger, was in the game. The Reese's Pieces made it in there, too. But aside from that, the rest of the movie was missing. There were a bunch of pits that you would fall into that you couldn't climb out of. That was fun. And cops or FBI agents or something that would pop on-screen at random times and capture you and end your game. That was fun, too.

I'm lying. It wasn't fun.

The game was a mess. Nobody knew how to play it, and the only way to really win it was to try to fall into every pit and see if it magically sent you in the right direction. Over and over again until you found enough pieces to build a phone. No, not Reese's Pieces, broken chunks of an actual phone.

Even the Reese's Pieces were disappointing. They looked like stale muffins.

All in all, the game got its bad reputation the old-fashioned way. It earned it. But like all tragic stories, there is more here than meets the eye.

Allow me to set the dial on the time machine back a little to help you get a good picture of the mess that was E.T. the Extra-Terrestrial.

The year was 1980, and the Atari 2600 was selling so fast that Nolan Bushnell and company had a hard time keeping up with demand. They were making games as fast as they could for the 2600, and gamers were gobbling them all up. All of them! Then Atari made a big announcement that Space Invaders would be coming home on the Atari 2600 for the first time ever, and fans lined up. Atari doubled the number of consoles in the world, and it looked like there was no end in sight.

By this time, Bushnell had been running the company for nearly ten years, and he was ready to move on. He sold the company to Warner Bros., who had big dreams for Atari and lots of money to make them happen.

But soon after Bushnell left Atari, a few old-time designers split and started up another company you might have heard of, Activision. And Activision really opened the floodgates, because not only did these guys know how to make games, they knew how to make games for the Atari 2600!

This might not sound that crazy to you nowadays, but back then it was HUGE news. Nobody saw it coming, especially not Atari. For the first time ever, a game developer was making a game for someone else's console. And Activision didn't just make good games, they made GREAT games, like River Raid, Kaboom!, and Pitfall!

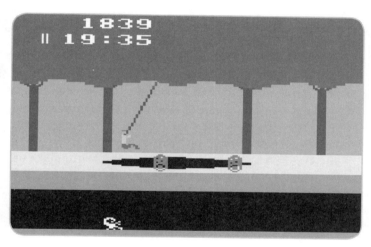

Pitfall! © Activision

David Crane's Pitfall! (1982) went on to be the second-best-selling game on the Atari 2600 (after Pac-Man), with over four million copies sold.

Things were good for Atari, but they were just as good for Activision.

Let me put it this way. In 1981 Atari became the fastest-growing company in the history of the United States. And the very next year, 1982, Activision replaced them by stealing the crown and becoming the fastest-growing company in the history of the United States.

Video game companies popped up overnight like a crop of zits on a teenager's forehead after an all-night pizza party. Problem was, most of these companies had no idea how to make good games. And by the end of 1982, not only did you find great games like Pole Position and David Crane's Pitfall!, you would also find total stinkers like I Want My Mommy, a Donkey Kong clone where you played as a teddy bear trying to avoid dream demons.

The real problem here wasn't that there weren't any good games, it was that the good games were getting drowned out by the bad ones. Gamers started seeing the Atari 2600 as an expensive garbage delivery system. Atari had to fix this problem, and in typical Atari fashion, they wanted to fix it fast. So they decided they needed to make games that would rise above the clutter. Big, A-list games that players would recognize and flock toward.

They tried Pac-Man first (1982), and gamers were pumped! Unfortunately, Atari thought that just having the name Pac-Man was enough, and the product itself was not that great. The ghosts popped in and out in random places, the sound effects were bad, and the game didn't really look like Pac-Man. Pretty much every place they could have failed on the game, they did. In the end, Pac-Man ended up being the bestselling game in Atari 2600 history, selling seven million copies. But that left five million unsold cartridges sitting on shelves, gathering dust.

But Atari had a plan that they thought would make up for Pac-Man's failure. It was that lovable alien E.T., the extraterrestrial.

They decided to make the game in July of 1982, and they wanted the game in stores in time for the holiday buying rush. To make a quality game for the Atari 2600 back in the day, it would take around six months of serious pizza-slamming, sleeping on the couch, and overtime work.

Atari gave their team six WEEKS.

Well, actually it was more like five and a little change, and it wasn't a team, it was just one man. Howard Scott Warshaw.

And they picked the right guy. Warshaw was a monster engineer, and he'd already put out two great games for Atari, Yar's Revenge and the movie-inspired Raiders of the Lost Ark. He had wizard-level coding skills, he nearly built these games by himself, and he'd earned quite a reputation as a go-to guy at Atari.

And to make a bad situation worse, Warshaw had only two days to design the game before he was to fly to Los Angeles to meet with Steven Spielberg.

After Warshaw pitched the concept to Spielberg, his first response was "Couldn't you do something more like Pac-Man?" Warshaw was shocked by this, but looking back, Spielberg might have been onto something.

To make the best use of his time, he had Atari install a development workstation in his home. He didn't work twenty-four hours a day, but he has said that it was the most grueling five-week period of his life.

It's hard to blame Howard Warshaw for the poor quality of E.T. But in the end, gamers didn't really care. They thought the game was horrible, and they'd had enough from Atari.

In the end, over two million E.T. game cartridges were returned to retailers. Truckloads of cartridges made their way back to Atari, so they took out the trash. Literally. Atari paid to have the unopened E.T. the Extra-Terrestrial boxes delivered to a landfill in Alamogordo, New Mexico. They dug a big hole, filled it full of cartridges, then covered E.T. the Extra-Terrestrial with a massive slab of concrete and tried to forget that it ever happened.

Atari New Mexico Dig © taylorhatmaker

This was a huge blow to the hearts and minds of Atari players, and just like that, the golden age of Atari was over. By 1983, Atari had completely tanked, and in the end they had lost over 530 million dollars. Most of us freak out if we lose our lunch money, and in a single year Atari lost over half a BILLION bucks! That'll ruin your weekend, not to mention your company.

On April 26, 2014, remnants of E.T. and other Atari games were unearthed in the New Mexico landfill. This finding proved once and for all that the stories of burying copies of the epic fail were true. In December 2014, the Smithsonian Institute added an excavated E.T. cartridge to their collection.

E.T. © Atari Interactive, Inc.

So with that in mind, here are five mistakes that led to E.T. the Extra-Terrestrial being known as the worst game of all time.

1. **IT'S ABOUT QUALITY, NOT QUANTITY.** There were so many games out there that it was impossible for gamers to tell the good from the bad.

2. **GAME PLAY IS MORE IMPORTANT THAN STAR POWER.** I mean, having E.T. or Shaq or Michael Jackson on your video game cover might get some attention, but nothing beats a good game. NOTHING.

3. **YOU CAN'T RUSH ART.** And video games ARE art. There's a big difference between a quick scribble on the back of a napkin and the *Mona Lisa*. Good things take time.

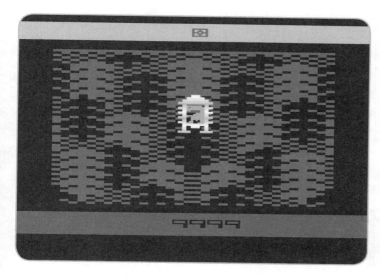

E.T. © Atari Interactive, Inc.

4. **IT'S OKAY TO MAKE THE GAME HARD IF THE RULES ARE EASY.** E.T. wasn't knocked because the game was hard; it was bad because nobody knew what to do. You can make a game so hard it makes a gamer cry, as long as you play by the rules.

....

5. And most important . . . **NEVER UNDERESTI-MATE A GAMER!** If your game stinks, gamers are going to let you know. Gamers are smart, passionate, and unforgiving. And smart. Did I mention gamers are SMART?!

Being by far the biggest player in the video game world at the time, this hit to Atari sent the entire industry on a downward spiral that nearly tanked video games forever.

Super Mario Bros. © Nintendo

Sometimes the world needs a hero.

After the mess that Atari made, gamers had had enough. Nobody trusted video game companies anymore. And who could blame them?

I mean, you save up all your hard-earned cash. Hours and hours pushing a rusty lawn mower around your neighbor's overgrown lawn or babysitting the wild Brooks brothers, only to blow your money on a game that is less fun than throwing rocks at the sidewalk.

The game industry was in trouble, and it seemed like video games were nothing more than a passing fad.

It wasn't that other companies hadn't tried. Plenty had. Atari even kept at it by releasing another console, the Atari 5200 Super System, in 1982.

In fact, in 1982 more consoles were released by more companies than in any other year in video game history. Emerson released the Arcadia 2001, Coleco shipped the

ColecoVision, Milton Bradley got into the game with their Vectrex, and just to keep it interesting, Coleco put out a second console, the Gemini. 1982 was a busy year.

But to be honest, all of those consoles just added to the problem. Gamers were confused, so instead of buying another console, they continued to drop their hard-earned quarters at the arcade.

But Nintendo had a plan, the people, and a plumber.

THE PLAN: Stay creative, and don't give up. EVER. When the home video game craze had all but vanished in the early 1980s, Nintendo kept trying to introduce the world to their new system. They tried to sell their system into every department store, electronics store, and toy store in the US, but nobody would take the risk. That didn't stop Nintendo. They believed in their ideas, and kept trying until a store in New York City gave them a little bit of shelf space for their Nintendo Entertainment System. They sold only a few hundred consoles that first year, but it was the sign the company needed to keep going.

THE PEOPLE: It is widely thought that a company takes on the personality of its leaders. Hiroshi Yamauchi, the president of Nintendo at the time, was a brilliant man. He was great at recognizing talent in people like Miyamoto and his teammate Gunpei Yokoi, who worked together so well on Donkey Kong and the Mario Bros. arcade games.

And **THE PLUMBER:** While the rest of the video game world was spinning down the drain, Nintendo continued to put their lovable, hardworking underdog Mario in the arcades. Not only had Donkey Kong been a major hit, but Miyamoto's next arcade game was an even bigger smash: Mario Bros., which starred Mario as well as his little brother, Luigi.

So, armed with the three *P*s, Nintendo got to work. They followed up the success of Donkey Kong with a second game starring Jump Man, who had undergone a name change to Mario. The two-player game, called Mario Bros., took place under the sewers of New York City and was a big hit.

So successful, in fact, that it caught the eye of Nintendo president Hiroshi Yamauchi, who had been quoted many times saying, "Great games sell consoles." Yamauchi

The name Mario didn't appear until Mario Bros., and it is now widely known that Miyamoto named his character after Nintendo of America's Italian-American landlord, Mario Segale. The story goes that Mr. Mario Segale barged into a staff meeting where they were discussing Jump Man and demanded rent. He left such an impression on Miyamoto that he borrowed their landlord's name on the spot.

trusted his rising star, Miyamoto, and recognized that Mario was just the thing he was looking for to sell the Nintendo Entertainment System.

Miyamoto loved Mario Bros., but he knew his next game needed to be even more unique. Miyamoto left the dark sewers behind and began work on a new home for Mario: the Mushroom Kingdom. And it made perfect sense. Who wouldn't want to play in a land of spiked turtles, flaming flowers that transformed you into a fireball-chucking tough guy, squashable mushrooms, and destructible bricks?

Remember, until this point, most video games were created by engineers. They were talented and creative programmers, but Miyamoto was an artist, and his approach was a visual one. At a time where most games were small white spaceships on black star-filled space scenes, Miyamoto brought bright colors, cute characters, and blue skies.

Today, Mario is more recognized by American children than Mickey Mouse. He's jumped around and squashed Koopa Troopas in over two hundred games. He's launched consoles, saved an entire industry, and led the charge into true 3D console gaming.

In fact, six of the top ten bestselling video games of all time are Mario games.

Orchestras have performed his theme music. Operas have been written and sung about him. And Mario has even starred in his own cartoon series and his own live-action film.

The Super Mushrooms in Mario are based on a fungi called *Amanita muscaria*. They are red with big white spots, just like they are in the famous Nintendo game. However, eating one in real life will make you very sick and cause you to see funny things. One common hallucination is that you will feel as if you have grown to twice your actual size. Sound familiar?

No matter how they dress the mustached hero, Nintendo's superstar always looks like Mario. And to prove it, he changed costume a lot in the early years. Mario changed his pants for his big solo debut for Super Mario Bros. In Donkey Kong and Donkey Kong Jr., he wore a blue shirt with red overalls, but the color scheme was swapped to a red shirt and blue overalls when Mario Bros. hit the arcades. He swapped again for the launch of the NES to red overalls and a brown shirt, and made his final switch for Super Mario Bros. 2, where he went back to red shirt and blue overalls. He has not changed since.

The Mario theme song is one of the most covered tunes of all time. Hundreds of YouTube videos star thousands of musicians playing the memorable song on everything from accordions to glass bottles.

When Miyamoto's vision for Mario and the Mushroom Kingdom was combined with the unforgettable music of Koji Kondo, the final piece of the puzzle came together. Kondo's memorable tunes are so familiar that they've been used in NBA basketball games, music videos, and TV commercials. In fact, I bet you're humming the Mario theme song in your head right now. Come on, tell the truth. It's there, isn't it?

The plot was simple but golden, and it became the story for every Mario game since. A grumpy, spiked turtle-dragon named Bowser (aka King Koopa) kidnapped Princess Peach (aka Princess Toadstool) and conquered Mushroom Kingdom. Undersized Mario leapt to the rescue, literally. You just couldn't help but root for Mario, the ultimate underdog.

King Koopa's name is also hotly debated. Some believe that it is based on a Korean food dish, while others claim the name is inspired by Kappa, a Japanese mythical beast that looks like a humanoid, four-legged reptile with a hard shell and webbed toes. I don't know what the Korean dish looks like, but I'm sure the description of the Kappa is a pretty good match.

Nintendo Entertainment System © Evan Amos

Super Mario Bros. turned out better than anyone could have imagined, and Yamauchi's philosophy of "good games sell consoles" also proved true. By February of 1985, millions of Nintendo Entertainment Systems were plugged into gamers' TVs. And before long, forty million Super Mario Bros. games had been scanned through the checkout line. That's ten million more than the nearest competitor at the time, and it was a sales record that would stay in place for twenty years. Nintendo was on top of the world, and the video game crash of 1983 was coming to a close. People were crawling out of the dark arcades to sit on the couch to play games again. And we owe it all to a little man with a big nose, a bigger mustache, and an even bigger heart.

Thanks, Mario.

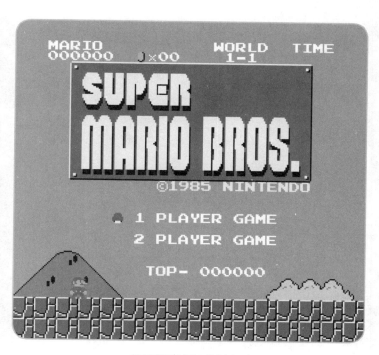

Super Mario Bros. © Nintendo

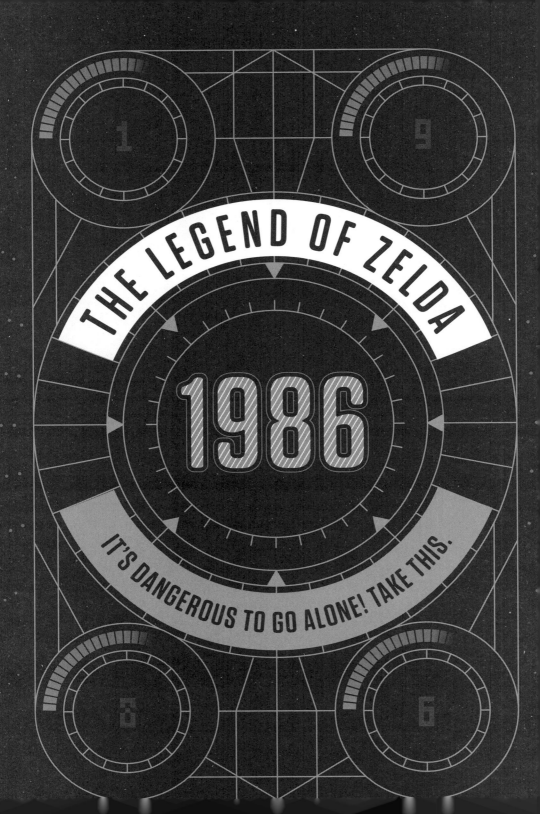

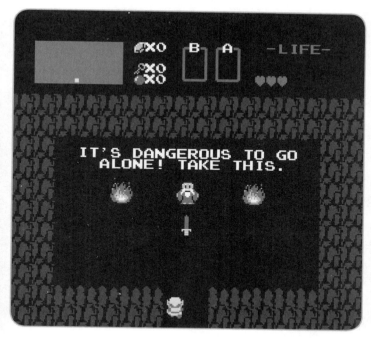

The Legend of Zelda © Nintendo

While Mario was helping the NES break records every day, sales of the Famicom (kind of like the Japanese version of the NES) weren't so hot. Nintendo of Japan had poured so much energy into winning in the US that they had fallen behind with their new disk-based console.

So, Nintendo of Japan challenged Miyamoto and his team to do what they had done so well in America: build a game to sell their Famicom. Luckily for gamers

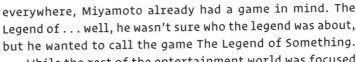

everywhere, Miyamoto already had a game in mind. The Legend of . . . well, he wasn't sure who the legend was about, but he wanted to call the game The Legend of Something.

While the rest of the entertainment world was focused on realistic TV shows and movies like *Magnum, P.I.* and *Top Gun*, Miyamoto and his creative team at Nintendo continued to dream up fantasy worlds that nobody had ever seen before.

With his experience creating Super Mario Bros. for the NES, Miyamoto knew that the best way to sell the Famicom was to take advantage of the unique features of the system. The Famicom was similar to the NES in many ways. It had more memory, but not enough to make a huge difference. The sound chip was similar, and the controllers were basically the same. But what really set the Famicom apart was its new disk system, which meant that not only could players load their game from a disk, but they could save their game on the disk, too.

The Famicom disk system needs a little explaining here, because today we think of disks as something entirely different. Today we mostly think of DVDs, Blu-ray, or CDs when we talk about disks, but the disks back in the time of the Famicom were more like huge SD cards you might see in a camera. They were about the size of a piece of toast.

Nintendo Famicom © Evan Amos

This changed everything for Miyamoto and for gamers around the globe, because for the first time in gaming history the player could save EXACTLY where they left off. Until then players could save only basic info, or not save at all. This reduced the size of the worlds that game developers built because it was frustrating for players to die and have to go back to the start of the level over and over again.

With the new hardware in mind, Miyamoto designed the largest game a console had ever seen. Miles and miles of dungeons, valleys, mountains, and swamps, and he tied them all together in a vast land called Hyrule.

One of Miyamoto's goals with The Legend of . . . *Something* was to create a garden for players to explore and get lost within. He wanted hidden entrances to caves and secret rooms that would lead to wonder and treasure. With this in mind, he designed Hyrule, and if you've played the series at all, you'd have to agree that, once again, Miyamoto nailed it.

Now that Hyrule was under way, Miyamoto needed a hero. This time he turned to Disney's *Peter Pan*, and you can definitely see the influence of the flying green boy and his fairy friend, Tinker Bell. Once again, Miyamoto went with the underdog: a small boy with great potential who fights against all odds to do the impossible. And in this case, the enemies were creatures and mazes, and an evil blue pig-beast named Ganon.

Okay, let's go back and see where we are.

- **A magical and wonderful land filled with hidden secrets. Hyrule—CHECK**

- **An unlikely hero with a sword, white tights, and a green tunic. Link—CHECK**

- **An angry, unlikable bad guy with blue skin and large tusks. Ganon—CHECK**

- **A princess worth saving . . . Oh yeah, that's what we are missing.**

To finalize the design and give Link something worth risking his life in the goblin-filled dungeons beneath

There are many similarities between Link and Navi, and Peter Pan and Tinker Bell. However, one major difference is that in *Peter Pan*, Peter talks and Tinker Bell is silent, while in Zelda, Link is silent (except for a lot of grunts) and Navi is a never-ending chatterbox.

Legend of Zelda fans like to point out all the changes Link has made over the years, but no character in the history of the series has changed more than Ganon. He's been everything from a bright blue warthog to a sword-wielding knight. One thing is for sure, he's always kept his bad attitude.

Koji Kondo reunited with Miyamoto once again to write the soundtrack for The Legend of Zelda. Many claim it to be his finest work. The music changed dramatically based on the mood and the player's location in the game, making it a truly emotional experience that had not been seen—or heard, I guess—until then.

A bit about RAM. It actually means *random access memory*, which kind of explains it, and kind of makes it more confusing. But basically, RAM saves things for you, memories like where you were when you died, your character's nickname, what type of sunglasses you wore to the king's ball, and so on. It saves them all in a big stack of numbers, in kind of a random order. Then the player can access these memories whenever they need them. So, Randomly saved piles of Accessible Memories, or RAM.

Hyrule, Miyamoto introduced us to Zelda, the most wonderful princess a boy could ever hope to rescue. Link would be a fool not to chase after the evil Ganon to save Princess Zelda and restore balance to Hyrule. I mean, this princess is amazing, and her story, or dare I say LEGEND, will live on forever. Oh, wait—now it is all coming together. The Legend of ZELDA! The story told by the people of Hyrule about their innocent princess, kidnapped by the evil Ganon and rescued by that guy in the funny green hat. It's all about Zelda!

I thought so.

Okay, admission time. When I first played Zelda, I called the main character Zelda for like a month, until a childhood gaming buddy corrected me and told me his name was Link. I know, I know. I'm the only guy on the planet that made this mistake. Right? Probably not—in fact, it's fairly common. Or at least that's what I tell myself.

So, Miyamoto built The Legend of Zelda for the Famicom, with this amazing disk system that let Japanese gamers run through a massive world, save, turn off the Famicom, do their homework, then pick up right where they'd left off. And it was exactly what gamers wanted. It did very well in Japan, so of course the next thing to do was to bring Link across the ocean to America.

One small problem. Actually, make that one HUGE problem. The NES didn't have a disk drive.

There was no way for players to save their data, and The Legend of Zelda was just too big to play in a single game session. The NES itself didn't have any writable memory. The cartridges of the day couldn't handle that kind of information, and without this, playing The Legend of Zelda was nearly impossible.

So Nintendo innovated once again. For the first time ever, Nintendo went to the extra cost of adding built-in writable memory in the cartridge. They also had to add a small battery to the cartridge to power up the RAM, but it was worth it. Now The Legend of Zelda became a legend of its own by being the first console game to be able to save.

Many players today still have their original cartridge for The Legend of Zelda, but very few have a battery that has survived.

Legend of Zelda cartridge © David B. Fant

Like the games Miyamoto had done in the past, The Legend of Zelda defined a new genre. Donkey Kong launched the platformer, while Super Mario Bros. perfected the genre and added more depth. And now The Legend of Zelda was defining a genre of its own. The action RPG—or *action role-playing game.*

For the first time, players were sent on long, open-world adventures, responsible for inventories, upgrading, and searching for new items to continue quests. More than that, players could watch a character change in ability as the game progressed. Today it might sound a little simple, but back then, if you were a red-suspendered, mustached carpenter on level one of a game, you were that same red-suspendered, mustached carpenter on level 100. Zelda changed that, too.

Not only that, Miyamoto blended multiple genres in the making of The Legend of Zelda. He borrowed from the rich storytelling of games like Zork, he built upon the arcade action of Mario Bros., and he improved on the epic size and scope of projects like Activision's Pitfall!. Miyamoto had created the first action RPG, and the genre blend is one that is still thriving today.

The first Legend of Zelda game for the NES sold over one million units. At the time, that was more than any game not packed right in with the system (Duck Hunt and Mario Bros. sold more as pack-ins). The game was new and fresh, and eventually topped out at 6.5 million units sold.

In a few carefully chosen locations in the Legend of Zelda series, cryptic text could be found in the Hylian language. Gamers were told in interviews, as well as in the game itself, that the Hylian text could not be decoded. Well, gamers don't take no for an answer, and an especially diligent gamer named Sarinilli cracked the text in Skyward Sword. Thanks to this very dedicated gamer, we can now translate all the ancient Hylian in Skyward Sword.

If your hearts were fully charged in The Legend of Zelda, your sword gained a cool ability. It would fire out a flaming dart that would clobber anything in its path. This was also accompanied by a very satisfying sound, making this in-game upgrade one of the most talked-about features of the game.

The Legend of Zelda ended with quite a long list of firsts in the home video game console market.

- **The first console game to have a save feature.**

- **The first game to blend and combine genres.**

- **The first left-handed video game character (Link).**

- **The first open-world game on a console.**

- **The first console game with RPG-style items and inventory.**

All of these innovations put Link and Zelda on the video game map, and they were there to stay. They have starred or at least cameoed in seventeen titles to date, and we know that Link will be back again and again.

In 2016, Netflix announced that they are working on a Legend of Zelda series for their popular video streaming service. There are a lot of hurdles to cross before Zelda is streaming on your TV or computer, but you'd better believe gamers around the world are going to watch the progress of this one.

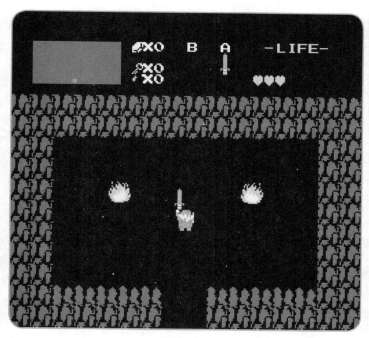

The Legend of Zelda © Nintendo

LEFTIES UNITE!

● ● ● ● ● ● ● ● ● ● ● ● ● ● ● ● ● ● ●

I know you lefties get left out (see what I did there?) all the time, but video games have got your back. Here are a few of the many famous left-handed video game characters that totally feel your pain when using right-handed scissors.

LINK from the Legend of Zelda series. The first and arguably the most famous lefty in video game history. But you can't bring up Lefty Link without mentioning that his creator, Shigeru Miyamoto, is also a lefty. Co-incidence? I'll let you be the judge.

SHEVA from Resident Evil 5. Talk about a tough woman. Don't mess with her, especially if you're a zombie.

KAIN HIGHWIND from Final Fantasy IV. A great villain that you kind of root for. He wields a massive spear with his left hand, and he's more than happy to use it on you.

MEGA MAN. Sure, his gun switches hands based on which way he's facing in the game, but he's left-handed on the box art, so this blue space junkie makes the list.

MIRANA from Dota 2 shoots her bow right, but does everything else left-handed. Even guiding around her owl-faced wolf-horse beast. What else would a Beastmaster ride?

AKIHIKO SANADA from Persona 3 is a southpaw boxer. We know for sure he's left-handed because he uses left-handed chopsticks to slurp up ramen noodles. Wait, are there left-handed chopsticks?

DISCO KID from Mike Tyson's Punch-Out!! on the Wii is a flashy, disco-loving lefty that throws a mean left hook and will drive you nuts with his left jab.

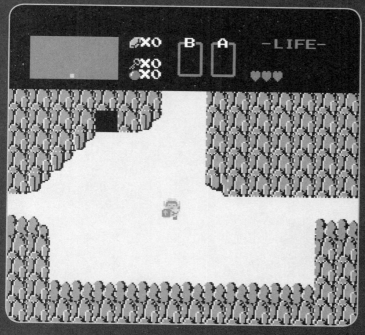

The Legend of Zelda © Nintendo

John Madden Football '93 © Electronic Arts

Everybody loves story problems in math class. Right? Well, here's one for you.

A video game executive and a Super Bowl champion coach board a train in Denver, Colorado, and head west at 85 mph. How long will it take them to design a video game series that will earn over four billion dollars and change the way gamers think of sports games forever?

The answer: eight hours and twenty-one minutes. But that's only the beginning of this story problem. And *problem* is the perfect word to describe the launch of the Madden NFL franchise.

The year was 1984, and EA's founder, Trip Hawkins, bought a train ticket from Denver, Colorado, to Oakland, California. He was sitting in a chair next to John Madden, giving him the pitch of a lifetime, and before they unpacked their bags in California, the idea for Madden Football was hatched.

Back then, before Hawkins and Madden became friends, sports games were very different. I mean, there was Pong, which was tennis—kind of. Well, that is if you squint your eyes and pretend really hard it looks like tennis. And Atari Football (1978) was a big hit in the arcades, especially in

Trip Hawkins and John Madden met on the train because of Madden's well-known fear of flying. For years Madden kept up with his hectic NFL travel schedule by way of train, until the Madden Cruiser—a very comfortable motor coach crafted for him that soon became a legend of its own.

bars and bowling alleys, but the only players you saw were painted on the side of the cabinet. The characters were nothing more than Xs vs. Os. If you didn't know you were playing football, you might confuse it with a fast-acting game of tic-tac-toe. Nintendo's 10-Yard Fight (1983) had better graphics because you actually saw players on the field, but the game play was very slow and didn't feel much like football. Hawkins wanted to fix this, and during his ride with John Madden, he convinced the coach that they could.

Now, you need to know a bit about John Madden to really get an idea for this story. Before he was head coach of the Oakland Raiders, he was a lineman. Those are the big guys that stand in front of the quarterback and try to keep the other big guys from smashing him while he gets all the glory. Yeah, it's kind of an unfair world. He was tough. REALLY tough. So tough that he took one of the worst teams in the NFL and pretty much scared them into being great. He didn't take any guff from anyone, and he only knew how to do one thing. WIN.

Well, win and eat ten-legged turkeys on Thanksgiving, but that's another story altogether.

All right, back to games.

It didn't take long at all for EA to have something they were excited to show John Madden. Partly because they were excited and really good at their jobs, but mostly because they had already started building the game before Hawkins had pitched it to Madden. A few short months after the train ride, Hawkins called up his new buddy and invited him to visit them in their studio in California. A limo was booked, lunch was planned, and the gruff, demanding coach was on his way.

Hawkins knew that Madden would be pleased, and he had already pictured selling John Madden in stores across America in 1985! Everything was working out perfectly.

That was, until Madden saw the game and flipped out.

Sure, there was green grass. There were players. There was even crowd noise and a referee. There were hash marks on the field, and music, and there were players wearing helmets and not just Xs or Os zooming around. But there were problems, too. John Madden's favorite part of the entire football experience had been left out.

There were no LINEMEN!

That's right. The computers of the day were pretty great for their time, but the Apple II that they showed Madden his new game on wasn't fast enough to display eleven players per team. EA had to reduce it to seven players per team, and you can't delete the quarterback. He'd call his agent and be traded to a new team before the game loaded. EA had decided to cut the linemen to make room for the flashier players.

Madden was not pleased, and before the meeting was over any thoughts Hawkins had of launching the game in 1985 had been punted.

But this didn't discourage Hawkins. In fact, it encouraged him. Okay, sure, getting the game out early would have been cool, but getting the game right was more important to Hawkins, and he knew now more than ever that John Madden was the perfect partner. The coach expected perfection, and that was exactly what Trip Hawkins wanted, too.

So, they went back to the drawing table. Or the design table, I guess. Madden went back to broadcasting NFL games on TV, and EA went back to making games. Each year for the next three years, EA presented their game to Madden, and each year they got a step closer, but they weren't quite there.

They added four more players per team, but that wasn't enough.

They added realistic plays and formations, most of which came directly from John Madden's very own playbook, but that wasn't enough.

They added weather conditions so you could play in the cold, rain, snow, and blazing sun, but THAT wasn't enough.

They added better crowd noise, player noises—even the tone of the referee's whistle was argued over and tuned until it sounded perfect.

If it was on the field of an NFL game, Hawkins and Madden wanted it in the computer game.

It took them three years, countless hours of game development, and visit after visit with John Madden, but in 1988, John Madden Football finally hit the shelves, and fans lined up.

In follow-up meetings with Madden, he shocked EA by bringing along his official playbook. He wanted to make sure EA understood the difference between a goal line and a dive play, and this attention to detail is what really set EA on the track to stardom.

If you add up all Madden sales, it has sold more copies than Zelda, Halo, and even Pac-Man. Over 100 million copies sold to date. If you could stack them up end to end, it would make a line long enough to reach from the EA office in Orlando, Florida, to Greece and back.

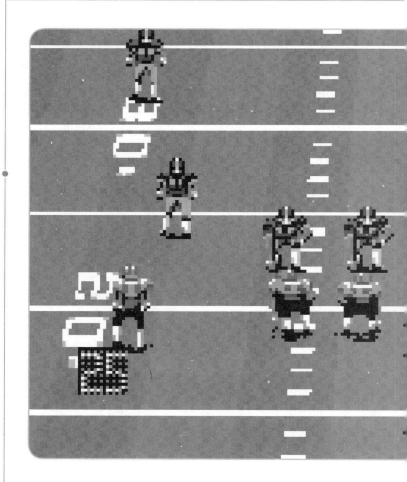

John Madden Football launched in 1988 for MS-DOS, Commodore 64, and Apple II, with Madden's smiling face right there to welcome you in. And in true Madden fashion, the game was a winner with a long list of firsts that have stood the test of time. Things like:

- **The first sports game to feature weather conditions that actually had an impact on the game. You could play in the hot sun, rain, snow, or cold and wind.**

- **The first game to allow you to choose how long you**

John Madden Football '93 © Electronic Arts

wanted to play. Quarter length could be eight, ten, twelve, or fifteen minutes.

- The first game to offer player fatigue. Your players would actually run slower or make more mistakes if they were tired.

- Not the first game to allow injuries, but the first to allow you to turn them off, along with penalties. Which made for some awesome and crazy matchups, let me tell you that.

- The first annual game to be aligned with a sports season. Players soon counted on the next version of Madden coming out every year.

- And while the game didn't have the NFL license, EA was pretty sneaky about putting in teams and players that were recognizable. Teams like the "Eighters" from San Francisco that looked just like the San Francisco 49ers, and players with initials like JR, the wide receiver, and JM, the quarterback. But the real innovation here was the addition of a BLANK team that allowed you to create any team you wanted and name it whatever you'd like.

The game wasn't the best sports game of all time, but it was good enough to kick off a franchise that is still killing it today. And that wasn't all Trip Hawkins had in mind. He wanted more than just John Madden—he wanted the entire NFL. And the NFL players. He'd felt that having the actual players and NFL franchises was the key to having long-term success in the sports gaming world, and he was willing to bet the future of his company on making this happen. Unfortunately for EA, getting the NFL to agree that it was a good idea was more difficult than taking your flag football team to the Super Bowl.

It took EA a few years to get the NFL involved. In fact, it wasn't until 1994, ten years after Trip Hawkins and John Madden boarded that train in Denver, Colorado, that you could play as an official NFL team, but once it happened there was no looking back.

Before long not only were kids across the country playing the game, NFL players were playing it, too. And EA followed up the game two years later on the SEGA Genesis and SNES, which took sports gaming from the arcades and personal computers and dropped it right on the very same TV gamers used to watch football.

Sports and video games were a perfect match—nearly as perfect a match as EA and John Madden.

EA not only launched the genre of sports simulation, they perfected it. They took what they learned with John

NFL players also love playing the game, and some have used it as a training tool. With under a minute to go in the first game of the 2009 NFL season, the Denver Broncos' wide receiver Brandon Stokley made a great catch at the goal line with only a few seconds to spare. Instead of jumping into the end zone, Stokley turned and toed the goal line, draining six seconds off the clock to make it harder for the Bengals to mount a comeback. Later, in the postgame press conference, Stokley admitted he had learned the trick from playing Madden.

Madden and pumped it into every sport, from cricket to FIFA, and in every sport, if it's in the game—it's IN THE GAME.

Well, not everything is in the game. The NFL has asked EA to focus on the ideal football experience when presenting their product to the fans. This means toning down over-the-top touchdown celebrations that would get flagged in real life, and reducing impacts on tackles that might cause concussions. Also, the NFL asked EA to take out a fan favorite a few years back by having them remove the ambulance. Starting in 1992, when a player was injured, an ambulance would zoom on field, pushing (running over) healthy players out of the way to help the injured. It was a lighthearted feature, and while it was a fan favorite, it wasn't the most sensitive approach to an injury. The ambulance last appeared in 2001.

Not only has EA built the best football simulator on the planet, they have even used their simulation engine to predict the Super Bowl winners at a crazy-high rate. How high, you ask? High enough you'd swear they can see the future.

Between 2004 and 2013, EA ran a full-season simulation before the first kickoff to predict the winner of each Super Bowl. They nailed it seven out of nine times. That's better than most Vegas bookies can do, by far.

Their closest call was in 2009. Madden predicted the Steelers 28 vs. the Cardinals 24, and in real life the Steelers ended up with 27, while the Cardinals scored 23. That's only two points off. To make it even more impressive, that year Madden NFL also predicted the exact number of receiving yards (131) for the Steelers' Santonio Holmes.

THE MADDEN CURSE

We all know that the Madden NFL franchise has been a major hit for EA and gamers alike, but it hasn't all been touchdown celebrations and Super Bowl parties. Madden has had its fair share of fumbles along the way.

For the first decade of the game, John Madden himself was on the cover of every game. Then along came Garrison Hearst, and a new, unexpected tradition was born. And when I say *tradition*, I really mean *curse*.

In 1998, the first NFL player replaced John Madden on the cover of his own game. Garrison Hearst was racking up yards for the San Francisco 49ers, and EA knew that putting the fan favorite NFL player on the cover would increase sales. Madden agreed, but unfortunately the football gods did not.

Before he even stepped a foot on the field that season, Madden's new cover boy broke his ankle. He didn't play a single minute for the NFL while he was on the cover of the game, so EA decided to go with the one and only Barry Sanders for their next cover. He was unstoppable, and one of the healthiest players in NFL history.

It wasn't an injury that kept Barry Sanders from playing this time. Out of nowhere, Sanders decided to hang up his cleats and retire from the NFL, becoming the second Madden NFL cover boy to never play a down after securing the cover. And thus, the Madden curse was born.

Of the next eighteen NFL players to be showcased on the cover of EA's Madden, seventeen have had season-ending injuries or other strange things that have kept them off the field soon after they appeared on the Madden NFL cover. There are theories about why this has happened, like all-star players pushing themselves too hard and causing injuries, but you'll have to be the judge. Seventeen out of eighteen is a pretty high number to just be a coincidence.

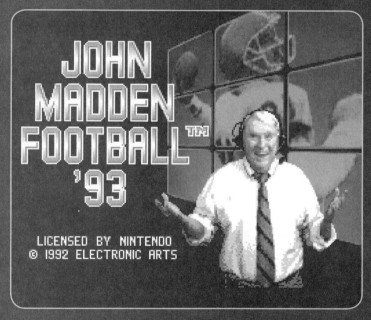

Title Screen featuring John Madden from John Madden Football '93 © Electronic Arts

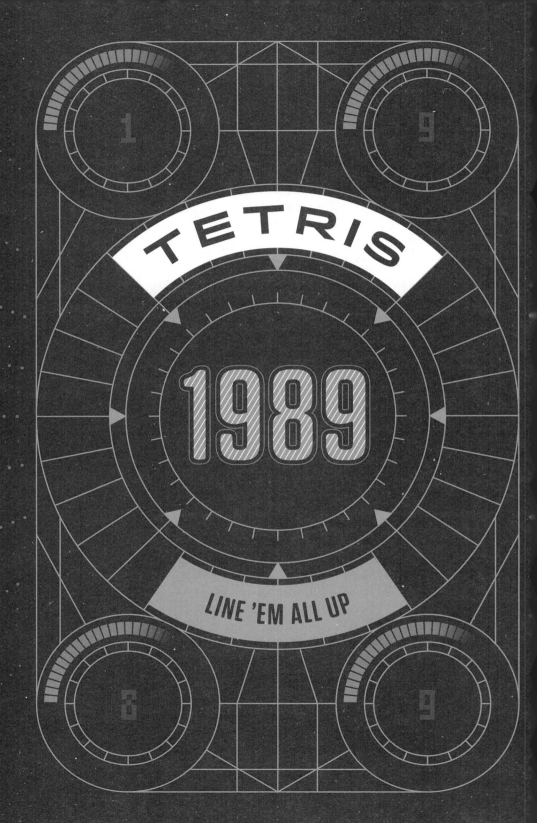

Tetris © Nintendo

Nintendo didn't invent handheld gaming, but they sure showed everyone how to do it right.

In 1989, the NES was the undisputed champion of video game consoles, and Mario was on the cover of every video game magazine out there. Gamers were loving what Nintendo was cooking up, and the Japanese video game company was starting to be known outside of the video game circle. *Inside Edition*, the number two TV news program at the time, did a five-minute segment on Nintendo, then ABC News, the number one TV news program, outdid them by doing a ten-minute piece about how crazy fans were to get their hands on new games.

For the first time, families were starting to have more than one TV in the house, so parents could watch *Seinfeld* while their kids hung out in Mushroom Kingdom.

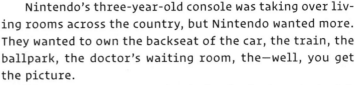

Nintendo's three-year-old console was taking over living rooms across the country, but Nintendo wanted more. They wanted to own the backseat of the car, the train, the ballpark, the doctor's waiting room, the—well, you get the picture.

They turned to Gunpei Yokoi, who had worked with Miyamoto on games like Mario Bros. and Super Mario Bros. and who was the lead designer on Duck Hunt. They asked him to help solve the problem, and his solution was a black-and-white handheld gaming system called Game Boy. It was bulky and pretty boring on the outside, earning it the nickname "the Gray Brick," but Yokoi's Game Boy was exactly what Nintendo was looking for. Now all they needed was the perfect game to help sell their new handheld console. Who knew they'd end up traveling to Russia to find what they were looking for?

The Game Boy was the first game system played in space. In 1993, Russian cosmonaut Aleksandr Serebrov blasted off for a trip to the Mir Space Station with his trusty Game Boy in the pocket of his spacesuit. Of course he brought along a copy of Tetris, and the trusty handheld spent a total of 196 days in space, orbiting our little blue planet over three thousand times. The very Game Boy Serebrov took along for the ride sold at an auction for $1,220.

Nintendo Game Boy © Evan Amos

The game they were after, even if they didn't know it at the time, was a puzzle game featuring a sound track based on a 100-year-old folk song, falling bricks, and zero mustached plumbers. Not your typical Nintendo product, but Tetris did have something in common with previous Nintendo greats. It was SUPER addicting.

At first, the power players at Nintendo wanted something more Mario-ish. They knew that Mario would sell a console; he'd done it before. But a man by the name of Henk Rogers had been playing Tetris on his personal computer for years, and he could see the addicting awesomeness inside. He's the one who convinced Nintendo to take a chance with one simple argument: If Nintendo wanted to sell the Game Boy to kids, pack in Super Mario World. If they wanted to sell the Game Boy to every man, woman, child, and puzzle-solving chimpanzee, pack in Tetris.

Alexey Pajitnov, a Russian engineer, made the game to show non-computer nerds that computers were actually fun AND easy to use. And he nailed it, because the game was simple. Bricks called tetrominoes fall from the top of the screen, and the player rotates them, then drops them into spaces to pack them in as tightly as possible. If a full line is filled in across the screen, the line will disappear, leaving more room for more blocks. Simple.

Remember, these were the days when the original *Teenage Mutant Ninja Turtles* action figures were considered high-tech toys because you could bend their elbows AND their knees. And computers were pretty much thought of as two things—expensive typewriters, or scary machines that only glasses-wearing software engineers could control.

Pajitnov wanted everyone to start loving computers as much as he did, so he thought making a game was the way to get them interested. Two years before Tetris found its way to the Game Boy, Pajitnov made a PC version while working at the Soviet Academy of Sciences (now the Russian Academy of Sciences). And as it turned out, at the time, when you made a game while living in the Soviet Union, it belonged to the Soviet Union. No exceptions. So the thought of Tetris being a big success, let alone something that could make him enough money to build his

The seven pieces that fall from the top in Tetris are called tetrominoes. Each tetromino is made out of exactly four small blocks, and each has a letter-based name that defines its shape—O, I, S, Z, L, J, and T.

Tetris © Nintendo

"Korobeiniki," the Tetris theme song, is a nineteenth-century Russian folk song. However, the song is more widely known now as the Tetris theme song, rather than "Korobeiniki." Partly because of Tetris's success, but mostly because nobody outside Russia can pronounce the word.

own empire, never crossed his mind. Pajitnov decided to give the game away for free to his friends and colleagues.

And as is often the case in gaming, when something is really great it has a way of spreading. Before you could say *borscht*, one of Pajitnov's coworkers shared Tetris with a family member in Hungary. Next thing you know, someone made an Apple IIe version of the game and was showing it at a trade show in Budapest. A man named Robert Stein saw Tetris at the trade show and thought the game was GREAT.

So, without finding out who owned Tetris, Robert Stein began selling the rights to make Tetris all around the world. For those of you keeping track, that's called stealing.

Basically, Stein created fake deals and contracts with unsuspecting companies who thought he owned the rights to Tetris. Companies like Microsoft, Atari, and Spectrum HoloByte. He was basically trying to sell the rights to make Tetris to as many companies as possible before Russia found out that he was selling their property and had him sent on a cold train to Siberia.

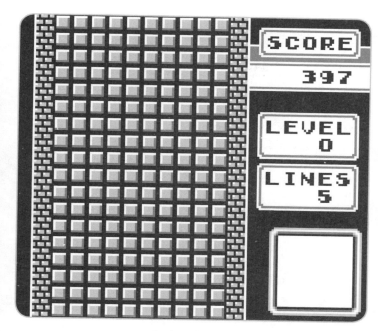

Tetris © Nintendo

The companies Robert Stein "sold" the rights to began selling *their* rights away, and before anyone could organize a four-line Tetris, the game had spread across the globe. The whole thing became a gigantic mess. By the time anyone actually tracked down who owned what, Tetris had already become the bestselling PC game in the UK and in America.

This is how guys like Henk Rogers got to know the game, and when he showed Nintendo how fun it was and how successful it had become, it was pretty easy to talk them into giving it a shot. And in 1989, Nintendo shipped their Game Boy with Tetris packed right in. The game, and the Game Boy, were overnight successes.

The game was doing great, but Rogers and Nintendo wanted to make things right, and they knew the only way to do it was to get a meeting with the officials in Russia and cut them in on the deal. So Henk Rogers and Nintendo showed up in Russia with the game in hand, literally, and they showed it to the Russian officials.

They were not pleased. In fact, they had no idea the Game Boy even existed, and here was their game helping make the system a worldwide phenomenon. Nintendo thought they owned the rights, but they had been duped by Stein, just like everybody else. So to make up for their mistake, Nintendo pulled out their checkbook and wrote Russia a big, fat check to pay for back royalties.

Russia was so impressed by Nintendo's honesty that they granted them exclusive rights to all handheld and console games on the spot. Now, not only could Nintendo continue to ship Tetris with the Game Boy, they could keep competitors from putting Tetris on their consoles as well. See? It pays to be the good guy.

The Game Boy went on to be the bestselling handheld device ever. That is, until it was knocked off the top of the hill by its little brother, the Nintendo DS. And Tetris went on to become the most widely ported game in the history of video games, appearing on over seventy gaming platforms and still counting.

And Tetris hasn't just appeared in the gaming world; it's pretty much everywhere you look. There's a good chance your dad has returned from the grocery store and stacked the cereal in the cupboard perfectly, then said something like, "I've always been good at Tetris." Tetris has been on everything from TV to T-shirts. Here are a few examples of Tetris invading television.

1. **Human Tetris.** There is a HILARIOUS Japanese game show that has an event called Human Tetris. Large blocks of foam zoom down a conveyor belt and the player has to shape their body like a tetromino to squeeze through a hole in the foam or get knocked off the platform.

2. *Futurama.* This FOX animated cartoon from the late 1990s featured Tetris in a very funny way. Fry and Leela (the stars of the show) had traveled to a bot planet, and in one scene a robot was trying to build a wall with tetrominoes, but he was too good at his job. Every

Tetris fans in Philadelphia played the game on a 437-foot skyscraper in 2014 in a stunning stunt, creating the world's largest game of Tetris. The event was created by game designer Frank Lee. The world's smallest version of Tetris was played on an electron microscope using forty-two glass microspheres as the tetrominoes.

time the wall was nearly complete, he'd fill in a line and the wall would disappear.

3. *The Simpsons.* In an episode from 2003, Homer uses Tetris block-stacking tricks to get his family's stuff packed into the car. "This is what all those hours of playing Tetris were for," he says before stuffing his family in the car as well.

All the pieces were falling into place for Nintendo and Tetris, but what ever happened to Alexey Pajitnov, the creator of Tetris in the first place?

Well, it took over ten years for Pajitnov to receive any money for his massive worldwide hit. But he's been quoted many times saying he was fine with it in the end, because his goal was accomplished. Everyone who played Tetris learned that the game was addicting and—more important—that computers were nothing to be scared of.

A game like Tetris comes around only once in a lifetime, but it stays around forever. My guess is that long after we've all stopped playing Assassin's Creed, we'll still sneak in a few games of Tetris every year.

The sales of the Game Boy weren't the only thing that went to extremes. In 1990, an American soldier's Game Boy withstood an explosion during a bombing raid. The Game Boy's case melted, but it still operated just fine. In fact, it still runs today and is on display at the Nintendo store in New York City.

Melted Game Boy on display at Nintendo Store © Lordcolus

GAMES FOR BRAINS

• • • • • • • • • • • • • • • • •

Tetris became such a huge hit that it jumped the gap from being just a game to becoming a part of our everyday lives. In fact, it is proven that simply playing Tetris can improve our brains and maybe even make us thinner!

Yup. You heard that right. Playing Tetris can make you thin and smart!

In 2009, research journal *BioMed Central* published a paper that proved that playing Tetris for thirty minutes a day increases the thickness of the gray matter in your brain. This gray matter increases the flexibility of the brain and leads to more cognitive thinking and reduces episodes or flashbacks of traumatic experiences. In other words, playing Tetris for as long as it takes to clean your bedroom makes your brain bigger!

This led researchers to implement Tetris playing for soldiers returning from war, and it had a very positive effect in reducing post-traumatic stress disorder.

In a separate test, conducted by England's Plymouth University, researchers found that playing Tetris for as little as three minutes before eating reduces cravings by 24 percent. It's like the anti-couch potato. Who knew playing games could make you lose weight?

Oh, now you want to give it a try. Fine. There is a free version of my personal favorite version of Tetris online. Go ahead, search for "Tetris-Nintendo NES" online and you'll find a full, official emulator ready to help you grow your gray matter.

SONIC THE HEDGEHOG

1991

SO FAST, YOU'LL NEED A BARF BAG

Sonic the Hedgehog © SEGA

Things were going well for Nintendo as the 1980s wrapped up. So well, in fact, that nine out of every ten dollars spent on home video games went to Nintendo. But 1990 was a new decade, and SEGA wanted to get into the mix.

They had already launched a console in Japan, the SEGA Mega Drive, a couple of years earlier, but it wasn't the hit they had hoped for. It was faster, had better graphics than the NES, and had a slick new controller that fans seemed to like, but they were missing something . . . something like Mario.

SEGA needed a mascot, and they needed one FAST!

So, they tossed the challenge to their employees to come up with a new mascot character for the SEGA Genesis, and the employees responded. There were a lot of entries, everything from a pajama-wearing rabbit to an evil clown, but the one that caught everyone's attention was a bright blue, spiky hedgehog with red running shoes named Mr. Needlemouse.

We learned from the comic books that Sonic's blue coloring is actually the result of a science lab experiment gone wrong. His brown spines turned blue after Sonic ran faster than the speed of light. Later, the evil scientist, Dr. Ivo Robotnik, invented the now-famous bright red, frictionless Power Sneakers, which allowed Sonic to run even faster.

Originally, Sonic and his band were supposed to do a sound check when you started up the SEGA Genesis. There were plans for a fully animated sequence to show off Sonic's break-dancing skills and introduce you to his friends and the cast of characters. One of these characters was a bass-playing crocodile named Vector. Vector later showed up in a few Sonic games, including Knuckles Chaotix and Sonic Heroes, where he was a fully playable character.

Yup, that's right. Sonic the Hedgehog's original name was Mr. Needlemouse.

Mr. Needlemouse was the brainchild of SEGA artist Noato Oshima. And by the time SEGA asked for concepts for their new mascot, he was already prepared. He'd been sketching Mr. Needlemouse for quite a long time. In fact, he'd been doing it so often that he got into a little trouble with his boss, who had been telling Oshima for more than a year to stop goofing around with his hedgehog and get back to work. But Oshima was so sure that Mr. Needlemouse was the next mascot for SEGA, he talked his boss into helping him with the hedgehog rather than reporting him for slacking off.

His boss, Yuji Naka, took a bit of convincing, but after spending some time with the little blue hedgehog, Naka fell in love with him, too, and the two game developers started right in on Sonic like it was already a real project.

When the time came to present the ideas to SEGA, most presenters showed sketches and drawings of their characters, but Oshima and Naka were WAY beyond that point. Not only did they have beautiful drawings of Sonic, they had a backstory, plush toys, stickers, and homemade marketing material to hand out to the decision makers. It was a slam dunk. Everyone loved Sonic, and they gave Oshima and Naka a large team and plenty of time to make a blockbuster title.

Oshima and Naka knew that their new game had to be different from Mario in every way possible, and they also knew they had the hardware to pull it off. Naka squeezed every bit of performance out of the new SEGA Genesis, as the team of artists animated Sonic through his colorful world environment at speeds so fast even Superman would have had a hard time catching up.

Within a few short months, the game was ready to try, and when the SEGA of America marketing team came over to play the game, they realized immediately that they had a hit on their hands. However, there was one small problem. The game was so fast that most of the first-time players got motion sickness. At first this worried Oshima and Naka, but they knew that speed was what would set them apart, and they also knew that gamers would get used to the fast graphics.

A few chapters back we talked about The Legend of Zelda needing to have a special cartridge to save the game on the NES. Well, nearly five years later, this was STILL a problem. Aside from Zelda, no other NES game shipped with the special cartridge, and the SEGA was going to face the same problem. It didn't allow players to save the game when the console was turned off.

This meant you had to beat the game in one sitting. Because of this, players replayed the early levels of games hundreds of times before they could get everything right. As a result, gamers became very good at the early levels of the games they played most, and Naka and Oshima took advantage of this by using Sonic's speed to allow players who had memorized levels to burst through and move on to new areas in the game like a blue speeding bullet! It really was the birth of speed running, a competitive technique that became very popular ten years later, where gamers try to beat entire games in record times.

Sonic's amazing speed and the polished graphics of the SEGA Genesis were right on track to zoom into the hearts of gamers around the world, but SEGA knew that all the slick game play and fancy graphics would be nothing without music to match. They went after Japanese boy band singing sensation Masato Nakamura, and he jumped at the chance.

Nakamura was a natural, composing unique and memorable tunes for each of the worlds in Sonic the Hedgehog. His music went on to inspire Naka and Oshima, pushing them to make things a bit more edgy, and yes—even *faster* than it had been before.

The game was nearly ready, SEGA of Japan and SEGA of America were aligned on how to make it a hit, and it was time to present the launch plan to the head cheese of SEGA, Hayao Nakayama. The problem was, the plan to beat Nintendo was a risky one, and Nakayama was known for being a hard guy to please.

To keep our timeline in perspective, the NES had been a huge hit, the SEGA Mega Drive was bombing in Japan,

While in the title sequence of Sonic the Hedgehog, you can press down-down-down-left-right-A to unlock a series of illustrated screens. Some of them are totally normal, like the first-ever-seen image of Tails informing players that he'll see them in Sonic 2, and an illustration of Sonic with gray metallic eyes with "You are cool!" written in Japanese. But there are some strange images in there as well, including a bizarre tribute to Batman and an image of distorted Sonics, lined up behind an antipiracy slogan. Still, it's a fun unlock and one worth checking out. Especially if you can read Japanese.

and just to make things worse, Nintendo was launching the Super Nintendo Entertainment System (SNES) a few months before SEGA was ready to ship Sonic and the Genesis in the United States. SEGA had to make a big splash, but the SNES boasted more colors on-screen and a faster processor. They also had a new Mario game, Super Mario World, which was already getting a ton of press.

Nintendo also had deep pockets and was willing to spend ten times what SEGA could afford to get their new machine in the hands of gamers. The cards were stacked against SEGA from the start, but SEGA of America had a plan.

Go head-to-head against Nintendo. Be young, aggressive, and a bit punky about it. Oh, and give the game away.

WHAT?

Yup, for FREE.

SEGA knew they had to sell a ton of hardware, because if the console wasn't out there, Sonic would never have a chance. A young marketing genius named Tom Kalinske had a plan, he just had to get it in front of SEGA CEO Hayao Nakayama. A meeting was scheduled, and Kalinske presented his plan. His crazy, brave, perhaps career-ending plan.

While the SNES was selling well at $199, the SEGA was set to launch for $189. Kalinske didn't think that was low enough, so he suggested that they drop the price to $149. But wait, that's not all! He also wanted to bundle SEGA's speedy new mascot's game with the system and STILL beat Nintendo's price by fifty bucks.

Hayao Nakayama was not impressed. In fact, he stood up at the end of the presentation and yelled at Kalinske, telling him that SEGA made their money on software and he was foolish for wanting to give away their best game EVER for FREE. Kalinske stood firm. Then Nakayama threw his chair against the door. No joke! And after that, Kalinske started to worry that he'd never work for SEGA again.

Nakayama was so angry that he walked toward the very door he'd just clobbered with his chair. Just before he exited, Nakayama turned to Kalinske and told him he had hired him to build SEGA into a massive gaming system, and that if he thought that giving Sonic away was the way to do it, he had his support.

Turns out, Kalinske was right.

Sonic was a massive hit, and the SEGA Genesis was a great system for such a good price. So good, in fact, that the SEGA Genesis became the second-best-selling console of the early 1990s.

SEGA Genesis © Evan Amos

Not only was he the fastest video game character at the time, but Sonic went on to break new ground over and over again.

- Sonic was the first video game character to partner with McDonald's. Over fifty million Sonic Happy Meal toys have been handed out worldwide.

- Sonic the Hedgehog 2 became the first video game to have a worldwide release on the same day—a day they called Sonic Twosday, and for the first time ever, gamers lined up outside video game retailers to wait for a midnight release.

- When SEGA introduced the SEGA Dreamcast, Sonic Adventures introduced gamers to DLC, or downloadable content, for the first time. They released expansions from day one, but the one that sticks out in gamers' minds was a pack called "Christmas in Station Square," which allowed you to sit beneath a massive Christmas

Part of what makes Sonic so fun is his personality. He's not only fast and loves to celebrate when he wins a level, he's also very impatient. If the player puts down the controller, it only takes a few seconds before Sonic will stare right at the screen, cross his arms, and start tapping his toe. If the player ignores Sonic for three minutes, he'll say, "I'm out of here." Then he'll jump off the screen, giving the player a Game Over, regardless of how many lives the player has at the time. Yeah, he's a pushy little hedgehog.

tree while listening to a Boyz II Men a capella song called "Dreams" that was included on the sound track.

· Sonic was the first video game character to have a balloon in the Macy's Thanksgiving Day parade, appearing in 1993. Unfortunately, things didn't turn out so hot for Sonic that day, as the massive balloon collided with a telephone pole that ripped a hole in it and caused it to crash to the ground. Two people were injured in the accident, a child and a police officer, so SEGA retired the balloon after one attempt. In 2011, Sonic returned to the famous parade and sailed through without a hitch.

Sonic has gone on to sell over seventy million units and star in sixty-five games on both SEGA and Nintendo consoles. He was also the star of his own animated cartoon, and was the leading hedgehog in the longest-running comic book series based on a video game character. The comic book series ran for over twenty years and is highly collected today. Sonic still has a huge fan following, and the Sonic games hold up great.

The character who started out as Mr. Needlemouse on the desk of an artist in Japan ended up running full speed into the hearts of gamers, where he still lives today. I know he lives in mine.

EVERY HERO NEEDS A VILLAIN

There's no doubt Sonic was one of the all-time great video game mascots. He had great speed, he was spunky, and he had cool shoes, but what really made Sonic cool was defeating the evil Dr. Ivo "Eggman" Robotnik.

I remember doing that for the first time when I was young(er), and it was SO SATISFYING to finally knock him out of the sky. So I got to thinking, what are the most satisfying villains to pummel in video game history, and I came up with my top ten list. I wonder how close it is to yours.

10. M. Bison from Street Fighter II

In true villain form, this tough guy wants to take over the world. Not only does M. Bison have an awesome blue cloak, rippling muscles, and "Psycho Power," but he can take a punch, or fifty. Who's counting? You always know when you start a Street Fighter game that M. Bison is waiting for you, and when you finally knock him out you feel like a champion.

9. Sephiroth from Final Fantasy VII

This villain is only part human, being that he had alien DNA injected into him when he was a baby. He is a master swordsman with sweet hair, and his calm personality only makes him more terrifying. It also helps that his theme song will give you the chills.

8. Arthas Menethil from World of Warcraft and Warcraft III

There's something great about a villain that used to be a righteous hero. Especially if we get to watch him fall from greatness. You knew things were falling apart when he slew his own father, which made him the Lich King. I'll bet Father's Day around his house is a drag.

7. The Joker from Arkham Asylum

The voice. That laugh. Those awful purple pants! And don't get me started on that smug smile and green hair. Few things feel as good as being Batman, but clobbering the Joker while you're Batman is the best!

6. Dark Link

When your enemy knows your every thought and can copy all your moves, it makes them super-hard to destroy. When they look like the nightmare version of you, well, let's just say it can get a little creepy.

5. Team Rocket from the Pokémon series

Oh man, do I even have to say it? These annoying siblings are just BEGGING to be shut up. Not to mention they perform tests on their Pokémons to make them stronger. Now, that's just wrong.

4. Dr. Robotnik

Maybe I have him a bit high on the list, but I'm blaming that mustache! That or the fact that he's always trying to blow stuff up or turn Sonic into a Werehog. Whatever it is, beating the Eggman is always worth it.

3. Bowser

Every evil reptile in the history of the world looks up to Bowser. He's covered in spikes, he's probably wanted for arson and kidnapping, and whether you're crossing the finish line first in Mario Kart or knocking him out in Mushroom Kingdom, you leave the game feeling a true hero.

2. GLaDOS from Portal

There's nothing quite like the calming voice of GLaDOS to totally lull you into more trouble than you can handle. She sounds so kind, motherly even, but she'll do anything she can to ruin your day. No other villain on this list will sing to you, promise you baked goods, tell you jokes, then laugh as you meet your demise.

1. Ganon/Ganondorf from the Zelda series

He is definitely my number one. Partly because he's dark and mysterious, but mostly because he's stood the test of time. It's been over twenty years, and Ganon is still creepy. He'll stop at nothing to control Hyrule, and there is just something great about going in with your humble weapons and green tunic and taking down the armored man with his massive sword.

So, what do you think? How close did I hit the top ten of your all-time baddies?

Street Fighter II © Capcom

In 1985, a young hotshot artist, Akira Yasuda, showed up to a job interview in his pajamas and a tie.

He had left his portfolio at home, which didn't seem like a problem to him because he said that fans stole his work all the time anyway because he was just THAT good. When his interviewers asked him why he'd worn his pajamas, he said it was because he wanted to look his best, and his pajama top was the only shirt he had with a collar.

Capcom developer Yoshiki Okamoto was sitting on the other side of the table with a smile on his face, because he knew he'd just found his new artist. Yasuda was exactly the type of guy he was looking for. Eccentric, not worried about taking things seriously, and extremely talented.

Yasuda got the job.

Little did Okamoto know at the time, but he was building a team that five years later would make the most influential and popular fighting game of all time, Street Fighter II: The World Warrior.

Probably the most recognizable special move in Street Fighter II is the hadouken. It's a move that Ryu and Ken use to "force push" their enemy back with a ball of energy. It has become so popular that the Internet is filled with hadouken memes. Check them out. Heck, make your own. It's fun! Everyone should feel that kind of power now and again!

If Okamoto were a character in his own video game, he would have been named "The Prankster." He had a reputation not only for being a very smart, creative leader for Capcom, but also for being a legendary joker. For example, one time a fellow Capcom employee fell asleep in a meeting, and Okamoto quietly set the clock in the room ahead to three o'clock in the morning, then told all the people in the meeting to sneak out. When the poor guy woke up, he thought he'd slept for HOURS and the team acted like he'd missed some very important news.

As you can tell by the *II* that follows Street Fighter, this game wasn't the first fighting game ever made. In fact, if you made a list of every fighting game ever made, Street Fighter II would fall somewhere in the middle. It's an old genre, with a ton of games, both in the arcade and on home consoles. But until Okamoto assembled his team of talented (and sometimes a bit loony) developers, fighting games were small potatoes compared to what they are now.

So, what changed it all, you might ask? And if you didn't ask that, you should, because it's a good question. Well, let me tell you. In a nutshell, what changed it was a team of creative geniuses who weren't afraid to make a mistake. They were brave. Not like fireman, police officer, and middle school science teacher kind of brave, but "I'll just go ahead and wear pj's to a job interview" kind of brave.

Before Street Fighter, fighting games were basically one-on-one matches where you squared off against an opponent with the same fighting abilities as you. You stood toe to toe and took turns punching and kicking until one of you had had enough. That was pretty much it. One button punch, one button kick, and a bit of dodging here and there.

Well, Capcom's Street Fighter introduced something totally different by offering players not just one punch button and a joystick, but six buttons. A soft, medium, and hard punch, and a soft, medium, and hard kick. They also added a cast of unique characters that you had to fight, each with a unique set of moves and skills that they would throw at you to keep the game fresh.

It's important to know these two things, the complicated six-button controls and the unique characters, because they are the only things that remained from that early Street Fighter. Even the team that built Street Fighter evaporated after it hit the arcades.

Okay, now that you're caught up, it's back to Street Fighter II and the guy that Capcom put in charge, Yoshiki Okamoto.

Okamoto and his team set to building a game right away. They liked—actually, LOVED—Street Fighter, and they couldn't wait to get Ken and Ryu back in action. However, instead of continuing on where Street Fighter left off with its one-on-one fighting style, they made a game in the other popular fighting game style at the time. They built a side-scroller fighting game.

Capcom did not approve, but they liked the team and the game enough to give them another shot.

So, the team went back to the design room and took a deep look at what they could add to or change in Street Fighter to make Street Fighter II the best game they could dream up. It took time, but eventually what they designed changed fighting games forever, and the rules they established are still the standard for fighting games to this day.

- Street Fighter II was the first fighting game to allow you to fight in multiple fighting styles. Everything from boxing to Brazilian capoeira was covered as the player traveled around the world to fight opponents on every continent.

The first game the Street Fighter II team created hit the arcades as Final Fight. A side-scrolling street brawler that didn't feel, look, or even smell like Street Fighter. However, the game was still fairly successful, and is now a highly collected stand-up arcade machine.

Street Fighter II © Capcom

- Street Fighter II had the first character selection menu in a fighting game. No, seriously. Before SFII,

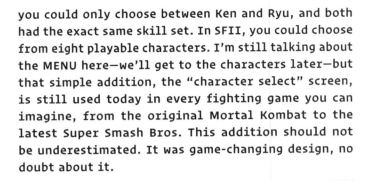

you could only choose between Ken and Ryu, and both had the exact same skill set. In SFII, you could choose from eight playable characters. I'm still talking about the MENU here—we'll get to the characters later—but that simple addition, the "character select" screen, is still used today in every fighting game you can imagine, from the original Mortal Kombat to the latest Super Smash Bros. This addition should not be underestimated. It was game-changing design, no doubt about it.

- Not only could you select your character in Street Fighter II, each character you selected was unique and had his or her (or its—not really sure what Blanka is) own player controls. While most of the controls were shared across all characters, the timing and how you defended, fought, and used your special moves was unique for each character. This made the game superaddicting, because once you mastered Chun-Li, you could drop in another 100 quarters to learn the yoga fighting style of Dhalsim. Once again, other games quickly borrowed this design idea and STILL borrow it today.

- The game was a button masher with a lot of depth. By this I mean, anybody could drop in a quarter and slam the six buttons, wiggle the joystick back and forth, and have a pretty great time. On the surface, the game was super easy. But the more you played Street Fighter II, the more you learned about the game. Complicated special moves could be fired off by each character, and if you got the timing down just right, you could pull off some unreal combo moves that not only looked cool as HECK, but would totally destroy your opponent.

- Street Fighter II was the first fighting game to add a deep backstory to each of its characters. Guile was a former United States Air Force special forces dude who was seeking revenge against the guy who killed his best friend, Charlie. The man who killed Charlie is one of the Grand Masters you face at the end of the game if you defeat all the other playable characters. His name is M. Bison, and he's a ruthless killer bent on taking over the world. Knowing this story makes beating M. Bison at the end even more satisfying, and that is just one example. There's an equally deep story for each character in the game.

As you can see, fighting game fans owe a ton to Street Fighter II. It revolutionized fighting games forever. Street Fighter II is still Capcom's most profitable arcade game today, raking in over thirty-five million bucks so far and still counting.

The game, which was a huge success in arcades, went on to find its way to home consoles. When Street Fighter II hit the Super Nintendo in 1992, the game was a hit as well. But that was only the beginning. Street Fighter II: The World Warrior went on to ship on every console in the 1990s, then continued on to multiple generations, shipping on the PS2 and the Xbox, and the Wii U virtual console. And I'm not talking about other games in the Street Fighter series (there are simply too many of those to cover), I'm JUST talking about Street Fighter II, a game made in 1991 that is still being ported to this generation's consoles. It's just that good.

They say that the best houses are built on good foundations, and since the foundation of fighting games is Street Fighter II, there is no doubt in my mind that the fighting game genre will stand the test of time.

When a game is made, it usually is created especially for one gaming system. For example, Street Fighter II was originally made as an arcade game. But when a new system comes out, if a game is still successful, video game publishers love to have their old game "ported" over to the new system. It isn't as easy as just slipping a disk into the DVD drive and voilà—it works. It takes a huge effort, and a team of engineers and artists, to move, or *port*, the game from one system to the next.

MORTAL KOMBAT

1992

FATALITY!: VIOLENCE AND THE ESRB

Mortal Kombat © Midway Games, Inc./Warner Bros. Entertainment, Inc.

Home gaming systems were taking off in a big way by the early 1990s, and the arcades were starting to empty out.

But when Street Fighter II became an overnight success, it wasn't a big shocker that other arcade companies jumped on the fighting game bandwagon. There were a bunch of copycat games in the arcades in less than a year, some good, some not so good, but there was no doubt that fighting games were the wave of the future.

During this time, Midway, a midsized developer known for bringing popular Japanese arcade games to the United States, was itching to build an original idea they could call their own. Midway and Williams, another arcade company, merged, and this marriage made in arcade heaven introduced John Tobias and Ed Boon, the dynamic duo who would soon become the creators of Mortal Kombat.

Scorpion's fatality sequence from Mortal Kombat
© Midway Games, Inc./Warner Bros. Entertainment, Inc.

The photographs had to be digitized because the digital camera technology was just starting to come to life. The quality of digital cameras at the time was very poor, so film photos were taken, then scanned in and touched up in a painting program called DPaint. To do this, real martial artists and actors were hired and extravagant costumes were built. Some of the actors, like Kerri Ann Hoskins Branson, who played Sonja, kept the original costumes and will show them off from time to time at cons and events.

The original Mortal Kombat was created by just five guys. Boon and Tobias, one programmer, one artist, and a sound guy. Impressive!

Tobias had already built quite a name for himself, working as an artist on some of Williams's biggest hits, like Smash TV and Total Carnage. Programmer Ed Boon started his career working in Williams's pinball department, working on classics like Funhouse and Black Knight 2000 (which had one of the most memorable music themes of any pinball game ever—I can still hear it now). The two visionaries began working on a football game called High Impact Football, where they were dabbling with using digitized photographs to make things look more realistic.

The football game was cool enough for Tobias and Boon to see the potential realistic photos had in games, and they moved on before the football game was even finished. Add in layered effects, a specialty of Tobias's, and a fighting game that blurred the lines of reality and fantasy was born. And it was just what the public wanted.

Influenced by 1980s kung fu action movies with over-the-top violence, Mortal Kombat was one of the darkest

Scorpion's fatality sequence from Mortal Kombat
© Midway Games, Inc./Warner Bros. Entertainment, Inc.

things on the market. It wasn't the most violent game out there—a light gun game called Chiller made Mortal Kombat look like a *Teletubbies* episode—but something about the pairing of real, live actors and gallons of blood made people take notice.

Midway noticed, too, and decided to make the gore and violence their focus, adding "Fatalities" at the end of battles that did nothing for game play but encouraged players to celebrate victories with decapitations and other gory deaths.

Tobias and Boon had a hit on their hands. In a time where games didn't really get massive attention until they hit the home consoles, Mortal Kombat had gamers lining up in the arcades to watch Kano rip the beating heart out of Scorpion.

Mortal Kombat drew the attention of both SEGA and Nintendo before it even hit the arcades, and development was long under way by the time gamers were dropping

Next time you watch the X Games, watch for a rollerblading trick called the MK. It's a trick where the blader kicks out his foot and strikes a pose in midair. The trick is in reference to Liu Kang's special move where he launches an awesome flying kick from across the screen.

quarters into the machines. And gamers, teens mostly, LOVED the game, but parents and the media HATED it. Before the game was released for the Genesis and the SNES, there were cries for the home version to be censored. Midway tried. In fact, they even censored the blood in the arcade version for a while, but nobody played the bloodless version of Mortal Kombat, so Midway happily put the blood back in.

In the end, SEGA and Nintendo decided to censor their games by removing the blood. Nintendo did it for real, recoloring the blood to gray in an attempt to make it look like sweat (gross). They also had Acclaim, who developed the home versions, remove some of the more graphic fatalities. But SEGA's attempts were not quite so honorable. They asked Acclaim to turn the blood off, then quietly released the code to turn the blood and gore back on to the public.

SEGA did do something else to warn people, however, and it was another industry first. They started the voluntary SEGA Videogame Rating Council, and gave the game a rating of MA-13. SEGA thought that video games should be held to the same standards as the music and movie companies, and they pioneered a rating system to match. Unfortunately, nobody else followed suit. That is, until the United States Congress got involved. The public outcry for censored video game content was at an all-time high. Concerned parents were unhappy, and they wanted someone to be responsible.

In 1992, with the impending release of a Mortal Kombat arcade game and the recent release of a SEGA title called Night Trap, a game where a slumber party goes wrong and nightgown-wearing sorority girls are threatened by terrifying Peeping Toms, Congress took action. Headed by US senators Joe Lieberman and Herb Kohl, the hearings lasted for months and resulted in an ultimatum for the game industry: Form your own ratings and review system for video games, or the federal government will do it for you. The threat of government regulation was real, and in no time the Entertainment Software Rating Board (ESRB) was formed.

The purple ninja in Mortal Kombat, Rain, claimed he was a prince, as a reference to pop music icon Prince's current album at the time, *Purple Rain*.

The Mortal Kombat characters all had code names during development. The developers must have been hungry, because they named them after condiments. For example, Cyrax and Sektor were known as Ketchup and Mustard before their names were finalized.

Mortal Kombat was the first game to receive an M (for Mature) ESRB rating, and the news only helped to stir up the frenzy. On "Mortal Monday," September 13, 1993, Acclaim packed stores with two million copies of the game, and they flew off the shelves in record numbers. And the timing couldn't have been better for SEGA. Sonic was really crushing it, outselling Mario even, and the sales of the SEGA Genesis were climbing every day. The censorship of Mortal Kombat tipped the scales even more in SEGA's favor. Violence sold, and Mortal Kombat helped the Genesis maintain its lead over the Super Nintendo in America. Nintendo's attempts at trying to keep their system family-friendly backfired.

The game continued to grow in popularity, making it to just about every system available, from the Game Boy to the PlayStation, in 1995. The series's popularity came to its peak in the summer of 1995, when New Line Cinema released an action film based on the game. The movie was the first film based on a video game to be openly accepted by gamers. It received a PG-13 rating, and it premiered at number one in the box office and went on to earn over 120 million internationally.

The Mortal Kombat series sold over 32.5 million copies worldwide, putting it easily in the top fifty bestselling game franchises of all time. The arcade version ranks in as the number nine all-time bestselling arcade game, pulling in a total of 570 million dollars, or 2,280,000,000 quarters. That's approximately 750 tons of quarters!

The series returned to the public in 2015 with Mortal Kombat X. Fans of the series were excited to see that Ed Boon was still involved. And yeah, it received an M rating as well. Boy, did it ever.

The character Noob Saibot is named after the creators of the game. His name is simply Boon and Tobias spelled backward.

In 2011, 1980s horror film icon Freddy Krueger made an appearance as a downloadable character in Mortal Kombat. With his nightmarish attitude, handful of sharp claws, and cult following, he fit right in with the rest of the cast.

ESRB BREAKDOWN

ESRB ratings stamps

The ESRB stamp on the front of your favorite game is broken down into two areas: the letter-based rating and the content descriptors.

The letter suggests the age-appropriateness of the game, while the content descriptors tell you a bit more detail about WHY the game got its rating.

Here's a breakdown for you:

EC—EARLY CHILDHOOD, for young children, makes up less than 1 percent of all games sold. Usually educational games for children ages three and up.

E—EVERYONE. Pretty broad category. Great games for the whole family to enjoy. This is the largest category in gaming, making up nearly half of all games published. These games might contain "infrequent use of mild or cartoon violence" and some "mild language."

E10+—EVERYONE TEN YEARS OLD AND OVER. A bit too much for very young children to handle. Comic mischief is usually a suspect when it comes to pushing a game from E to E10+. Makes up 12 percent of all games. E10+ games might contain a larger amount of mild violence, mild language, and crude humor.

T—TEEN. Ages thirteen and up. Makes up 24 percent of all games sold. T-rated games can contain moderate amounts of violence (including small amounts of blood), mild to moderate use of strong language or suggestive themes, and crude humor.

M—MATURE games are for the over-eighteen crowd. Strong language, violence, and adult situations all fall into this category. Surprisingly, it's not a very big category, even though a lot of people over eighteen play games. Only 12 percent of all games sold get the M rating. M-rated games can include intense and/or realistic violence (such as blood, gore, mutilation, and depictions of death), stronger sexual themes and content, partial nudity, and more frequent use of strong language.

AO—ADULTS-ONLY games are pretty rare and usually contain . . . well, how about we cover that when you're an adult. Let's just leave it at that. They also make up less than 1 percent of games sold.

These guidelines are there for gamers to be able to make great choices and find games that will fit their age and play style. Both developers and the ESRB take the ratings very seriously, and they use the ratings as a guide to help them build the right stuff for the right gamer.

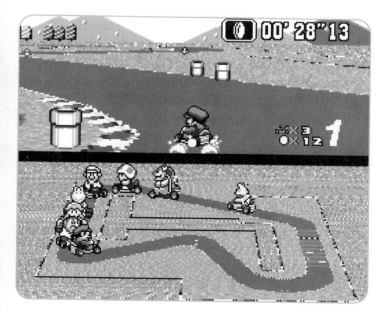

Super Mario Kart © Nintendo

In 1990, Nintendo put a great racing game on their SNES.

It was called F-Zero, and it was loved by all because of its super fast pace, its winding, impossible-to-build-on-Earth tracks, and its slick racing controls. Oh, and the game was HARD, and at times it revved up to nearly impossible, which, of course, drove gamers nuts and thrilled them at the same time.

Why do we do this to ourselves?

Anyway, F-Zero, the futuristic racing game, was great, but it had one small problem. It was single player only, and everyone knows that the only thing better than zooming over the finish line in first place is watching your best friend finish second.

Why do we do this to each other? Gamers are horrible (and by *horrible*, I mean the best!).

Nintendo loved the game, which was made by a handful of Nintendo partner developers, but they knew that it would be another megahit for them if they could only make it a two-player game. So Nintendo did what Nintendo does best. They called Shigeru Miyamoto into the office.

At first the goals were simple. Take what is great about F-Zero and add a second player. But soon the dev team at Nintendo discovered that it wasn't all that simple after all. The complicated tracks of F-Zero were out of the question because adding a second controllable player meant adding a split screen. There wasn't enough room to show the player what was coming down the track. And for all you racing gamers out there, you know that there is nothing worse than not being able to see what's around the corner.

They had to simplify the tracks.

Next they realized that the blazing high speeds of F-Zero were also impossible because the SNES hardware couldn't handle the graphics that fast if it was running in split screen.

Split screen is a cool feature for what gamers call "on-the-couch multiplayer." But it is really tough on console hardware because the console has to basically run the game in each screen independently. It's almost as if the game is playing twice on the same console, once in each window. Playing four-player split screen is even more demanding for your console.

Super NES © Evan Amos

The cars had to be slowed down.

So Miyamoto had a thought, and it was a good one. Instead of zipping through futuristic space tracks on nuclear-fueled rocket cars, just drive around on the street in a go-kart.

Wow, that sounds like a MAJOR DOWNGRADE when you say it that way, but that's what had to happen.

Miyamoto had been around the track a few times. He trusted his team, so they moved along. They built a prototype of a simple track and two racers in go-karts. At first, the racers were generic dudes in suspenders, but we all know what happened next. The dev team raced around the track a few times and thought it was pretty okay, but then someone (yeah, you guessed it, Miyamoto again) asked them to replace the generic characters with Mario, and immediately the game had a personality.

Now people weren't talking about how the game was a slow version of F-Zero with simpler tracks—they were calling it the Mario racing game. This little prototype launched a bunch of ideas, and the next thing you knew, the Mario racing game had a banana peel and a second character, Mario's brother, Luigi.

Battles ensued in the Nintendo office. The dev team discovered that the game wasn't only about getting across the finish line first, it was also about tripping up your opponent with a well-placed banana peel.

Before long, there were meetings to discuss who should be added to the game next. Yoshi was a new character in the Mario universe, recently introduced in Super Mario World, and even though he didn't have thumbs, he made the cut. Princess Peach wanted in on the game. And then there was the always-helpful Toad. And what was a Mario game without the baddies, only this time Donkey Kong Jr., Bowser, and Koopa Troopa were all invited over for a bit of kart-racing fun.

This lineup of characters was something that hadn't been done in games EVER. Now, not only were there familiar characters from the Nintendo games, but they were all mixing together. Donkey Kong characters were hanging out with characters from the Mushroom Kingdom, and it was, in a word—AMAZING!!!

There were also meetings and debates about how to add more traps and boosts to the game. The banana peel was no longer the only tool you had to ruin Bowser's day. Soon you had red shells, green shells, mushrooms for a boost, a star to make you invincible, and a lightning bolt that shrunk all of your opponents for a short time.

The game was super—so super that they had to add it to the name: Super Mario Kart.

It featured three racing modes, single player (which was largely ignored), multiplayer (which caused many fights on the couch), and battle mode (which usually ended in either tears or high fives all around).

Mario, Luigi, Bowser, Toad, Princess Peach, and Yoshi have appeared in all the Mario Kart games, while the only track to appear in all the games is Rainbow Road. However, the track has gone over some pretty major road construction from game to game.

The player select screen and the unique playing styles for each playable character are very reminiscent of the player select menu and unique player styles in Street Fighter II. I told you that was a big innovation. Do you believe me now?

But perhaps the most exciting and innovative thing that the game added was a concept called rubber-banding. It's something that Nintendo pioneered with Super Mario Kart, but it has become such a general term that you see it in every genre from real-time strategy games to fighting games. Here's how it works. When you are in last place, you get HUGE advantages to help you catch up to the front of the pack. When picking up power-ups, you'd get big boosts like mushrooms (speed boost), stars (smaller speed boost, but for a time you are invincible), and red shells (which allowed players to shoot self-aiming, or homing, shells at their opponents). And when you are in first, those advantages all but disappear, leaving you with mostly banana peels and eggs (which both worked the same, leaving small traps behind that caused opponents following you to lose control, or spin out, for a few seconds). This kind of game leveling really keeps the race close for racers of all skill levels.

There's a great lesson here for you future game designers, so pay close attention to what Miyamoto did. He was asked to do something impossible, but instead of tossing his hands in the air and walking away, he learned what the problems were, and he designed around those challenges. And here are the steps he used to get there.

1. **LEARN THE LIMITS. Miyamoto had to slow down the vehicles and simplify the tracks, so two of the best features of F-Zero were already cut.**

2. **PROTOTYPE AND LET YOUR MIND WANDER. Miyamoto created a simple version of his game first. Trying out a game, even if it is a total piece of junk you drew on the back of a paper bag stained with fried chicken grease, is the ONLY way you can make it better.**

3. **GET HELP FROM SMART PEOPLE. Nobody is perfect, not even the great Shigeru Miyamoto. Ask others to play your game, then**

ask for suggestions and ideas on how to make it better. Then, most important, listen to those ideas.

4. **THINK BIG THOUGHTS!** I'm sure when Miyamoto told his bosses that he wanted to add Bowser as a playable character in Mario Kart so that he could toss banana peels at him from a slow-moving kart while rushing down a simple track, they thought he was a bit loony, but look where it ended up.

5. **FIND THE FUN.** One of Miyamoto's mottos is "Find the fun," and Super Mario Kart is a perfect example, because he didn't just make it fun for the best racer on the couch—he made it almost as fun for the guy who finished in last place as it was for the guy who finished first. Genius!

Super Mario Kart launched the kart-racing genre, and everyone from Sony to SEGA had kart games out within a year, but there's no replacing this original masterpiece. Well, except for improving the game with a sequel, which Nintendo has done time and again. In 2014 they topped themselves by sending Mario Kart 8 into the world.

In Mario Kart 64, if you let the music on the results screen loop sixty-four times, the music will change to an alternate tune. I have two questions about this. One ... why? And two ... who took the time to figure this out?

Rainbow Road track in Mario Kart: Double Dash!! © Nintendo

WHAT IS AN IP?

You hear these little initials from time to time when people are talking about video games, but what do they mean? "Interesting piglets"? "Irish popcorn"? "Internet protocol"?

Okay, one of those is a real thing, but I'm not talking about Internet stuff here, what I'm referring to is intellectual property. Which is a fancy way of saying a game, character, or franchise that is the original property of a company or person.

Okay, that was too wordy. Let me break that down. An IP game is a game that belongs only to one publisher because they invented it. It's their very own creation, if you will. The game industry is FULL of examples of IP games, and while the term is occasionally kind of fuzzy in how it is used, the idea is still the same.

For example, Mario Kart is an IP that belongs to Nintendo, while Halo is an IP that belongs to Microsoft.

Most of the time the IP belongs to the publisher, but there are some times when the IP actually stays with the game's developer. In cases like this, it isn't uncommon for a game to shift from one console to another. Final Fantasy is an excellent example of this. The first six Final Fantasy games shipped exclusively with Nintendo, but that didn't mean that Nintendo owned the IP. Squaresoft, the developer of the franchise, owned the IP. So, when things changed up a bit for Squaresoft, they decided to ship Final Fantasy VII on the PlayStation.

BTW, you don't have to be a billion-dollar megacorp to create an IP. In fact, you can create one yourself. Make something creative and unique that the world has never seen before, give it a name, maybe do a few drawings of your idea, then blammo—congrats. You've created your own IP.

MYST © Cyan, Inc.

While most of the world was busy blasting gruesome bad guys or jumping across bright gaps in kingdoms filled with fungi, two brothers were dreaming up nearly impossible puzzles, while crafting a rich time-hopping story. And creating the most amazing 3D art the world had ever seen in the process.

The brothers were Rand and Robyn Miller, and the game they were hammering away at was MYST. Standing on the shoulders of interactive fiction games like Zork way back in 1977, Rand and Robyn saw their new project as an opportunity to bring storytelling back to gaming. Storytelling was something the brothers felt could be improved in video games. Or at least Rand saw it that way. Before creating MYST, Robyn Miller had played a grand total of ONE video game. EVER!

The Miller brothers came up with the name for MYST during a thirty-second phone call. Robyn Miller said the conversation went something like this: "What should we name it?"—Rand. "How about MYST?"—Robyn. "Okay, sounds good."—Rand. Not bad considering it took months of debating to name the sequel, Riven.

The game that Robyn Miller had played was Zork II. I guess if you're going to make a fiction-based adventure game and you can only play one game to get you ready, Zork II isn't a bad place to start.

The Miller brothers started working on the game months before the rest of the small crew at Cyan, Inc., joined in. They drew maps and concept art sketches of the game on everything from chalkboards to yellow notebook paper. At first they planned on drawing the entire game by hand. Animation studios do this all the time. They draw hundreds—wait, make that thousands upon thousands—of drawings for a single movie. But this was only a few guys, a storyteller, an audio designer, and a couple of artists. They just didn't have the staff to reach their goal, so they looked at technology to help them out.

Now, a couple of really cool things were happening during this time period that are important to this story. The most important thing was the rise of computer-generated (CG) graphics and how they were impacting the movie industry. One movie in particular was blowing minds all around the world. That movie was *Jurassic Park*. While it had its share of puppets and robots disguised as dinosaurs, it also starred a lot of digital dinos. Part of this is that the Pentium processor was invented in 1993, which allowed artists and engineers to create and "render" images on computers at much higher speeds and much lower costs. The computer-generated animation phenomenon was born, and before you knew it, just about every movie company on Earth was trying to get their ideas on the big screen.

Why is this movie info in a book about video games? Glad you asked.

The software created to make these movies made its way through the film industry and into the game world. One piece of software in particular, StrataVision 3D, was priced just right for small developers, students, and even amateur hobbyists to give it a shot. And if you had a fast computer and a good brain for using software, you could make something pretty cool right there on your desktop.

Knowing that hand-drawing the game wasn't an option,

Cyan, Inc., began building the mysterious island Rand and Robyn had sketched in the new 3D software. It took months, but they built every inch, every hidden library, every mysterious building, every tree and rock. Now, without too much effort, Rand and Robyn could fly a digital camera around in space and, well, the best way to explain it is to say they could take a picture.

All these beautifully rendered images gobbled up a lot of space—more space than was available on your run-of-the-mill floppy disk (a flat five-inch-square removable storage disk used by early computers) or video game cartridge. This was the next problem for the Miller brothers. The game they had in mind, combined with the eye-popping graphics they were building, was so amazing that they weren't about to let storage space get in the way. At the time, they were developing the game on some pretty slick Macintosh Quadras. These fancy new machines had a neat new peripheral (fancy word for a doodad you hook to your computer to expand what it can do). This new peripheral was known as a CD-ROM drive, and while it was slower than a cartridge, it held a TON of content, and it would allow you to play CD-quality music.

The brothers knew this was the way to go, and while there wasn't really a market for CD-ROM games at the time, Cyan, Inc., and the Miller brothers believed that their game was good enough to change that. And they were right.

The images created by the artists at Cyan were going to blow gamers' minds. The Millers were sure of this. But Rand knew that the game play and the story had to be the most important things. In order for that to happen, they needed a truly original idea. And Rand had one. The idea was to never introduce the main character to the player. Ever. In fact, he didn't want the player to even know the main character's name, so they called him "the Stranger."

The story centers around an unnamed player, the Stranger, who stumbles across a book called, yup, you guessed it, MYST. The Stranger learns about an odd island world called, yup, you got it again, MYST! But unlike your typical, boring school textbook, when the Stranger

It wasn't really as easy as snapping a digital photo. Each of the 2,500+ images took between two and fourteen hours to render! In comparison, today your smartphone could render the simple scenes in MYST at over sixty frames per second.

In the game industry, it's pretty common to use the word *content* to define everything that isn't programmer code in the game. So that would be things like audio files, speech, art, and videos. Basically, if you can see it or hear it, it's called *content*. If you play it, it's called *code*.

touches the last page of the book, he's zoomed away to a mysterious island. He finds himself all alone, and has no choice but to explore.

MYST © Cyan, Inc.

The story of MYST was so memorable that it still has fans today. Three novels were published in the late 1990s by British sci-fi writer David Wingrove. And recently Hulu, a popular streaming video service, announced an exclusive series based on the MYST story.

Eventually, the Stranger finds a library, and two items catch his eye—a blue book and a red book. Funnily enough, the books are written by two brothers. Huh. Imagine that. A game written by two brothers, starring two brothers.

The Stranger learns that the father of the two brothers is dead, and they blame each other for his death. There are pages missing from the red and blue books, and the Stranger has to explore the island in search of the missing pages. The more he finds, the more the story is revealed. Eventually, the Stranger discovers that the brothers are trapped, and finding the last pages of their books will free them. By now, the Stranger, which is actually YOU, in case you haven't figured that out by now, has had time to decide which of the brothers the Stranger believes, or if he believes either of them. And he also discovers one more book, a green book, which the brothers beg the Stranger not to open.

Of course, you, the Stranger, open the green book. The best way to get a gamer to do something is to ask them NOT to do it.

Inside the green book, the Stranger learns that the father is not dead but trapped inside his own island, actually NOT named MYST, and he asks the Stranger for his help to be freed so he can bring his terrible sons to justice.

Now the Stranger has a lot of choices to make. Free brother one, the blue book; free brother two, the red book; or free neither one and let the father go. Well, he could also choose to free nobody, I guess, but what's the fun in that?

In the end, the Miller brothers really came through. Not only was the game filled with difficult and visually awesome puzzles and traps, but the complex story stuck inside gamers' minds. And the best part: There were multiple endings based on what you chose. I won't spoil it for you because you can still play MYST today, and you totally should. But I will say that not every choice will end up giving you that happily-ever-after feeling you get from watching a Disney movie. You've been warned.

MYST went on to break all kinds of records and open up a new genre for games.

- **MYST was the first PC game to sell over five million copies. In the end it sold more than six million copies worldwide, ranking it currently the number three bestselling PC game of all time.**

- **MYST had a huge influence on visual puzzle games. In fact, it had such an influence that for years slow-paced puzzle games that made you think were referred to as "MYST clones."**

- **MYST was the first game to be called *art* by many critics. It opened up a big dialogue about the importance of art in video games, as well as recognition that video games are actually an art form.**

- **MYST was so popular that it introduced the CD-ROM device. Until this point, most computers still relied on floppy disks, but the game was so beautiful and engaging that gamers around the world joined in, adding CD-ROMs to their home computers.**

When the Millers were creating MYST, they knew that another way to take advantage of the CD-ROM was to include video. By the time it was finished, MYST had more than sixty-six minutes of video. An impressive first for the gaming industry.

DOOM © id Software

Looking back, 1993 was epic.

I mentioned this before, but it's worth mentioning again. The Pentium processor was invented. It's basically your computer's internal math nerd, and it makes things run fast. At the time, nobody could really afford one, but now they are totally affordable, they rock, AND they make your games run supersmooth.

Bill Nye, the Science Guy aired its first TV episode. At the time it was pretty neat because Nye made science cool. Shows like *MythBusters* and the Vsauce channel on YouTube would probably not be around if it weren't for Bill Nye.

The World Wide Web was launched. At the time, www.NobodyKnewWhatToDoWithIt.com, but today www.WeCantLiveWithoutIt.com.

Even the *Mickey Mouse Club* was way ahead of its time, because a superyoung Justin Timberlake, Britney Spears, Christina Aguilera, and Ryan Gosling were on the show. They were just kids back then, but those four kids went on to be MAJOR stars later on.

While DOOM ended up being the game that caused the first-person shooter craze, the game most people consider the first modern FPS game was also created by id Software: Wolfenstein 3D.

It was the year to launch influential media for sure, but this list wouldn't be complete if it didn't include DOOM. John Carmack's visionary game started off pretty quietly, but it spawned the first-person shooter genre, which would dominate games for the next decade.

DOOM started in 1992 when a young genius, and I don't use that word lightly, named John Carmack developed a basic frame for the game, or *game engine*, that he named the DOOM engine. Oh, and he did it all by himself while the rest of his team at id Software worked on the sequel to their hit game Wolfenstein 3D.

John Carmack is kind of a digital cowboy. A code-writing wizard. A lone wolf engineer that breaks from the pack and makes cool stuff that nobody else can quite understand. Add the fact that he is an ACTUAL ROCKET SCIENTIST, and you'll agree that I did not use the word *genius* lightly.

To give you an idea of what made Carmack's DOOM engine so special, it's helpful to know what came before. FPS games had been around for a LOOOONG time by 1993. In fact, some of the very first games ever written were first-person shooters. A full twenty years before DOOM, Steve Colley created a game called Maze War, a black-and-white game where you stepped through the hallways of a maze, looking for a floating eyeball that you would then shoot for points.

There were a lot of others along the way. Some would say that Battlezone, a vector-based arcade tank game, is an FPS (I know I would), and then there was MIDI Maze, which looked pretty much like Maze War except with some strange music component added on and floating smiley faces instead of floating eyeballs. It was weird, but there was no doubt it was a first-person shooter.

Then in 1992 Carmack's group, id Software, made Wolfenstein 3D and the modern shooter was born. For the first time players could move through an environment and shoot guns at other characters. The graphics were miles ahead of anything that came before. Wolfenstein 3D also introduced us to some of the staples of the modern shooter, like health and ammo packs and the ability to switch weapons on the fly.

The game was great, but Carmack, who had written the game engine for Wolfenstein 3D, wanted improvements for his next game that the old game wouldn't allow. For instance, Wolfenstein 3D was played on a flat surface. Think a large warehouse full of hallways, and no stairs, with square walls and corners that only allowed for ninety-degree turns. But Carmack's new DOOM engine allowed for multiple levels and detailed textures on the floors and walls. It was more like running around in a five-story building full of winding turns, stairs, animated floors and traps, and maybe even some lava just for fun.

Carmack knew that adding this kind of awesomeness would allow DOOM-level designers to make the environment itself an enemy by introducing danger. For the first time in a 3D game, players could fall into lava pits, get smashed by movable ceilings, and plummet to their deaths on moving bridges.

With all these innovations, 3D really started to look, well, 3D, and the term *immersive* was being used to describe the game. Which is WAY more than you can say about a musically controlled smiley face bobbing through flat, shaded maze hallways.

That in itself would have been enough to make the game innovative, but that was just the start. After John Carmack had polished the game engine, it was time for another John to get involved: John Romero.

Romero was to level and game design what Carmack was to game programming. And I don't say THAT lightly, either.

Working closely with Carmack, Romero designed levels that were fun to play even before enemies were added. Unlike previous FPS games, players could move freely in the space, running around long swooping bridges, sprinting up stairways, and balancing on thin walkways above lava pits.

And the environment wasn't the only challenge facing the level designer. You might think that pickups like health and ammo could be scattered around randomly and the game would work out just fine, but that isn't the case.

The pickups in DOOM were so legendary that they were copied over and over by other developers. You can still see them in just about every shooter today—pickups like the first aid kit to restore health, a backpack to increase ammo capacity, night-vision goggles, soul spheres that increased your health to 200 percent, and even the Berserker, which rammed your health back to 100 percent and increased your punching ability to superhuman strength.

Before DOOM really got moving, a previous id Software developer, Tom Hall, wrote a detailed story and backstory about the game. Carmack felt that the story wasn't important to the game play, and while Tom's work was beautifully written, in the end Carmack won out and a simpler story drove the game.

By 1995, DOOM was estimated to be installed on more computers worldwide than Microsoft's new operating system, Windows 95. Bill Gates briefly considered purchasing id Software before deciding that it would be better to fund a port of DOOM to promote his new operating system as a gaming platform.

Romero knew that placing pickups in the perfect spot, just before the player enters a big brawl, or just after, to help them recover before the next wave of attacks, would be the key to designing an addictive game.

Of course, all those levels took a lot of in-office polishing, which the id developers were more than happy to do. Don't get me wrong, the team at id took their job seriously, but play testing the game over their network became more than just work. It became a party, and even before the game was ready to ship, something else had been hatched. The LAN party.

A cast of terrifying, demonic monsters was added, along with a simple story, and DOOM was ready to rock and roll.

And by *simple*, I mean simple. You are an unnamed space marine, sent to Mars as a punishment for beating the snot out of your commanding officer. You begin the game with only a pistol. If you run out of ammo, it's you, your right hook, and a knuckle sandwich. But, lucky for you, the abandoned space station you've been banished to is littered with shotguns, a chainsaw, and the most sought-after weapon on Mars—the BFG9000!

That was it. The entire story could really be boiled down to two words: Shoot stuff!

When Romero and Carmack felt the game was ready they released it. For free. That's right, DOOM was a shareware game. id Software encouraged people to share the game and play it over the network with their friends. All they asked was that if you liked the game you would buy follow-up chapters of DOOM. Or if you REALLY liked it, you could buy an official version of the shareware version as a way of saying thank you to id.

Even though most users did not purchase the official version, over one million copies were installed, and the popularity of the game drove future sales of DOOM games down the line.

DOOM had so many innovations it should have shipped with a dictionary. Here are a few of the terms DOOM introduced that we find commonplace today.

The world's largest LAN party at DreamHack Winter 2014 © Toffelginkgo

- **LAN PARTY:** A LAN is a local area network. Before Internet gaming really took off and people joined up online while sitting in their basements, people would pack their entire computers to a single location and connect the computers together over the LAN. This became so huge after DOOM shipped that entire hotel conference rooms were booked just to hold DOOM LAN parties.

- **PICKUP:** A pickup is an item in the game, usually floating a couple of feet above the ground, that the player can "pick up" by running over the item. In DOOM, these items ranged from health boosts to ammo packs to temporary invincibility.

- **MODDERS:** Modders are tech-savvy gamers who like to use the tools a game developer has provided them to transpose the game to make it feel different. DOOM embraced this idea by shipping software or modding tools that allowed players to build their own arenas and modify the effects of the weapons. It was a totally new concept back then, but the modding community is responsible for some of the biggest games out there today. League of Legends, for example, is a game built initially by the modding community. (More on League of Legends later on.)

- **FRAGS:** *Frag* is actually a military term, short for *fragmentation*, but in FPS games like DOOM, a frag is used to count how many times you clobber an opponent.

- **DEATHMATCH MODE:** Deathmatch mode is a multiplayer game mode where each player is out for himself. Blast away at your friends and collect frags. The gamer with the most frags at the end of the match is the winner.

- **ALPHA RELEASE:** DOOM was the first game to release the game to the public before it was finished. To be more specific, an alpha release is a build of the game where all the parts are in the game, but the game is still not fine-tuned or polished for final release. DOOM showed great bravery in releasing early, but the fans ate it up, and by the time the game was ready to ship there was already a huge number of gamers already playing. Pretty smart.

- **SHAREWARE:** A shareware game is a game that is given out for free. Gamers are encouraged to share it with their friends to get more players involved. After a while, additional features or maps might be added for a cost, but the bulk of the game will always remain free and shareable.

DOOM is often referred to as one of the most influential games of all time. It established FPS network play, cooperative story mode, pickup-driven level design, weapon pickups, and so much more. DOOM has blasted its way into the video game history books, and it will continue to influence the future of video games. Just remember: Every time you collect a frag in your favorite shooter game, you owe a little nod to John and John and their fantastic game DOOM!

In a press release in 1993, id Software predicted that DOOM would become "the number one cause of decreased productivity in businesses around the world." This prediction came true, at least in part. DOOM became a major problem at workplaces, both stealing away employees' time and clogging up valuable network traffic. Some companies even formed policies banning DOOM from being played in the office.

ART MEETS MATH

There are basically two ways to create art for a game engine: polygons, which are used in 3D games, and pixels, which are primarily used in 2D games.

They both have their advantages and disadvantages, and they both require totally different tools for artists to create them.

Pixels are two-dimensional art. Think of it like a graph or a grid. You've got a row of blocks across that run horizontally along the bottom, called *X*, and a column of blocks that run vertically, called *Y*. If you say that the block, or pixel, at X 5 and Y 5 is bright red, then the game engine will draw that red pixel at exactly that point. If you then move that pixel to X 7 and Y 7, the pixel will move up and over a bit, appearing to animate the pixel.

It's pretty basic algebra stuff when you think of it. If you haven't covered that in math yet, you'll soon be introduced to the fun of plotting graphs on a 2D plane. I'm serious. It's fun!

Luckily for artists in the game world, the pixels aren't charted in one at a time on a graph. They have really slick, high-tech computer programs, like Adobe Photoshop, that allow artists to paint digital images and the computers to do all the math. But as you can imagine, the larger the grid, the more detailed the images can be. The original Mario was sixteen pixels high (Y 0-15) by twelve pixels wide (X 0-11). Pretty challenging to make an animated character look good with only that many pixels to play with.

Polygons are totally different. A polygon is actually a triangle created by joining three points in space. You can draw one on your paper by drawing three dots, then connecting them, but here's what makes it really different. On a piece of paper, the polygon is actually still only 2D, when in reality, those three points in space can be anywhere. Try to follow me here, because this is really cool.

Imagine that 2D grid: X for width and Y for height. Now punch a new line back through that grid that we'll call *Z*. Z represents the depth. Now you can connect that triangle, which is actually a polygon, to another polygon, and you've made a true 3D shape. Attach another and another, and you can start to sculpt those polygons into a 3D object in space.

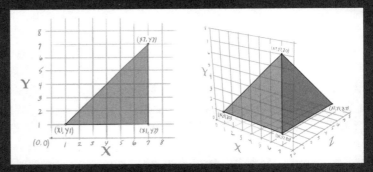

2D vs. 3D

This requires a different kind of math, one called geometry, where you plot objects in 3D space, discover an object's surface area, and translate an object in space. All really cool stuff, and also really exciting to learn about in math class. No, I'm serious! It's REALLY interesting stuff!

Once again, luckily for the art creators, there is software that helps them sculpt objects digitally. For example, Autodesk Maya is a tool that is used for creating 3D art for everything from video games to Pixar movies.

So, basically think of it this way: 2D art, or pixel art, is more like painting or drawing on a piece of paper, and can be explained using algebra. On the other hand, 3D art is more like sculpture, and is defined by geometry.

Pretty cool when you see how art and math work together like this, and believe me, your math teacher will be impressed when you can chart out the coordinates for the original Mario pixel art.

TOMB RAIDER

1996

A NEW FACE, A NEW SYSTEM, A NEW ERA

Tomb Raider © Eidos Interactive/Square Enix

By 1996 gamers were starting to line up behind their favorites and taking sides in what would become a big debate. There were Nintendo fans, PC elitists, and SEGA die-hards.

Atari had been shoved out and a host of other gaming companies had tried to break in, but nobody was able to crack the code and unseat one of the three gaming juggernauts.

Then along came a woman with two rapid-fire handguns, a brilliant wit, and a desire to find the most elusive treasures in the world, and all of a sudden people were starting to talk about a newcomer, the Sony PlayStation.

By the mid-nineties, technology was rapidly changing what video games could do. What had started out as an industry driven by engineers and game designers was now opening up to artists. The new tech and faster machines inspired a lead artist at British game developer Core Design by the name of Toby Gard to build something rich, complex, and full of life. Gard had a vision of something that looked more like a movie than a game, and he had an idea of how to make it happen.

Speaking of movies, Gard was a big fan of a certain hat-wearing, whip-wielding archaeologist who was a big

Tomb Raider was created by just six people. The game was cutting-edge, but back in 1996, *cutting-edge* didn't require a staff of hundreds of developers. The game was created over a three-year period by Core Design, which, at the time, was only a half-dozen developers.

First-person view means that the game is played through the eyes of the gamer. You can usually see a gun or steering wheel, but it is as if you are playing through the character's eyes. Third-person view pulls the camera back to show you the character you are controlling in the environment.

hit in movie theaters around the globe. In the early 1980s, when Gard was just a teenager, Indiana Jones was every child's hero. His adventures were over-the-top, he used knowledge and his own brute strength, rather than superpowers, and he only pulled out a gun when he absolutely had to. While dreaming up ideas for games, Gard kept coming back to *Indiana Jones* for inspiration. Gard started sketching out early ideas for an adventure game set in jungles, pyramids, caves, temples, and tombs. He added a hat-toting, leather-coat-wearing hero, and before he realized it, he'd created a character that wasn't just inspired by Indy, it looked like him, too.

Gard's game caught on fast and his project got the go-ahead. However, his character didn't. Everyone felt like it was just too close to Indiana Jones to go forward, so Gard suggested bumping up one of the female characters in the game to the lead role. At the time, female characters in games were mostly playing roles of princesses, hostages, victims, or all of the above. But instead of shying away from the challenge, Core embraced it, and a star was born.

A new story was crafted to fit the new character, Lara Croft. Instead of being a rough-and-tumble treasure hunter, Lara became an upper-crust thrill seeker. She was an eleventh-generation countess who left the life of tea parties and lacy dresses behind to seek adventure and the life of an explorer.

Core had never attempted to make a 3D game before—in fact, few developers had—but that didn't stop them from trying. And if that wasn't challenging enough, Gard wanted his character on-screen at all times. That meant that Core had to learn how to make a 3D, human-character-focused, over-the-shoulder, third-person game, which was something nobody had quite figured out yet.

Remember when we talked about polygons earlier? Well, in this new 3D game, every single thing you saw in the game used polygons. It was a true, honest-to-goodness 3D game. Every item in the game, from the rocks you climbed, to the enemies, to Lara Croft herself, was built from them. It took just over 540 polygons to build

Miss Croft, and great care went into animating her to make her come to life. She could jump, grab, shoot, dive, roll, climb, swim—you name it. At a time when most in-game characters were limited to a few animations, Lara Croft was a rich and complete character, and the more time they spent on getting her right, the more Core knew they had something special on their hands.

While the original Lara Croft was made up of 540 polygons, the 2013 version of Lara, who starred in Rise of the Tomb Raider, came in at more than forty thousand polygons.

Lara Croft in the 1996 Tomb Raider © Eidos Interactive vs. Lara Croft in Rise of the Tomb Raider 2013 © Square Enix

They polished the game beyond anything that gamers had seen in the past. They got involved with a publisher called Eidos Interactive, who immediately saw the potential in Gard's game and promised to help them

In the original Tomb Raider game, Lara's trademark braid had to be cut. The game simply couldn't handle the additional polygons and joints required to animate it. They kept it in for the cut scenes and all the marketing material, but the braid itself didn't make an appearance in-game until Tomb Raider III in 1999.

market Tomb Raider into the next hit. All they needed was a platform, and they thought that PlayStation was the perfect match. Not only was PlayStation looking for a character to help launch their new system, the PlayStation promised a faster processor, better memory, and a CD-ROM drive that would give the developers everything they needed to show off their new game.

Sony didn't agree. In fact, they thought the game was a bit on the boring side.

Sony PlayStation © Evan Amos

Did Core give up and go home? Did Core seek another publisher for their game? No way! Like their heroine, Lara, they were survivors. Core went into overdrive. They tightened the controls, found the perfect voice actor for Lara, hired a composer to write them an original music score, and added beautiful videos to help push the story to the front. They even gave Lara Croft herself a bit of a makeover to make sure she looked good enough to be on the cover of the game, and on the cover of any fashion magazine that might come calling.

As a way of paying tribute to *Indiana Jones*, the original inspiration for Tomb Raider, Core decided to hide something special in the foyer of Croft Manor, Lara Croft's mansion. Right where you'd expect a comfy couch, you'll see the biblical artifact Dr. Jones recovered in his first movie—the Ark of the Covenant.

Core also amped up the excitement. Instead of just running through the jungle shooting at wolves and bears, Lara was now racing against an evil woman named Natla and her henchmen as they tried to find an artifact called the Scion. By the time the twisted and compelling story was finished, Lara learns that the Scion and Natla herself originated in the lost civilization of Atlantis, and that Natla was doing some odd experimenting with reverse evolution, which ended up making a bunch of mutant creatures and even a T. rex, all under her control. The horde of mutant critters and the massive T. rex proved to be quite a challenge for Lara, but with her trusty sidearms and her ability to climb walls well enough to make Spidey raise an eyebrow, Lara comes out on top.

They went back to Sony, and this time they received what they'd hoped to get the first go-round. Sony loved the game, and Lara Croft was no longer in the doghouse. In fact, she was now a lead title for Sony's new system, the PlayStation.

Tomb Raider debuted in November of 1996, less than two months after Super Mario 64 and the N64 console arrived on the scene. By the end of the first day, it was easy to see that Lara was a hit. The game shot to number one in sales in a matter of hours and stayed there for months.

In the end, Core couldn't have timed things better. Gamers worldwide were looking for compelling 3D games, and here was Tomb Raider, an engrossing game with true 3D graphics and a fresh face that nobody had ever seen in games before.

Tomb Raider not only sold well, it helped launch the sales of the PlayStation. The space that was once dominated by Nintendo, with barely enough room for SEGA, was now starting to see PlayStation as a major competitor.

Lara Croft had become a true hero in the minds of gamers, but it didn't end there. Lara soon became a true pop icon. She appeared on the front page of the *Financial Times*, the top business paper in the UK. She had cover stories in *TIME* magazine, *Newsweek*, and, of course, just about every gaming magazine on the rack. But it was an eight-page cover article in *The Face*, Europe's premier fashion magazine, that really put her in the public eye.

Even before the sequel to Tomb Raider was ready, Lara appeared in commercials for Visa, energy drinks, and a Spanish sports car company. She'd been on a French postage stamp, made an appearance on U2's PopMart Tour, and recorded a single with Dave Stewart of the Eurythmics. And that was just the beginning of Lara's rise to fame.

- *Lara Croft: Tomb Raider* (2001), starring Angelina Jolie, became the highest-grossing video game movie of the 2000s, bringing in over four hundred million dollars worldwide. And it established that the crossover from games to film was here to stay.

- U2, the world-famous Irish rock band, recorded a song for the sound track of *Lara Croft: Tomb Raider* called "Elevation," and an animated version of Lara was featured in the rock group's music video.

- Lara Croft starred in her own animated TV show, voiced by British actress Minnie Driver. The show was called *Revisioned: Tomb Raider*, and the entire series can easily be found online today.

- An entire library of Tomb Raider novels has been published over the years. Most notably the first trilogy, *The Amulet of Power*, *The Lost Cult*, and *The Man of Bronze*, which were all bestsellers in 1999, but more recently, in 2013, *Tomb Raider: The Ten Thousand Immortals* kicked off a whole new generation of Lara Croft adventures.

- The first issue of the Tomb Raider comic book in 1999 became the bestselling comic book of the year, and they were released monthly by Top Cow Productions from 1999 to 2005, until things got a little messy when the comic book rights were chopped up and given to other companies. A French publisher, Glenat, also ran a twelve-part series called *Tomb Raider: Dark Aeons* during the same time, from 2001 to 2003.

- Action figures, costumes, lunch boxes, and even a replica version of Lara Croft's backpack hit the scene in the early 2000s, proving once and for all that the wealthy treasure seeker was here to stay.

Getting Tomb Raider in the hands of gamers wasn't easy, but it was worth it. Lara Croft became a bona fide franchise character, and loyal fans gobble up every adventure she offers up. She'll probably be climbing mountains, seeking treasure, and clobbering bad guys well into her nineties. Well, at least we can always hope.

ALL I NEED IS A HERO

● ● ● ● ● ● ● ● ● ● ● ● ● ● ● ● ●

So, I guess if I'm going to include my top ten villains, I am duty bound to share my all-time favorite video game heroes, too. So here it goes, my personal favorites. The most memorable and fun characters in video games—according to little old me. I'm sure your list will be different, but let's face it. We all agree on who's number one. Right?

10. Solid Snake

With a gravelly voice and eye patch, and the toughest gray hair in video game history, Solid Snake was destined to die in combat, but that never stopped him from being a hero. From the old 2D sprite days of 1998, to cutting-edge 3D graphics, this Metal Gear Solid hero has worked his way into the hearts of gamers for decades. He even found his way to Super Smash Bros. Brawl, where he became a fan favorite.

9. Cloud Strife

He's the most recognizable hero in the Final Fantasy series. Is it the golden, spiky hair? Is it his massive sword? Is it the totally cool name? Perhaps, but I think it's because he's a mercenary and ex-member of a genetically augmented military unit and that he fights for a resistance group called Avalanche. Cloud Strife is a true hero, always fighting for good, storming into battle, slashing his sword, and striking poses. Lots and LOTS of poses. Also, is it a coincidence that his nemesis, Sephiroth, shows up at number nine on my favorite villains list? I think not.

8. Lara Croft

She's been called the female version of Indiana Jones since her early days on the PS1, but this dual-wielding treasure hunter has been the star of more video games than Indiana and has become the most recognized female character in video game history. She's smart, tough, can climb a cliff like a man in a red spider suit, and packs more heat than a blockbuster action movie star.

7. Donkey Kong

He didn't make the cut on my all-time favorite villains list for a reason. It's because he's a HERO! Sure, he started off capturing the princess, but in Donkey Kong Country, this lovable ape swung, thumped, bumped, and jumped his way to the top. Sure, he's only concerned about his banana hoard, but you can't help but love the guy. Not to mention, he's made cameos in Mario Kart and Smash Bros., and he even had his own music game, Donkey Konga.

6. Sonic the Hedgehog

Okay, so it's been a while since Sonic was a leading man, or should I say leading hedgehog, but there was a time when this sneaker-wearing speedster was all the rage. He's packed with attitude, has a catchy sound track, and destroys the evil Dr. Robotnik without ever firing a single projectile. You just gotta love this little blue streak of awesome.

5. Master Chief

The confident and deadly star of the Halo series not only helped lead a rebellion, he became the face of the Xbox. Actually, it might go beyond just the Xbox; Master Chief, in many ways, has become the icon for a new generation of gamers.

4. Mega Man

The Blue Bomber has taken on the nefarious force of Dr. Wily for decades. In that time, he's saved humanity time and again, while showcasing the ability to absorb the powers of his fallen enemies. Yeah, he did that first. He's fast, dangerous, and this eight-bit hero has a blaster for an arm. It's a combo that is as fun to play as it sounds, and if you haven't given Mega Man a try, you really owe it to yourself to check him out.

3. Samus Aran

When I first played the NES hit, I thought this bounty hunter was the coolest thing I'd ever seen. She had a gun for an arm, like Mega Man, but could transform into a ball to zip through hallways and avoid enemies. And the best thing was how Nintendo held the reveal of Samus being a woman until the very end of the first game. Everyone was shocked and impressed, cementing her as one of the all-time most memorable heroes in video game history.

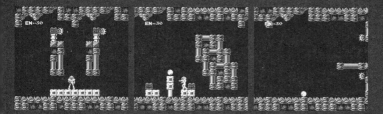

Samus Aran in Metroid © Nintendo

2. Link

How do you become my second-favorite video game hero of all time? Easy—make a green fashion statement, sport an awesome sword and shield, and become the Hero of Time. He's not only a hero as a child character, he also became a hero as an adult character. Not to mention he defeated my all-time favorite villain, Ganondorf, and has saved Zelda and her kingdom over and over again while staying humble. Oh, and he has a pony. Let's not forget the Epona factor here.

1. Mario

Yeah, you probably saw this one coming. This high-jumping, mustached plumber IS video games to me. Not only has he saved the princess and the kingdom countless times, but he saved the video game industry after the big crash in the 1980s. Way to go, Mario!

So there you have it. My top ten all-time great video game heroes. I'd love to compare it to your list. One of the greatest things about video games is that there really is no wrong answer to who the greatest video game hero is. I guess, in the end, it's actually you. I mean, where would Mario be without you behind the controller?

Gran Turismo © Sony Computer Entertainment, Inc.

In 1997, things were about to get real. And I mean REAL!

At a time when most games were celebrating fantasy and trying to give gamers the most unusual, out-of-this-world experiences they could dream up, Japanese developer Polyphony Digital was studying the benefits of all-aluminum vs. titanium bolts on the brake calipers of a 1997 Acura Integra Type R.

And if that's too much car info for you, well, then Gran Turismo is going to overwhelm your mind. But in all the right ways.

Gran Turismo is one of the most celebrated series in driving games—and in games in general. For car lovers it is an automotive heaven. The game was fueled by a love of cars and racing that can only be described as obsessive. It has consistently raised the bar for racers and thrilled digital drivers with unmatched realism, detail, and visual polish. Not to mention handling, which the guys at Polyphony Digital nailed. Each car handled uniquely, and it was all due to their deep understanding of physics and how cars work.

An exclusive is a game
or franchise that shows
up on only one console.
Mario for Nintendo, Halo
for Microsoft, and, of
course, Gran Turismo
for Sony are all good
examples of exclusive
video games.

To a motor head who dreams of driving a million-dollar sports car on a closed track in Germany, the game was a dream come true. Car nerds could swap out parts from real-life car part manufacturers, complete with the actual specs, and test out how small adjustments in their car's gear could alter performance.

But to the average gamer, Gran Turismo was just a fun racing game. To them, tons of tuning options and a long list of increasingly obscure, exotic car models meant less than just simply running the perfect race and crossing the finish line first.

But everyone agreed, the game was the most exciting visual racing simulation game they had ever seen, and it was only going to ship on the PlayStation, an exclusive for Sony, which was exactly what they wanted.

There really was nothing like it at the time, and it's difficult to imagine the gaming landscape had GT not hit when it did. At the time, Sony was trying to "age up" the gaming industry. For years the public opinion was that video games were only for kids—expensive digital toys that took up too much time and only appealed to young gamers. But Sony knew that they had so much more to offer, and they used GT to help them get there.

Sony wanted to get games into the mainstream; they wanted everyone to know that playing games was cool, regardless of your age. And the ultrarealistic, hard-core racing game was exactly what they needed to push their new idea.

Gran Turismo soon became the poster child for a new generation of teen and twentysomething gamers. Other racing games, like Wipeout and Ridge Racer, grabbed gamers' interest, but Gran Turismo did away with the fantasy and made driving games at once ultra-accessible and completely cool.

Built with a tinker-happy, home-mechanic-pleasing, car-guy-thinking attitude, Gran Turismo's 178 cars, eleven tracks, and thousands of modification options set a new standard. Gamers were building cars to fit their digital driving style and arguing over which shocks held up best at which tracks.

And, for the first time in a racing game, the feeling you got from collecting a garage of the world's fastest and finest cars was similar to leveling up a character in other games. It was a reflection of you, and the more you played the game, the more you felt like the garage you were assembling was yours and yours alone.

Gran Turismo also introduced another feature that really showed off the individual handling and performance of each car: license testing. At first glance, it looks a little boring, but if you look at it as a whole you will realize that it was a stroke of genius. Each time you purchased or were introduced to a new car, you had to take it on a test run and achieve a certain level of expertise with it before you could enter it into a race. It opened the world to the concept of a time trial in racing games, and better yet, it taught you how to handle your shiny new vehicle.

DualShock Controller © Evan Amos

And speaking of controls and handling, GT also ended up being the perfect way for Sony to show off their new hardware, the DualShock Controller. Sony's new controller was as fine-tuned and responsive as any of the 178 cars on GT's list, and the internal rumble device inside the DualShock meant that you got a real feel for every bump, twist, and collision.

Gran Turismo © Sony Computer Entertainment, Inc.

In gaming, RPG stands for *role-playing game*. It's a general term that you hear to describe a lot of games and genres, but they all have one thing in common: The player takes on a character, or role, and they build, grow, change, and behave in that role as the game progresses.

The list of innovations GT brought to us is an impressive indication of just how legendary this game really was.

- **Gran Turismo was the first game to allow players to tune and tweak every performance part on their automobile.**

- **GT introduced gamers to time trials by way of their license tests.**

- **GT became the first RPG racing game, where players collected, modified, and perfected their cars by entering racing circuits and using their winnings to continue their journey and buy more cars.**

- **Gran Turismo's replay mode became a legend of its own. The cinematic cameras made the game look beautiful, but that wasn't the only benefit. Racing gamers would watch the replays to learn from their mistakes and memorize the tracks for future races.**

Gran Turismo © Sony Computer Entertainment, Inc.

- **Gran Turismo changed the landscape of gaming, making it suddenly cool and acceptable for adults and teens to play video games.**

The list of innovations and Polyphony Digital's dedication to realism and quality show why Gran Turismo has lasted the ages. The series went on to be a HUGE seller for Sony, raking in over ten million sales by the end of 1998. It was a breakout success, and gamers have remained loyal to the franchise since.

Gran Turismo changed the face of racing games forever, introducing us to a pure simulation-based game with undeniable RPG elements. It was revolutionary at the time, and Gran Turismo remains today a how-to driver's manual for driving game design.

With over 80 million Gran Turismo games already sold in franchise history, Polyphony Digital launched Gran Turismo 7 in 2017 as a PlayStation 4 exclusive, and the game is fully approved by the FIA, the Federation Internationale de l'Automobile, the world's governing body for racing.

THE BATTLE ROYALE!

● ● ● ● ● ● ● ● ● ● ● ● ● ●

Every decade there is a show-down for the ages. In the 1970s, Muhammad Ali and George Foreman rumbled in the jungle for all the world to see. In the '80s, the Boston Celtics and the LA Lakers fought for the NBA Championship. And in the '90s, electronics juggernaut Sony decided to take on entertainment superstar Nintendo.

It all started out as good fun. In fact, before they became competitors, Nintendo and Sony were working together. Nintendo had asked Sony to help them add a CD-ROM drive expansion to their SNES system. Sony could see that Nintendo was doing great in the game world, so they jumped on board.

Well, to make a long story short, things turned sour days before the new SNES CD was to be shown to the public, and Nintendo started working with a company called Phillips instead of Sony.

However, by then Sony thought they had a good handle on things in the gaming world, so they continued working on their system until they came up with a console of their own: the PlayStation.

With their head start, Sony released the PlayStation in 1994, two years before Nintendo was ready to ship the N64.

Nintendo 64 © Evan Amos

But those two years gave Nintendo time to put together something great with the N64. It was faster than the PlayStation, and it had more RAM, which meant shorter load times, faster save times, and better all-around performance. But they did leave one thing off the N64 that ended up being their downfall. Once again, Nintendo shipped with a cartridge-based system rather than investing in a CD drive like the PlayStation.

A lot of developers would store the game's audio in a regular CD format. This meant that gamers could insert their game disk into a standard CD player, or even in their car CD player, and listen to the game's audio track any time they wanted to. This became the standard, and many devs started sneaking in hidden tracks as a fun unannounced bonus for hard-core fans. Tony Hawk's Pro Skater really took advantage of this by featuring music by the Dead Kennedys, the Ernies, Even Rude, Goldfinger, Primus, Speedealer, Suicidal Tendencies, Unsane, and the Vandals. Gamers and music fans rejoiced.

But this battle wasn't won on the speed of the hardware. The battle was won with software—GAMES.

When the N64 launched it had an impressive lineup of games that would go on to become classics. Games like Mario Kart 64, GoldenEye, F-Zero X, and Super Smash Bros. The quality was there for Nintendo. Nobody could deny that, but only for games made by Nintendo. One of Nintendo's flaws was that it was really hard for other companies to make games for the N64. But the same couldn't be said about the PlayStation.

The PlayStation was easy to develop for, and its beefy CD drive gave developers a chance to show their skills in a whole new manner. In the past few years, gamers had grown to expect so much more from their games. Cinematic masterpieces like MYST and Tomb Raider were selling fast, and fans loved the new deep experience they offered. Developers also loved the challenge of telling more complex stories, creating audio sound tracks that rivaled what was being done for movies, and giving players memorable full-screen, movie-quality video moments. The N64, despite all its greatness, just couldn't do this. Game developers lined up behind Sony and showed massive support. Games like Tomb Raider, Metal Gear Solid, Gran Turismo, and Tekken 3 were all Sony exclusives. These new cinematic games found a new, more adult audience that had grown up gaming and was looking for the next big thing.

As is usually the case, the winner was crowned at the cash register. The N64 sold a whopping thirty-three million consoles. That sounds like something to celebrate to me, but considering the Super NES sold nearly fifty million copies, it was actually a downer for Nintendo.

So where did all those lost sales end up? Had people stopped buying games? Of course not! They went to Sony, along with a whole lot of new video game sales. The PlayStation racked up 102.49 MILLION units. That's almost more than three times as many as the N64.

While Nintendo and PlayStation were the top dogs, SEGA wasn't ready to give up just yet. They launched the SEGA Saturn during this same time, but it sold only 9.5 million units, almost four million less than they sold with the SEGA Genesis, and less than one-tenth as many consoles as the PlayStation.

SEGA Saturn © Evan Amos

In the late '90s, the PlayStation thrived, but it was the loss of longtime Nintendo backer Squaresoft that really punched Nintendo in the gut.

Final Fantasy VI © Squaresoft/Square Enix

Your parents might not want you to know this, but Hironobu Sakaguchi was a college dropout.

He was in his second year of college, studying electrical engineering, when he got a part-time job working for Squaresoft, and he ran out of school so fast he left his books behind and he never went back, although he did have one close scare. Sakaguchi had been working on projects at Squaresoft for three years, and while they'd shipped a few smaller games, they struggled to make a game that made money.

Turns out, making money is how you stay in business. Funny, that.

Sakaguchi was terrified that they would fail, and that he'd be forced to run back to Yokohama National University and try to find his books again. But he had a dream—a fantasy, if you will. One last shot to try to make his vision come true. Sakaguchi and Squaresoft decided to follow their passion and build the role-playing game they all wanted to play. They named it Final Fantasy, fearing that it would be their last game together, but boy, were they wrong.

Final Fantasy saw overnight success on the NES in Japan, and within a few years the games grew a following in the United States as well. They were popular because they were good—no, make that GREAT—games of epic size, with complex stories and memorable characters, and by the time Final Fantasy VI came out, the games were being compared to movie releases.

Squaresoft teased players with Final Fantasy VI by taking a cinematic approach. They even opened the game like a movie by rolling opening credits over an epic sound track, and now they wanted to take it to the next level.

All the games to this point had been Nintendo exclusives, but Sakaguchi and Squaresoft had a problem. The Final Fantasy games grew as the series increased, and while the SNES had been good to them, their ideas for the next game were going to be too big for the Nintendo's new console, the N64. They wanted, heck, they NEEDED a CD drive to accomplish their goals.

Luckily for Squaresoft, Sony PlayStation was up for the challenge. With CD-quality audio, the ability to play near-DVD-quality movies, and a lot more space than the N64 cartridge, things were about to get interesting.

It's said that the game was originally going to be set in New York City, which would have been a major change from the previous games, but in the end FFVII ended up being set in a world very familiar to their fans.

The game itself was known as a JRPG, which stands for *Japanese role-playing game*, but perhaps the best short-hand for the game is to call it an interactive novel. Story unfolds in rich detail, then the player is presented with choices to unlock new areas of the world, travel, or enter into quick battle sequences. Squaresoft really made the genre popular with their Final Fantasy series, but it was Final Fantasy VII that proved that the JRPG was something everyone could enjoy.

While the success for the Japanese release of Final Fantasy happened almost overnight, it took a while for the US versions to find an audience. Part of the problem, a pretty big part actually, was that all the dialogue had to be translated. That takes a lot of time. So much time, in fact, that by the time Final Fantasy III shipped in the United States, it was actually the same game as Final Fantasy VI in Japan. This odd numbering system continued until 2015, when Final Fantasy XV was the first in the series to have a simultaneous worldwide release date.

The city of Midgar from Final Fantasy VI © Squaresoft/Square Enix

Set in a true fantasy world, with everything from a living energy that drives the planet, to half-human/half-tiger creatures, Final Fantasy VII has a story so rich it would capture the imagination of any Comic-Con-going, cosplaying nerd out there. The story is so complex and deep that the average playtime to finish the game is over sixty hours. Many gamers have put hundreds of hours into the game, because they enjoy searching around in every nook and cranny to find all the details of the rich story.

Remember earlier we mentioned that Squaresoft wanted to innovate and their new ideas made it nearly impossible for the game to work with the N64 cartridge? Well, here are some of the things they did that required a more media-friendly CD.

- **For the first time in the series, voice-over was used for the main characters.**

- **Some of the scripted scenes played out like movies: fully animated cut scenes, with movie-quality audio and flashy particle effects.**

- The music, composed by Nobuo Uematsu, was his biggest work to date. While he'd created original sound tracks for previous Final Fantasy games (IV, V, and VI), Uematsu pulled out all the stops with VII, creating fifty-one original tracks and themes, a total of over two hours of unique music.

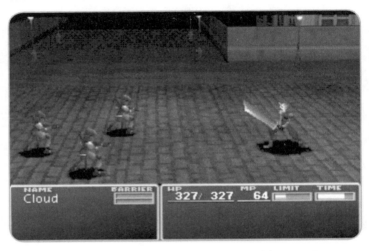

A Fight Scene from Final Fantasy VII © Squaresoft/Square Enix

- For the first time the characters for the fighting sections of the game were made from 3D models, and the number of unique animations in the game more than doubled from Final Fantasy VI. The extra space required for the animations alone would have blown their previous memory limitations.

The game was set to be a masterpiece, and things like that don't come cheap. It took more than 120 developers to build Final Fantasy VII. It was by far the most expensive video game development of its time, costing around forty-five million dollars. But in the end it all worked out for Squaresoft.

With the ease of developing on the new platform, Squaresoft was able to launch the American version of Final Fantasy VII a short nine months after the Japanese version. This was a major change from the past, where

Final Fantasy X was the first game to feature full voice acting all the way through in 2001, but it all started with the cut scenes in Final Fantasy VII, three games earlier.

sometimes it took two, maybe three years for the games to make their way across the ocean.

This new timeline even included Europe, where Final Fantasy VII not only shipped on the same day as the US launch date, but was the first Final Fantasy game ever to be sold in Europe.

Until this point, while the Final Fantasy games were loved by critics, outside Japan, Final Fantasy was really only purchased by hard-core collectors and JRPG fans. But with the release of Final Fantasy VII the game went . . . viral? I'm not sure that was a thing in 1997, but that was the concept.

Final Fantasy VII launched at the right time for Sony, too. They were riding high on the release of other, more mature games like Tomb Raider and Metal Gear Solid. The exclusive launch of Final Fantasy VII solidified the PlayStation as the must-have console, and Nintendo found themselves in an unfamiliar place. For the first time in their history, Nintendo wasn't making games about an underdog—it WAS the underdog.

Nintendo and Squaresoft were able to patch up their relationship eventually. There have been a few ports and spin-offs of the Final Fantasy games on the handheld Nintendo devices, and while rumors have spun for years about Final Fantasy VII making its way to the Wii U, so far it remains a Sony exclusive.

I CAN'T REMEMBER WHY I CAME HERE

Memory is a strange thing when you think about it. Actually, even thinking about memory creates a memory about thinking about memory, even though there's no guarantee that you'll remember thinking about memory tomorrow. Heck, you might even remember what memory is, but forget about how you learned about memory in the first place.

It's easy for me to remember big things like my birthday. I can remember the first time I beat a video game. I can even remember the name of my high school art teacher (Hi, Mrs. Criner), the name of my first dog (Hi, Skippy), and the first time I saw *Star Wars*: in the theater in 1977.

I can remember how to read, how to spell, how to tie my shoes, how to eat, what my favorite foods are, what color my car is, how to dial a phone. I can remember all kinds of useful things. Heck, I can even remember some pretty useless things as well, like the combination to my high school locker (24-36-16), the score of the 1997 Western Conference Finals game and who hit the big shot (Utah Jazz 103, Houston Rockets 100; John Stockton hit a three at the buzzer to send the Jazz to the finals).

I never forget to breathe. My heart never forgets to stop beating, unless I'm playing Silent Hill. Sometimes when I play that game I forget to breathe and my heart stops for a second or two. Are these part of my memory, too?

So why, oh, WHY can't I remember why my wife sent me to the grocery store? Why can I only find one shoe in the morning? Why can't I remember that I have a dentist appointment on April 3 at three thirty p.m.?

Yeah, it's confusing and strange. But if the power has ever gone out in your house just before you saved your game, you know exactly how important memory really is.

But how does it work on a computer or a console, and is it anything like OUR memories? Let's take a look and see how it compares to computer memory and see if we can make sense of things.

So, there are basically three types of memory. RAM, which means *random access memory*. ROM, which means *read-only memory*, and what we'll call storage space, which you probably think of as your hard drive or disk space. Each of these types of memory does something special, and they are actually very similar to the way your brain/memory works.

Let's start with the easy one, ROM, OR READ-ONLY MEMORY. ROM is the stuff that is always there for you. The basic starting instructions for how your PS4, your computer, or your 3DS starts up and runs. Anything that your computer needs to just keep things going is stored in ROM. This type of memory is pretty slow, but it's stable, and NOTHING can change it. That's why it's read-only. It's always there running in the background, and you probably never even think about it. Just like breathing or your heartbeat. It's just . . . there, ticking away and keeping things smooth.

The next one is DISK SPACE, OR YOUR HARD DRIVE. This is where big chunks of data are stored. Let's say you buy the latest version of Minecraft for your Xbox 360. Before you can play it, you need to download it and save it somewhere safe. It's pretty big, too, maybe a few gigabytes. I mean, you've got all those textures, models, rules, audio files, code. You name it. It takes a lot of parts to make a game. It might take hours to download the new game, and you don't want to have to do that every time you play. That would be HORRIBLE! Hard drive to the rescue. It's a big, empty space waiting to store video game content and data. And once it's there, it's there for good. And it will stay there until you delete it, even if you turn your computer off, unplug it from the wall, and ship it to your older brother in college a thousand miles away. The data is safe.

This is kind of like those big memorable moments in your life. The important things, like birthdays, and celebrations, and family get-togethers, that stay with you for the rest of your life. You don't forget these things because they are meaningful and important to you. You don't want to lose them because they are difficult to replace.

And the last, but certainly not least, type of memory is RAM—RANDOM ACCESS MEMORY. RAM is special because it is lightning fast. It is where the in-the-moment stuff happens, and where what you are seeing on-screen is being stored. What RAM does is grab the part of the game that you need immediately, and it loads it up so it's right there ready for you almost instantly. And not only that, small things that you do during the game are also saved in RAM. Your score, your position on-screen, your controller input information, all the stuff you are doing at the moment are saved right there for you, even if you aren't aware of it.

RAM is awesome. The more RAM your device has, the faster it is, because the bigger chunks of the game saved on your hard drive can be loaded up into your instant memory, or RAM. But . . . RAM has one major drawback.

RAM is totally forgettable.

In fact, the minute you turn off your computer or console, it's gonzo. Bye-bye. No save file.

That's why your games will usually ask you, "Hey, do you want to save before you quit?" What it's actually asking is, "Hey, do you want me to take this RAM memory stuff and pack it down onto the hard drive so I can remember it later? Or do you want me to just flush it out of my mind?"

This, to me, is like forgetting where you left your shoes after you go to sleep at night. Or getting to the store and forgetting why you came. The information is short-term, not really that important, but still, there's nothing worse than getting home after a trip to the store and remembering that you forgot to buy the dish soap. Well, there's something worse: losing a save file because you forgot to save your game to your hard drive. Yeah, that's worse by FAR.

Half-Life © Valve Corporation

In 1996, Gabe Newell was helping build operating systems at Microsoft, and he was bored.

Now, don't get me wrong. Few things in the history of American ingenuity and invention hold as much importance as Microsoft's Windows operating systems, but that doesn't mean it's the most fun job on the planet, either. And if you're a guy like Gabe Newell, finding fun is almost as important as building an empire. And, as it turns out, if you're a guy like Gabe Newell, you might be able to do both.

Newell is a true entrepreneur. A visionary who understands not only how to make great software, but how to build huge communities and systems to deliver content. It is perhaps his biggest takeaway from his time at Microsoft, and a huge influence on his work at Valve (especially the invention of Steam—more on Steam later, I promise). Gabe is great at noticing trends in the gaming world, and new things on the horizon, so back in 1996, while working at Microsoft, Gabe started noticing what id Software was

At first glance, you might think Valve is a strange name for a video game company, but there is a special meaning behind the name. They came up with the name Valve to represent how their company works: They see themselves as a valve that is used to control the flow of an entertainment experience. And after you play a Valve game, you'll see how they truly are masters at deciding when to turn down the action or intensity, and more important, when to crank it up.

doing in Texas, and he thought it looked like a whole lot more fun than making operating systems.

It was time for a change for Mr. Newell, and he wasn't the only employee at Microsoft that felt that way. Another developer, Mike Harrington, shared his curiosity and passion about games, so after a few discussions and a whole lot of planning, Harrington and Newell left Microsoft and founded Valve down the street in Kirkland, Washington.

They had one goal in mind. They wanted to make great—not good, not okay—GREAT games, and with millions of Microsoft stock dollars in the bank, they had the money to do it.

Unfortunately, as they found out the hard way, money isn't the only thing you need to make great games.

Valve grew quickly as Newell added talent to his new team, hiring engineers, artists, writers, and designers, but remember, Newell and Harrington were used to building operating systems, the thing that lives on your computer that allows it to, well, operate, or do things like open windows, launch programs, and turn off and on. And while this was great experience, it didn't really teach them how to make games.

So, Newell reached out to ANOTHER ex-Microsoft developer, Michael Abrash, who had previously left Microsoft to join up with id Software in Texas. Abrash loved what Newell was trying to do, and he had one big piece of advice: Come to Texas and see what id was working on.

Newell listened, and he jumped on a plane right away. His visit to id Software was eye-opening, and one thing that he learned really quickly was that building games and building business software were two different things for sure. John Carmack and his crew at id had invested millions of dollars developing their first-person-shooter engine, the Quake engine, and Newell saw it as a huge shortcut to realizing his dreams of making a quality game. So, after a bit of negotiation, Gabe Newell thanked the guys at id and climbed back on a plane to head back to Seattle. Only this time, he had a CD containing the Quake engine with him.

Now Valve had employees. They had an office. They had an engine. All they needed was a game idea, which, it turned out, they had under control as well. Inspired by the compelling environments of DOOM, the team at Valve focused on making a FPS of their own, only instead of relying solely on high-paced action, Valve wanted to slow things down a bit and make story a HUGE part of the experience.

To prove their point, as much to themselves as anyone else, Valve started right away, and before long they had something they could play. Half-Life started off in a revolutionary manner at the time. From the moment you started the game, you were locked into the experience, and they did everything they could not to break that illusion of *being* the character in the game. Things started off quiet and normal. No weapons, no sense of peril, and no decisions to be made. Just you, a scientist named Gordon Freeman, who was showing up for a day at work at Black Mesa Research Facility.

But your so-called normal day goes totally wonky as an experiment goes horribly wrong, and in a matter of minutes, you go from mild-mannered scientist to crowbar-wielding savior of the universe. Or, at least, savior of the Black Mesa Research Facility. It's a perfect story setup for what then becomes a fight for survival.

The team at Valve was excited about how things were progressing, but Gabe Newell took a long look at the game about a year and a half after the company had started, and he wasn't thrilled. In fact, he was worried. The game was fine, but there was no way that what they currently had in place was going to hit Newell's vision. He wasn't okay with just fine, he wanted amazing, and their current plan wouldn't get them there.

They had a hard decision to make. Finish up and launch the current version of Half-Life, hoping that it would do okay, or throw the WHOLE thing away and start from scratch, hoping that the new end result would match the company's lofty goals. After much debate, Valve decided that the game was missing the mark, and deleted everything.

You'd think that having a project ripped out from under you would really hurt after spending more than a year of your life cranking away at it. I mean, that is a LOT of time to put toward something, only to have it scrapped and never see the light of day. But the Valve employees saw this as a great sign—an indicator that Newell was committed to quality first, and that he recognized how important it was to get things done right, not just get things done.

After the cancellation of their first attempt, the team refocused and set their sights on being the best they could be.

Probably the most significant thing Valve added in the new version was the role of the NPC, the nonplayable character. These characters filled the halls of the Black Mesa Research Facility. They were your colleagues before the accident—nerdy scientists, buff security guards, lab-coat-wearing assistants—and there was something about being among them as you tried to rid the world of mutated bad guys and slithering, crab-like beasties that made you feel connected, even responsible for them.

Barney in Half-Life © Valve Corporation

The NPC characters follow you around or stop you in the hall to ask you questions. They join you on missions, lead you to new places in the game, and even help you against the enemies from time to time. But the most important role your coworkers at the Black Mesa Research Facility play is that of storytellers. They are how Valve

Barney, a loyal security guard character type in Half-Life, became a fan favorite for gamers. And I say *type* because there wasn't just one Barney, there were quite a few. Some players became such Barney fans that they would do everything they could to save and collect all the Barneys in the game, trying to finish the experience with a small army of Barneys joining them at the game's finish line.

progresses the story, one little hint at a time.

In 1997, the game was ready to be shown to the public. It wasn't finished yet, but Valve was confident that their decision to start over was the right one, and that they had something special. They took the game to E3, a popular video game show in California. They didn't have a big, fancy booth, or a light show like some of the big publishers, but eventually, by word of mouth, people started finding their game and giving it a try. Before the show was over, Half-Life ended up winning the E3's Action Game of the Show.

Valve finally released Half-Life in November 1998, and it took the industry by storm. For many gamers and reviewers, it was more than just a video game. It was like a playable movie that you starred in, and fans LOVED it. And so did reviewers. So much so that Half-Life was named Game of the Year by fifty publications. FIFTY! FIVE-OH!

At a time where console games were ruling the industry, this computer game went on to sell eight million copies worldwide and bring in more than 100 million dollars in sales. That's a lot of cash!

Valve went on to build two expansion packs and, of course, the game fans were begging for, Half-Life 2, but perhaps the most important and longest-lasting legacy that Half-Life created was what it did for the modding community.

At the time, modding games, or taking the original content of a game and tweaking it with your own art, rules, and level designs, was something that was only done by a small fraction of the game-playing world, modders. But Valve, who always encouraged modding, made it easy for users to alter their content, and boy, did the community respond. Hundreds of mods were being made, ranging from Half-Life clones to totally original pieces like Afraid of Monsters, a pure horror game, or Wanted!, a Western gunslinger mod.

These mods kept Half-Life at the forefront of PC gaming for years. In fact, new mods are still being made almost twenty years later, but none of them compare to the quality and sales of a popular military-based mod, Counter-Strike.

A modder/designer named Minh "Gooseman" Le built a multiplayer, military-based shooter on top of Half-Life in 1998, shortly after the game released. It quickly rose to the top of the list of mods being played. In fact, it grew so popluar that Valve took notice and started helping Gooseman build the mod. Not all mods grow to see the success of Counter-Strike—actually, most of them are only played by the people creating them—but with Gooseman's design and the backing of Valve, Counter-Strike grew from being a mod to an actual product released by Valve in less than a year.

Valve truly innovated in the first-person-shooter genre, leaving behind a trail of important additions to the history of video gaming.

Counter-Strike was so popular, in fact, that by its fifth beta, the mod actually surpassed Half-Life in number of players online, becoming the most-played online game in the world in 1999.

- **DYNAMIC WORLD DESTRUCTION.** The brilliant programmers at Valve pioneered in-game destruction. In Half-Life, when you shot a gun, you left bullet holes on the wall; when you hacked away at a mutated scientist, you left his blood splatter on the wall; and you could even spray-paint the walls, leaving behind a mark so you could find your way back. These marks not only showed up when you created them, but they stayed around forever, changing the environment as you played and making it feel that much more realistic.

- **NPC SCRIPTING.** I touched on this above, but here's a bit more detail. Not only did the nonplayable characters interact with you, the big change and innovation here is HOW they did this. Earlier games had stopped the action for cut scenes (where developers pull you out of the game experience and show you, the gamer, a movie) to advance the story. But in Half-Life, the NPCs never interrupt game play—it happens in game, while you are still playing, and it made things very immersive.

- **ADVANCED WORLD SCRIPTING.** Similar to the NPC scripting, but in Half-Life, not only did the characters help tell the story, the environment did, too. Massive machines went haywire around you, walls crumbled, wet floors caused you to slip and fall through glass ceilings, and much more. The world was scripted, or predetermined by the game developers to change and alter your game-play experience. Truly awesome and unexpected at the time, although many games now use this.

- CONTIGUOUS EXPLORATION. This is one of those big things that you don't notice until someone points it out to you. Before Half-Life, it was very common for games to pause and load frequently. Heck, it still is today. But the Valve level designers worked together with programmers to pioneer a nearly load-free gaming experience. They did this through cleverly placed hallways, elevators, and shafts that would mask the fact that as you traveled, new areas of the game were being loaded in the background.

- MORE SOPHISTICATED AI. While games had enjoyed artificial intelligence for years, Half-Life took this to a whole new level with their AI system. It was especially noticeable in the enemies. Soldiers would flank you, toss grenades, seek cover, engage aliens, and communicate and plan with one another. This was a HUGE step up from previous games, where AI generally consisted of "find the player; smash him."

Half-Life put Valve on the map, solidifying them as one of the most important and well-loved game developers on the planet, and Valve is still thriving today. Half-Life 2 moved the series to new heights with better graphics, more complex AI, and even better in-game storytelling. But the big question still remains: *When will we get to play Half-Life 3?*

Gabe Newell: Let Off Some Steam

• • • • • • • • • • • • • • • •

Gabe Newell learned a lot about business from his first employer, Bill Gates. You know, the Microsoft guy. Mr. Gates told Mr. Newell that success in software comes from getting someone else to make a program or game that will help sell more copies of *your* program. You know, like Windows. Microsoft doesn't make all the games that work on their computer or Xbox consoles, but those games couldn't run without Microsoft. It was a lesson that would stick with Newell for decades—one he's still learning today.

He was one of the first three hundred employees at Microsoft, number 271 to be exact, and he worked with the software giant for years, becoming the producer of the first three releases of Windows. But in 1996, Newell and coworker Mike Harrington left Microsoft and started a company of their own: Valve Corporation.

Gabe Newell signed the official papers to start Valve on his wedding day.

Two years later, Valve released their first game, a sci-fi first-person shooter called Half-Life. According to his bio on Valve's website, Newell's biggest addition to Half-Life was this statement. "C'mon, people, you can't show the player a really big bomb and not let them blow it up."

He had a point. But we know his contribution was much bigger than that. Newell is the managing director of game development at Valve, but his true love and focus is on technology. And being a techy guy, trained alongside Bill Gates, Newell saw an opportunity early on to build something that every gamer would need. Or at least thirty million of them would. Although, at the time, even gamers didn't know they needed what Valve was about to offer.

Gabe Newell directed and managed the creation of Steam, a digital video game store that allows players to buy, launch, and play games without ever having to leave the couch!

Steam is a digital distribution tool. What that means is that Steam is basically an online store where you can browse for new games, buy them right there within Steam, and download them directly to your computer. But that was only the beginning. Steam also checks to make sure your game is up-to-date. If a developer changes something in the game, fixes a bug, or adds more free content, Steam automatically delivers that to the gamer, too.

This was all very innovative at the time, but as Newell is known to do, he kept innovating. Steam tracks all of your game-playing history, awarding you badges and achievements that you can display to show off your gaming awesomeness. It also encourages you to make friend lists, groups, and private gaming parties with your gamer buddies.

Steam was released in 2003, and it was a big hit from day one, but Newell knew that for it to really be great he needed other game developers to make software that he could sell in his Steam store, so he started looking.

If Gabe Newell is good at anything, it's finding good talent. He pays close attention to the modding and independent game communities, and because of this he discovered games that have gone on to be hugely successful. Newell and Valve discovered Counter-Strike, Team Fortress, Portal, and Dota 2 in this manner.

Gabe Newell has a reputation for being a very open and honest guy, especially for a company owner. He often responds to e-mail questions from fans, and he also relies on his community of gamers for ideas, suggestions, and feedback. And Gabe not only listens to his audience, he jokes with them as well. Especially when it comes to rumors of games ending at number two. For years fans have clamored for Half-Life 3, Portal 3, and Left 4 Dead 3, but the running joke is that Mr. Newell can only count to two. He's very good-natured about this, but I say we keep bugging him about it. Who knows, he could break, and we'd get a chance to enjoy more of our favorite games. (Please, Mr. Newell. Please!!!)

Gabe Newell is credited with more than twenty-five games as of 2015. I won't list them all here, but here are some of Gabe Newell's greatest hits.

- Half-Life

- Half-Life 2

- The Orange Box

- Team Fortress

- Dota 2

- The Counter-Strike series

- Homeworld 2

- The Portal series

Steam © Valve Corporation

DANCE DANCE REVOLUTION

1999

STEP IN A NEW DIRECTION

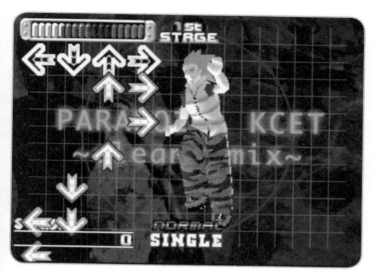

Dance Dance Revolution © Konami

The home PC and console gaming business was booming.

The TV cabinet was being overrun by gaming systems and games. Gamers were spending big bucks on fancy gaming PCs. And the slumber party had been replaced by all-night gaming sessions. Gamers were working on their hand-eye coordination. They pounded buttons with fury, they slammed joysticks with precision, and they timed jumps and turns in racetracks like professional drivers, but Japanese arcade developer Konami had a new idea. They wanted gamers to play with their feet.

So Konami introduced Dance Dance Revolution in Japan in 1998, then they brought DDR to the US arcade stage in 1999. And it was a game that truly lived up to its name. After all, you danced, you danced some more, and it was a revolution in gaming.

DDR, as it came to be known by everyone who stomped to the beat, had a huge impact on the culture of games just before the turn of the century. Instead of just a few die-hard gamers blasting aliens in a dark arcade, Dance

Dance Revolution came along, and suddenly *everyone* was stepping in and giving it a try.

The game spawned the beginning of the Konami Music Group, also known as the Kukeiha Club, Konami's in-house band. The game didn't push the limits of graphics or game play, or even contain a plotline. But it provided gamers with endless amounts of fun, and isn't that what games are supposed to do?

When the game was introduced in Japanese arcades in 1998, it was an instant hit. The culture of arcades in Japan was different from in the US. It was more social. It was cool to just go and hang out with friends in the arcade, so when a game came along that was as inviting as DDR, Japanese gamers were more than happy to give it a try.

Konami started to move the game to America the very next year, but US arcade owners thought it was too different to catch on with their less social gamers. Not to mention, at a time when most arcade cabinets cost around $2,500, Dance Dance Revolution cost arcade owners between $15,000 to $17,000. It was a steep price to pay, so it took a while for it to catch on. However, a few arcades in California gave it a shot, and the popularity of the machine caught on like wildfire. By 2000, DDR cabinets could be found in just about every decent arcade across the country, not to mention in movie theater lobbies and pizza parlors.

DDR was easy to learn how to play, and it was also easy to describe. There was a big screen with brightly colored arrows that appeared at the bottom, then made their way to the top in perfect timing with the loud dance music pumping from its high-quality speakers. There was a safety rail behind the dance pad that you could use to help you balance if you had two left feet, and four arrows embedded in the floor in front of the arcade. All you had to do was step on the right arrow at the right time, and before you knew it you were dancing.

As gamers really began to learn the game, different play styles emerged. Part of this was due to the way the songs were selected and organized in the game. For twenty-five cents, you would be able to pick any three songs on the list. The difficulty was up to you. If you wanted to take it easy, maybe drop in some sweet spins and dance moves, you'd pick something from the Beginner or Light category. If you were more about trying to push yourself to get a perfect score on a difficult song, you'd choose a song from the Standard or Heavy list.

Dance Dance Revolution Extreme Machine © True Tech Talk Time

While there were plenty of gamers that just wanted to jump on the pad, groove out to some cool tunes, and have a good time messing around, the "serious" players started to divide into two camps: freestylers and PAs (perfect attack).

The challenge of getting a perfect score on the most difficult songs was such a drive for some players, they did everything they could to mimimize any extra movement. They focused solely on their feet, timing every step exactly to the corresponding arrow on-screen. These DDR players were often called techs, technical, or perfect attack players. And the more technical a song got, the more the player used minimalistic movements in order to hit all the arrows with perfection.

The freestylers took a totally different approach. They prided themselves on being able to add flashy or complex dance moves using their entire bodies, while still trying to get a great score in the game. Some freestyle players developed intricate dance routines to perform during a song. In general, freestylers chose songs on lower difficulty levels to be able to add more moves without being tied down to too many arrows on-screen.

There was quite a debate between freestylers, who claimed that PAs took the fun out of the game, and the PAs, who claimed that freestylers were more dancers than gamers. But in the end, it didn't really matter how you played the game—what mattered was that it was FUN. And it was fun to watch.

Another interesting phenomenon to pop up from DDR was that not only did gamers like playing the game, but they LOVED watching others play as well. There was something funny about watching your friend tumble her way through the first (easy) tune, and it was just mesmerizing to watch someone really good at the game tap their way through a super challenging song.

Watching people play DDR became such a big thing that soon there were DDR competitions popping up all over the place. Arcades hosted battles that drew hundreds of people—people who wouldn't normally play games. And some of those people would give other games a try and realize they were fun and stick around.

Not only was DDR fun, it was good for you, too. In fact, in 2007 the *New York Times* did an article about Dance Dance Revolution being used as a physical education tool. It started with a few schools in West Virginia, but when PE teachers were reporting how excited kids were to get up and move with the game, it spread. The *New York Times* estimated that by the end of the decade there were 1,500 schools using DDR as PE. Now, that's my kind of sport.

Dance Dance Revolution changed the way we thought of games, and it paved the way for an abundance of music games over the next twenty years. Without DDR, we might never have had Guitar Hero, which would be a TRAGEDY!

But it was more than just music: Dance Dance Revolution innovated in other areas as well.

- DDR was the first arcade game that was considered exercise. At a time when parents were growing increasingly concerned about their kids spending too much time sitting on the couch with a controller in their hands, DDR inspired a generation to get on their feet.

- The home versions of Dance Dance Revolution introduced the gamer community to large game pads, or peripherals, paving the way for everything from plastic drums to virtual tennis rackets.

- DDR was the first arcade game to become an official sporting event. The entire country of Norway was so engaged in DDR that they formed professional DDR teams that competed for a national championship.

Gamers around the world were stepping to the beat, as the flashy Japanese arcade game introduced a whole new generation of gamers to a new hobby of dropping quarters in machines with friends. I guess all we have to say is, "*Domo Arigato, Dansu Dansu Reboryūshon!*"

Not only was DDR a global craze in the arcade, it launched a dance style called *jumpen* or *jumpstyle*, where gamers, mostly freestylers who memorized the steps in the game, took those steps and moves out into the wild, where they performed DDR-style moves away from the arcades. It's really crazy to watch a very good jumpen dancer. You should give it a shot. youtube.com/watch?v=uteGXChtVTc

A "Perfect" being scored in Dance Dance Revolution © Konami

LET'S GET PHYSICAL

. . . .

Have you ever heard this? "Playing video games makes you fat."

I have. In fact, I'll admit that I've even said it a time or two to my video game-playing kids. And while it's true that simply sitting around all day with a bag of Cheesy Poofs, a two-liter bottle of Sparkling Caffeinated Nitro Glow, and a controller in your hand is not the healthiest thing in the world, there have been some great advancements in the last ten years to address this issue.

As games become an even bigger part of our lives, it's good to know that there are ways to improve our fitness AND still have fun.

The DDR dance pad really helped start this craze, and if you've ever tried to beat some of the more difficult songs, you know why. But it didn't end there. The Wii came along, and everyone, from toddlers to grandpas, was waving their arms around like mad. Then the PlayStation Move and the Xbox Kinect joined the party. Soon, there were motion-activated games on every platform, and every living room was potentially turned into a gym.

Exergames—yeah, they even have their own category now—have come a long way since the early days of the dance pad, and it isn't just gamers that have taken notice.

In fact, Dance Dance Revolution has become a regular part of physical education (PE) in elementary schools around the country. Add to that, the *Journal of Pediatrics* (a very fancy doctors' magazine) actually recommends using exergames to improve your health. Imagine that: a doctor telling you to play video games! Very cool!

So, if you're wondering where to start, here's a quick list of ten great games that will raise your heart rate AND keep you entertained. Oh, and just another suggestion: Swap out the Cheesy Poofs and Nitro Glow soda for something healthy, and you'll be looking like a video game character yourself in no time.

10. Wii Fit U—Wii U

This game comes with a Balance Board that can measure your weight and balance, and the new Fit Meter will allow you to track your fitness in and out of the house. The games are really fun, too. There's everything from Yoga to Dance, but I really like the Aerobics activities. Rowing, Puzzle Squash, and Boxing are all a blast. But my favorite has got to be Trampoline Target. And don't kid yourself, if you turn up the settings on these games, you'll get a real workout.

Oh, one last note. The Wii Fit Trainer even made an appearance in Super Smash Bros., but don't worry, you don't need to use the Balance Board to play her character in the game. Now, THAT would be tough.

9. The Biggest Loser

Based on the hit TV show, this game brings world-famous fitness trainer Jillian Michaels right into your living room. Whether you're playing on your Xbox or your Wii U, you'll break a sweat, and if you don't, Jillian will start yelling at you. Oh, and it comes with a diet plan as well.

8. Kinect Adventures!

This game kind of plays like an adventure reality show. The graphics are appealing and fun, and you do everything from extreme river rafting to obstacle courses. This is a real family game, and with their tournament mode it can get really competitive. It is superfun, and superactive.

7. Dance Central

This game not only uses your feet, like the original DDR, it uses your whole body. The game teaches you actual dance moves that you can break out to impress people, and it uses the Kinect camera to make sure that you're really nailing it. Seriously, if you memorize a few steps from this game, you'll be a hit at any dance party.

6. PlayStation Move

This game was bundled with the PlayStation Move controller. It ships with eleven sports, including boxing, tennis, archery, skiing, and more. The PlayStation Move controller didn't really take off, but the game was pretty fun and, in my opinion, had the best boxing game of all the motion-controller games. You really have to work it to be good at this game.

5. Zumba Fitness

Not only is *Zumba* a fun word to say, it's actually really fun to do. Or at least that's what I've heard. Okay, I'm not the guy for this game, but I tried it out, and it was really hard. And really fun. But mostly, really hard. I was lying on the floor like a puddle of goo by the end of the first workout, but the music was cool, and I totally got my Zumba on. Whatever that means.

4. Wii Sports

This one was such a massive hit that it simply has to be on this list. Believe it or not, it became the bestselling Nintendo game of all time. (It even surpassed Super Mario Bros.!) That's incredible. It sold so well because it is easy to play, superfun, and yeah, it gets you off the couch. It really did change how we play games.

3. Dance Dance Revolution Max 2

This one *has* to make the list. It's fun, the music is great, and it will really get you moving. This is the seventh version of DDR, and it really amps up the tempo on songs, as well as introduces players to a new step-and-hold move that totally changes the way the game is played. Not only does your heart rate go through the roof, but it is so much fun you barely notice you are getting a workout.

2. Just Dance 4

Okay, you might be thinking . . . "Another dance game," but this one is just awesome. Funky graphics, great music, and cool dance moves are all in the game, but the best part is that it's a four-player game. This one really takes party games to a whole new level, and it takes photos of you and your friends during the game and plays them back as embarrassing moments at the end. Lots of exercise and lots of laughs.

1. UFC Personal Trainer

If dancing isn't your style, then step it up with UFC Personal Trainer for Xbox or Wii U. This game is serious fun, and if you put your time into this one, you'll be toned, tough, and tired out. You know, just like a UFC athlete.

POKÉMON YELLOW

1999

GOTTA CATCH 'EM ALL

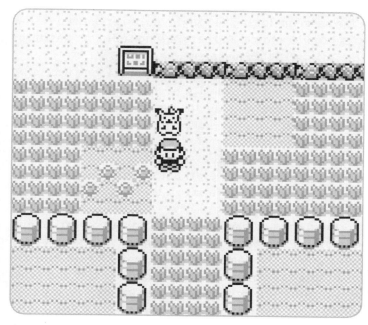

Ash and Pikachu in Pokémon Yellow © Game Freak, Inc./Nintendo

In 1998, when the first Pokémon games, Red and Blue, hit the United States, a lot of people claimed Pokémon was just a fad.

Two decades, sixteen main games, a handful of spin-off games, seventeen feature films, over one hundred television episodes, and more than seven hundred Pokémon later, I'd say they were wrong.

But before we get to all of that, it's important to know the story of how this huge pop culture phenomenon came to be. And to best do that, we should go back to Japan in 1981, where a seventeen-year-old named Satoshi Tajiri was so in love with arcades and arcade games that he made his own magazine about them called *Game Freak*. The magazine was written and stapled by hand, not full of glossy photographs and advertisements like his competitors, but that didn't stop it from gaining

In 1989, Tajiri transformed his magazine company, *Game Freak*, into a video game company of the same name, and he and Sugimori pitched their first game, an arcade-style shooter called *Quinty*, to Namco, who would eventually publish the game on NES.

Tajiri was such an avid bug collector as a child that his schoolmates nicknamed him *Dr. Bug*.

a fan base—including Ken Sugimori, an artist and fellow arcade game addict, and before long Sugimori was helping Tajiri with his magazine.

By the late 1980s, Tajiri and Sugimori were becoming disappointed in the quality of new games being made, and they decided the solution was to start making games on their own.

So now it's 1990. Game Freak has published their first game, and Tajiri is still as passionate about making and playing great games as ever. But nothing they try seems to be just right. Until Tajiri starts messing around with the Game Boy Link Cable.

The Game Boy had been out for about a year, and it was doing great. But there weren't many successful games using one of the Game Boy's most unique features, the Link Cable. Gamers could use the cable to link two Game Boys together. Now, remember, this was back in the days before Wi-Fi, before you could even hook a handheld gaming system to the Internet at all, so this was a pretty big deal. But unfortunately, developers weren't really taking advantage of it.

The few games that *were* using the Link Cable, like Street Fighter II in 1991, were mostly focused on combat and fighting, but Tajiri thought there might be a better use for the Link Cable.

Sharing.

Inspired by the Link Cable and his favorite childhood activity of bug collecting, Tajiri imagined a world where you collected and shared small monsters with your friends, and Pocket Monsters was born.

Well, *born* might be an exaggeration at this point. In fact, it would take another *six* years after Tajiri had the idea before the Pokémon games were ready to launch. But, lucky for him and his small company, Game Freak, Tajiri had a mentor who believed in him and his Pocket Monsters: Shigeru Miyamoto.

When Nintendo first saw Tajiri's idea for Pokémon, they couldn't quite grasp the concept, but they liked Tajiri and trusted him as a developer enough to give him a chance. Miyamoto began to mentor Tajiri, guiding him during the creation process, which took so long that it nearly bankrupted Game Freak.

But if we've learned anything from reading about the history of video games, it is that nothing stays the same, and here's another example. In 1990, when Tajiri came up with the idea for Pokémon, the Game Boy was a shiny new handheld gaming system. It was in the news, being advertised on TV, and new games were being made for it all the time. But, six years later, not only was the Game Boy dying away, but handheld gaming in general was on a major decline. Home consoles were the rage, and SEGA, Sony, and Nintendo were all trying to outdo each other with stunning new games. And not only that, there was a nice arcade revival going on with games like Dance Dance Revolution, Gauntlet Legends, and Time Crisis II—all three celebrated cooperative play and lots of action.

Handheld gaming was fading fast, which caused Tajiri to think that his game would never get a chance. Luckily for him, and for us, Nintendo saw things differently. They thought that Tajiri's game was just what they needed to save handheld gaming, and their little gray Game Boy.

So, on February 27, 1996, Nintendo launched Pocket Monsters Red and Pocket Monsters Green in Japan. It took a while for the games to catch on, but when they did, it was obvious that they were going to be huge. So big, in fact, that Nintendo decided to put a third game into the mix that same year. On October 15, 1996, they released Pocket Monsters Blue, a game that has since become quite a collector's item. Mostly because Nintendo revised Pocket Monsters Red and Green for releases in the United States as Pokémon Red and Blue, but the original Pocket Monsters Blue only released in Japan.

By 1997, more than ten MILLION copies of Pocket Monsters had been sold in Japan, totally bringing the Game Boy and the underutilized Link Cable back from the dead. Pocket Monsters, as it was known in Japan at the time, became a national craze, but on April 1, 1997, the franchise took it to a whole new level. That was the day the first episode of the Pocket Monsters anime TV show aired in Japan.

Satoshi Tajiri owes a lot to his parents, because during the six years it took to bring Pokémon from a concept to an actual game he did not take a paycheck from Game Freak, his own company. He lived in his parents' home, and off their generosity.

One of the most important details of the Pokémon universe that really set the game apart from other games at the time was the game's tame take on violence. It was very important to Tajiri that Pokémon only fainted when defeated in arena battles, and this is a feature that still lives on in the Pokémon game two decades later.

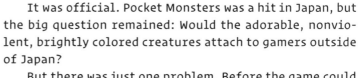

GAME ON!

It was official. Pocket Monsters was a hit in Japan, but the big question remained: Would the adorable, nonviolent, brightly colored creatures attach to gamers outside of Japan?

But there was just one problem. Before the game could be released in the US, the game needed a name change. The name Pocket Monsters had already been trademarked by another company, so they shortened the name to Pokémon, and the name was such a hit that it eventually made its way back to Japan as well.

Pokémon Red and Blue launched in September 1998 in the United States, and in less than a year the game had sold nearly as many copies as it had in Japan. Gamers fell in love with the unique personalities of the Pokémon. They knew all 151 of them by name, could tell you which Pokémon matched up best with one another, and traded and built up their collections until they had "'em all."

Pokémon's tagline, "You gotta catch 'em all," was seen as a challenge in early games, because players had to find, trade, and collect all 151 Pokémon. In order to keep this straight, the game had something called a Pokédex, a digital catalog of each of the Pokémon in your collection. But, if you think that was a challenge, try filling in your Pokédex in Pokémon Alpha Sapphire or Omega Ruby. There are 721 Pokémon required to fill your Pokédex. Be ready for some serious trading to make this happen.

Pokédex entry for Pikachu from Pokémon Yellow © Game Freak, Inc./Nintendo

By then the Pokémon franchise had single-handedly brought the handheld gaming market back to life. The

Game Boy was seeing a nice second life, but Pokémon wasn't done yet. In fact, it had just started. The TV series was a massive hit in Japan, and it made its way to the United States in record time, filling the eyes of American fans in 1998.

Pokémon had become a cultural phenomenon around the globe. Kids everywhere were toting plastic Pokéballs around with them in their pockets and backpacks, and loving Ash and his little yellow friend, Pikachu. They loved the collection and exploration in Pokémon Red and Blue, and the companionship and deep story of the anime. All they needed was a game to tie them all together, and in 1999, gamers got what they wanted. All this buildup led to the launch of Pokémon Yellow.

Pokémon Yellow was a HUGE hit for Nintendo and Game Freak, because not only did it have updated graphics, it was based almost entirely off the TV show. In the show, Ash is known for being followed around by his "pet" Pokémon, Pikachu. This behavior showed TV viewers that not only was Ash funny, clever, and the best young Pokémon trainer in Kantō, but that hard-to-catch Pokémon, like Pikachu, loved him. So, in the new game, a pixelated Pikachu followed your character around the game.

Pokémon Yellow also did something that game developers call *bridging the gap*. It was the last game to be launched for the regular Game Boy and the first to be launched for Game Boy Color. So Pokémon Yellow was first released on October 18, 1999, for the Game Boy, and one week later, on October 25, 1999, it was released for the Game Boy Color. Sounds crazy, huh? But it worked. In fact, the special-edition Pikachu-inspired yellow Game Boy Color shipped with Pokémon Yellow in the box was one of the hottest toys of that holiday season.

Pokémon Yellow did for Game Boy Color what its predecessors, Red and Blue, had done for the Game Boy. It boosted sales and kept gamers busy for HOURS collecting, battling, and trading Pokémon with friends.

We owe a lot to Satoshi Tajiri and his bug-collecting, Link Cable–inspired game. Perhaps no game in the history of gaming has gone on to have as big an impact

1999 also brought us the first Pokémon film, cleverly titled *Pokémon: The First Movie*. While the film suffered from poor reviews, the Pokémon fans LOVED it. They loved it so much that it became one of the most successful video game–inspired films of all time, grossing over 163 million dollars worldwide and giving way to a long line of Pokémon films. In fact, as of 2015, seventeen films have been released, and more are certainly on the way.

on worldwide pop culture as Pokémon. Here are a few examples of the literally hundreds of ways Pokémon has expanded beyond the Game Boy and found a place in our daily lives.

- In 1999, Nintendo and Volkswagen collaborated to create a yellow Volkswagen New Beetle, with some features taken directly from Pikachu, like black headlight surrounds and an optional lightning-bolt-shaped antenna.

- In 1999, *TIME* magazine ranked Pikachu as second on their "Best People of 1999" list, citing him as the most beloved animated character since Mickey Mouse.

- In 2001, Pikachu floated over downtown New York City as a balloon in the famous Macy's Thanksgiving Day parade.

- The Pokémon trading card game hit Japan early on in 1996, shortly after the video games became popular, but it didn't explode in America until 1999. The card game went on to be the defining trading card game of the 2000s. It was a massive hit, so much so that it became a distraction in elementary and middle schools across the country, and it was frequently banned from the classroom.

- Starting in 1998, Japanese airline All Nippon Airways decorated their massive 767 international jets with Pokémon characters. These colorful and fun jets were big hits when they landed in airports around the world, but unfortunately the last Pokémon jet was retired in 2013.

- Toys"R"Us, the American-based toy giant, signed an exclusive deal to distribute Pokémon toys in 2000, but the megastore couldn't handle the demand for Pokémon toys. Now you can buy Pokémon figurines, plush toys, clothing, backpacks, lunch boxes, Pokéballs, key chains, you name it, in just about every store in America.

- The Pokémon Video Game World Championships were started in 2004, bringing the series into a more competitive light. If you're a championship winner, Nintendo will give you a scholarship to a college of your choice.

- In 2014, the Pokémon characters showed up in the World Cup, as Pikachu became the official mascot of Japan's national soccer team.

- Pokémon's very own wiki page, Bulbapedia, is the second-largest video game index in the world, coming in close behind the World of Warcraft wiki. This fan-built reference page is the best and only place to go for accurate, up-to-date stats and news about everything Poké-related.

- In 2016, Pokémon celebrated their twentieth anniversary by announcing it during the Super Bowl. The commercial inspired a whole new generation of Pokémon fans with its encouraging words "I can do that."

- Pokémon GO developers, Niantic, Inc., released thousands of real-world Pokémon into the wild in July 2016. Okay, not REAL Pokémon, but if you spied one through a smartphone, you'd sure think it was real. They partnered with Nintendo on the phone-based game, and it quickly jumped to the top of the charts as millions of Pokémon players explored the real world in search of augmented-reality Pokémon.

Pokémon GO © Niantic, The Pokémon Company

Pokémon GO also did something no other game to date has been able to do. It got players out of the house, exploring, running, walking, and even jumping in the real world. In fact, many gamers took to social media to joke around about their new Pokémon workout. Though I'm not so sure it was a joke. I know I felt the burn.

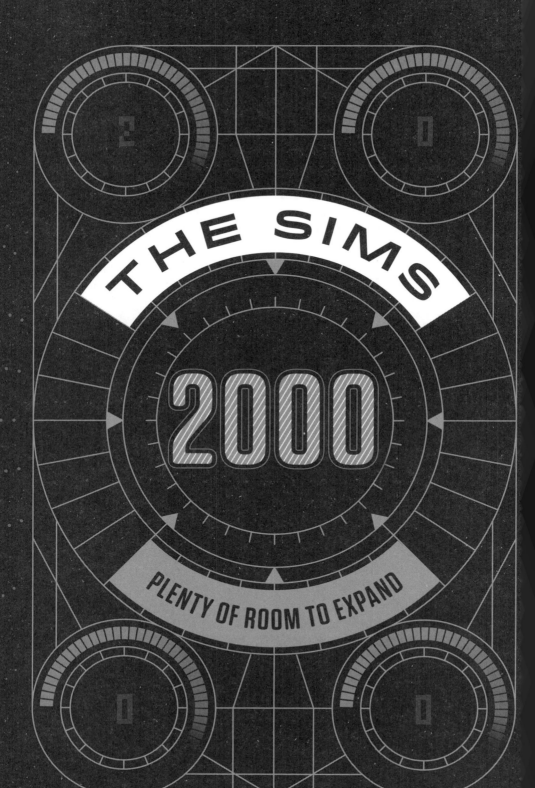

The Sims © Maxis/Electronic Arts, Inc.

Do you know about the phoenix?

No, not that online college, or the desert city in Arizona. I'm talking about the legendary fire bird, the phoenix. When the phoenix dies, this mythical bird bursts into flames and then rises from the ashes to be even more beautiful and powerful than before. In many ways, this is also the story of The Sims.

It all started in 1991, many moons before The Sims would hit the shelves. Will Wright had already found a lot of success for his game SimCity and was sitting in his home office finishing up his next simulation/building game, SimAnt (yes, you read that right, and it is incredibly fun to build a tiny ant farm!). SimAnt had just gotten to the point where Wright was ready to share it with the rest of the team at Electronic Arts, so he packed it up and relocated to his main office. Which was great timing, as in less than a week, his entire house had burned to the ground in the Oakland-Berkeley firestorm.

The firestorm hit so quickly that the only thing Will Wright had time to grab was his wife, a few photographs, and a neighbor who was stranded without a car. When

Wright returned to the site of the fire, the whole area had been burned clean and the only survivors were the ants who had burrowed deep beneath the soil to wait out the horrendous heat.

This might have been a poetic and fitting ending to the story considering the game he had just finished, but Will Wright dove right into rebuilding his life, piece by piece.

He began by designing his home. Then later, purchasing furniture and decorations that reflected his tastes and personality. Surprisingly, he had a lot of fun doing it. And all the while, a little idea tickled in the back of his mind: the idea that objects in a home become a reflection of who we are and what we aspire to be. From that idea sprang the most successful PC video game franchise of all time: The Sims.

Back at his newly purchased keyboard, Will Wright began working on a game he called Dollhouse. A house-building simulator, complete with human characters that walked around and reacted to the house you were building. He showed the idea to EA, who had recently purchased his company, Maxis, but they didn't get it. Unfortunately, this wasn't a new thing for Wright. In fact, it had become a pattern for him. When he built his first truly successful game, SimCity, he couldn't find a publisher for it at all and had been forced to form Maxis to publish the game on his own. Ironically, EA, which had passed up on publishing SimCity, had taken Maxis under its wing, in hopes that Will Wright and his group would build another hit.

Maxis had a feeling that his dollhouse game WAS that hit, but EA didn't see it that way. Still, Wright convinced them to give him a chunk of time and a small team, and got started working on Dollhouse right away.

After about a year, EA tested the name *Dollhouse* with a bunch of potential gamers, and they discovered that the name wasn't working. At all. And honestly, even the development team wasn't convinced the game was fun yet. Then, at the urging of two game designers on the team, Roxana Wolosenko and Claire Curtin, characters were added to the game, and The Sims was born.

While Wright was focusing his brainpower on building an amazing world and home builder, Curtin and Wolosenko continued to explore the impact that characters could have on the game. The designers felt strongly that having characters react to the things you purchased and placed in your house in a positive way would improve the overall game-playing experience, and they were right. Spot-on.

The Sims characters started off with a fairly small role to play in the game, but the more the Sims reacted to what you, the gamer, did to the game, the more interesting the game became. Soon everyone who played the game was talking more about how the Sims reacted, or what they were doing in their lives, than they did about purchasing new furniture.

The characters, not the house building, became the focus of the game, and suddenly everyone started to see the game through new eyes.

Well, not everyone exactly. EA trusted Maxis and Wright to make great games, but even so, it was hard for EA to be convinced The Sims was something gamers wanted.

You know, I guess in a way it's hard to blame EA for taking a cautious approach. When you hear the pitch for The Sims, it sounds a bit too much like everyday life. You have these little families and people you watch and you send them on jobs. They have to make dinner for themselves, read to become smarter, shower, use the restroom, call their moms on the phone, then repeat it all again the next day. And again, and again, and so on and so forth, until death comes for them and you start over. It does seem more like work than play.

But the team at Maxis wasn't finished with the design. They had so much more to add. Like Simoleons, a fake currency that the Sims would earn in their careers and spend on new goodies for their homes. Curtin, Wolosenko, and Luc Barthelet, a third designer on the team, added relationships and a gibberish language called Simlish. They added a fun sound track, art for the walls, clothing, and food. They added everything you could dream up, but EA was still nervous about introducing The Sims to the world.

The Sims' fictional language, Simlish, is based on mixed-up versions of Ukrainian, French, Latin, Finnish, English, Fijian, Cebuano, and Tagalog. There are many recognizable Sim words, but it doesn't qualify as an actual language because it has no grammar. However, there are Simlish language dictionaries out there on the web.

Not willing to give up on his idea, Will Wright came up with a new plan, one that would change the way publishers launched games forever. Wright suggested that they ship a game that was smaller than his complete vision, just to test the waters. In his mind, The Sims was destined to be a massive hit, and the game needed to be HUGE to support his vision, but he trusted EA's experience as much as they trusted his vision, so the two thought this approach was a smart compromise. Safe, even.

Remember, at the turn of the century, console games were really the biggest thing going. But PC games were also starting to take off. FPS games were, of course, a huge hit, but other, more complicated games like Sid Meier's Civilization, Will Wright's own SimCity franchise, and the Tycoon economic games (Railroad Tycoon, RollerCoaster Tycoon, and Zoo Tycoon) were all doing really well on home computers. Will Wright knew that with PC gaming on the rise, and his new idea of shipping smaller games with the promise of expansion packs later on, home computer games would be the perfect platform for The Sims.

EA/Maxis shipped The Sims for PC in 2000, and much to EA's surprise, Will Wright's prediction came true. The game was an overnight success. So big, in fact, that within two years, The Sims kicked MYST off the top of the PC game mountain before eventually settling somewhere around thirteen million copies.

Alice and Kev © Robin Burkinshaw

The fans got it. The game wasn't about just doing daily tasks, and it wasn't just about building a larger house, or filling your home with all the coolest stuff. It wasn't

The Sims games offered players a lot of freedom. So much, in fact, that some users actually created full backstories and lives for their Sims. One example created in The Sims 3 is still particularly moving today. It is the story of Alice and Kev. A dedicated Sim player and game design student in the UK created a blog about a homeless man and his daughter, chronicling the lives of her Sims in a deep and compelling way. The blog is still live today, and totally worth checking out to see how a game like The Sims can be used in the hands of an artist like Robin Burkinshaw (https://aliceandkev .wordpress.com/).

just about making your place so fun that all of your Sims' digital friends would want to come over to your house for a party. It was about crafting and building complex and interesting stories about your Sims and their daily lives. Somehow, watching your Sims on-screen felt like you were part of their lives. You wanted the best for your Sims. So gamers wanted more things to play with to improve the lives of their Sims.

Bed selection screen from The Sims © Maxis/Electronic Arts, Inc.

They wanted more wallpaper. They wanted more furniture. They wanted designer haircuts for their Sims. They wanted big-screen TVs, stereos, and a hot tub in the backyard. In short, they loved The Sims, but what they really wanted was Will Wright's original HUGE vision for the game. They wanted endless choices.

In less than nine months, EA heard their cries and shipped the first expansion pack for The Sims, titled The Sims: Living Large. Gamers gobbled up the new content and only asked for MORE! In March 2001, The Sims introduced The Sims: House Party. By November 2001, they were ready to ship The Sims: Hot Date, and so on and so forth for the next two years. By the time they were ready to ship The Sims 2, EA had shipped seven expansion packs and enough content to make any dollhouse junkie happy.

Will Wright's game would go on to influence both games and the way we purchase them forever, proving that, as I said at the beginning of this book, great games stand on the shoulders of the games that came before. But Will Wright showed us something else. Not only are great games inspired by other games, but they are inspired by everything around us. His house fire was just the beginning. Here's a list of some of the other things that inspired Will Wright while designing The Sims. I think a few on this list will really surprise you.

- Will Wright studied architecture, mechanical engineering, and robotics in college. These topics play a major role in The Sims, because not only did Wright find them interesting, he discovered that building, planning, and robots are just plain fun.

- Marc Gimbel, linguistics specialist, and Will Wright found inspiration for their unique Simlish language in the form of World War II code talkers, who spoke Native American Navajo in radio transmissions to confuse Japanese code breakers.

- The first-person shooters Quake and Quake II, which he played often during the production of The Sims, inspired Will Wright in many ways, but the most important takeaway was the gaming community. Wright was blown away by the countless hours gamers were spending building custom levels. He not only embraced this idea, but took it to whole new levels, providing gamers with the ability to modify everything in the game.

- The book *A Pattern Language: Towns, Buildings, Construction* was a big influence on Wright. It might not sound like the most entertaining book to you or me, but Wright claimed its exploration of architecture from a physicist's point of view was a major influence in how he planned out placement for everything from a toaster in the kitchen to a house within a city in The Sims.

- The Sims, the in-game characters, are actually really smart. But not as smart as the engineers who programmed their behavior. Wright wanted the game to feel as real as possible, so he looked to famous psychologist Abraham Maslow's Hierarchy of Needs pyramid for inspiration. The engineering team programmed The Sims to follow the needs. For example, when a Sim is hungry, they need food; if they are bored, they need entertainment; and so on. It's really brilliant stuff.

- Will Wright also studied the importance of time. One book in particular was a big inspiration: Robinson and Godbey's *Time for Life: The Surprising Ways Americans Use Their Time*. This book became the backbone for how Sims behave, and what they choose to do on their own when the player isn't telling them what to do next.

- And last, Will Wright was inspired by watching people do everyday things. He was known to spend hours in shopping centers, watching people make choices; he watched people at work; he observed people lounging around at home, hanging out with friends, mixing together at big events. And in the end, Will Wright's people-watching turned into the greatest people—Sims—watching game ever made.

The franchise has only grown bigger and better. The Sims 2 went on to take the title of the bestselling PC game. In fact, as of 2016, it is still at the top of the list. In April 2008, EA announced that The Sims as a whole had sold over 125 million units. That translates to more than 2.5 billion dollars, or to put it another way, more than the *Matrix* trilogy, *Titanic*, and *Avatar* movies combined.

THE KILLER APP

S o, there's a term that gets tossed around quite often in the computer world. You've probably heard it in reference to iPhone or Android games, but it's way older than that. The term is *killer app*, and it's short for *killer application.*

A killer app is a piece of software, or even a single feature in a piece of software, that is so amazing, so earth-shatteringly cool, it makes you want to run out and buy the hardware or console that is required to play the software. And most important, it can only be found on that one specific piece of hardware. It has to be exclusive or it doesn't meet the definition.

One of the first killer apps was actually a spreadsheet for the Apple II called VisiCalc. While it doesn't sound as exciting as squashing mushrooms in a fantasy kingdom, people still rushed out to buy the software for $100, then lined up to buy an Apple II that cost them anywhere from $2,000 to $10,000 just to run it. Sound crazy? Well, that's what a killer app can do.

So, here are a few games that are widely considered killer apps, ones that helped drive the sales of specific consoles. Some of them will look pretty familiar by now. It isn't a complete list, and sometimes it's impossible to name just one per console, but there's no doubt these games put a lot of game systems in front of a lot of TVs.

- Space Invaders—Atari 2600

- Star Raiders—Atari eight-bit computer

- Donkey Kong—ColecoVision

- Super Mario Bros.—Nintendo Entertainment System

- Tetris—Game Boy

- Sonic the Hedgehog—SEGA Genesis

- Super Mario World—SNES

- Final Fantasy VII—PlayStation

- GoldenEye—N64

- Halo—Xbox

- Super Smash Bros. Melee—GameCube

- Pokémon Gold/Silver—Game Boy Color

- Grand Theft Auto III—PlayStation 2

- Wii Sports—Wii

- Gears of War—Xbox 360

- Metal Gear Solid 4—PlayStation 3

- Mario Kart 8—Wii U

GRAND THEFT AUTO III

2001

HIJACKED!

Grand Theft Auto III © Rockstar Games

You've probably heard of Grand Theft Auto.

It's one of those games that people hear about, whether they are gamers or not. Also, it's one of those games that people either love or hate, even before they play it. It's controversial, to say the least.

It's your basic rags-to-riches story, but set in a dark, crime-filled world. Start off poor, work hard, and take what you want before anyone else can. Oh, and lie, cheat, steal, and shoot your way to the top. Okay, so maybe it's not the classic American dream, but fifty million players were willing to make it their American fantasy.

Strangely enough, the game's roots are actually planted in Scotland and the United Kingdom, where a genius software engineer, David Jones, met up with two young record producers from BMG. The trio of visionaries could see that there were a lot of similarities between mature video games and rock and hip-hop, and they wanted to make a game that would celebrate this.

David Jones had already made quite a reputation for himself as a developer. He'd been making successful games for years, eventually landing his company, DMA Design, a coveted spot with Nintendo's "Dream Team" to work on games for their upcoming Nintendo 64 console.

Jones was thrilled, but when Miyamoto got a look at the game he was working on, an open-world sci-fi shooter, one where you could take control of any vehicle you found lying around, Miyamoto wanted a game that was more puzzles and less big blood.

Jones saw things differently and kept working on his game. Eventually, Nintendo and Jones decided they just weren't a good fit, and parted ways. So Jones and his gang of developers started working on a new version of his idea, Race-n-Chase, without a publisher in mind.

During this time, two British brothers, Dan and Sam Houser, were working in the music business at a record label called BMG. BMG was really crushing it, digging into music culture. They decided to start a video game division, BMG Interactive, and Sam and Dan were just the guys to head it up. With zero experience in the game world, their first titles didn't resonate with gamers, but then they met David Jones and discovered Race-n-Chase.

The scope of the game is impressive. You play as a petty thug, making your play for the big time. You bash through contract murders, steal cars, commit aggravated assaults, and chain together as much collateral damage as you can. You can drive pretty much any car you can catch, and a sports car performs differently from a truck. All the while you watch your Wanted level rise, and face more and more police response, even ending in helicopters, street blockades, and SWAT teams.

The game was outrageous, and unlike Nintendo, it was exactly what BMG Interactive was looking for. They immediately signed Race-n-Chase, changed its name to Grand Theft Auto, and slammed it onto the scene in 1997. But much to the Houser brothers' surprise, the game, while it was selling okay, didn't make the splash in the media that they thought it would.

The Houser brothers were looking for something that would catch the attention of every media outlet out there. They wanted to make noise—GTA II was even more outrageous, with more carjackings, more innocent bystanders, more bank robberies and SWAT teams, but it was going to take a *big* change for Grand Theft Auto to become a household name.

The Houser brothers thought they knew what the problem was. GTA and GTA II looked like they were shot from a helicopter. The gamer's point of view was above the buildings, and it almost made the cars you were stealing and the banks you were robbing feel like toys. Then, Dan Houser had an idea. He left his full-time job at BMG to join the newly named Rockstar Games, and things were about to get a whole lot more real.

As GTA III's producer and writer, Dan Houser was about to take the game to the streets with a new third-person perspective that promised to put gamers in the middle of the action.

Grand Theft Auto III was ready to be as bold as it could be. No holding back. There had been plenty of backlash from their previous titles, but the team at Rockstar Games was not backing down. In fact, they turned up the heat.

Rockstar announced a ship date of October 2, 2001. Concerned parents and worried politicians were ready, and so were gamers.

Then, on September 11, 2001, the Twin Towers in New York City fell to terrorist attacks, and for a moment, the world stopped. Rockstar Games was within walking distance of Ground Zero, and suddenly there were some lines they weren't so comfortable crossing anymore.

Rockstar announced that the game would be a few weeks late. Then the team began searching through Liberty City, the fictitious city in GTA III, for anything that would be too sensitive or offensive under the new circumstances. Police cars were changed to look less like NYPD cars. An aircraft mission was scrapped. Elderly and child pedestrians were removed from the streets, and missions handed out by homeless anarchist Darkel got the chop.

When it was finally ready for the public, the reaction was mixed, to say the least. It seemed like you either loved the game, or HATED it. Nightly news TV shows talked about how over-the-top the violence and language were.

Anti-violence in video games groups shouted to anyone who would listen that GTA III was a horrible influence on society, and parents around the globe banned the game from their homes.

But gamers loved it. It was like nothing they'd ever seen, and many critics were forced to agree it had exceeded their expectaions.

It wasn't just the deep story line of the game, it was how that story line was delivered. The guys at Rockstar had really created a new style of game play, called *emergent play*.

Games like Final Fantasy VI tell great stories, but you can't really affect the world. In sandbox/builder games like The Sims, you can build whatever you want, but it's up to the gamer to create their own story. But Rockstar wanted to give players freedom to do whatever they wanted in their free-roaming game, and still provide them with a Hollywood movie–quality story.

The way they achieved this was by giving the player story-based challenges that were small, but added up to be one big, epic story in the end. Kind of like chapters in a book. But the tricky part, and in the end the most compelling part, is that Rockstar allowed players to choose if they wanted to continue the story, or just explore and see what kind of trouble they could get into on their own.

The game was like nothing gamers had seen. Not only did they enjoy the story, but they also used the city to create their own stories and share their experiences with friends. When the game shipped, it impressed gamers and exceeded their expectations, and critics agreed.

But even if the subject matter of the game isn't your kind of thing, you have to acknowledge Rockstar's innovative spirit.

- **GTA III pioneered the nonlinear story-driven genre. Players are allowed to cruise through the open world of Liberty City and move the story along at their own pace.**

- When you climb into a car, the radio is already blasting, and you can turn to any one of eight unique stations, ranging from talk radio, to adult contemporary, to underground hip-hop. Rockstar's relationship with BMG gave them the rights to their massive music library, and Rockstar used it perfectly.

- GTA III allows you to put your own MP3 playlists into the game to play your own music. Being that the game launched in the same year as the iPod, this game seemed right in line with cutting-edge technology.

- GTA III is loaded with small features or effects that were way ahead of their time. Things like when you wade into the water your clothes get wet, but only up to where the waterline hits your body, or that little *tink-tink-tink* sound a car engine makes when it cools down. These little details, which were so often overlooked before GTA III, made a huge impact on the overall quality of the award-winning game.

Walmart continued to sell the controversial game, but announced a new policy that all gamers who appeared to be under seventeen years of age would be required to show ID before they could purchase the M-rated title.

The timing for the game was also great for Sony. Their PS2 had been on the market for a year, and while the new system was selling well, Grand Theft Auto III became the must-have software. Sales of both the PS2 and GTA III skyrocketed. Over a decade later, Grand Theft Auto still remains one of the bestselling, best-reviewed, and most hated titles ever.

Grand Theft Auto III sold 14.5 million units, with nearly eight million of those sales falling on the PlayStation 2. The PlayStation 2, in turn, went on to become the bestselling console of all time, topping out at a staggering 155 million units sold!

WE'RE ALL A BUNCH OF CHEATERS

Everybody loves a cheat code.

It's true. Even if you are the type of gamer that just *has* to complete every little feature on your own, there's always a little comfort in knowing that if things get rough, you can always dig up a cheat code and bulldoze through the land mines.

But it isn't always about cheating your way to the end. At their core, cheat codes are about one thing and one thing only. FUN.

Yep. Cheat codes are fun, and they can be funny. But mostly, they are just awesome. I mean, who wouldn't want to drop a tank in the middle of downtown Liberty City in GTA III? That might be the very definition of *awesome*.

awe·some

adjective

Extremely impressive or daunting; inspiring great admiration, apprehension, or fear.

"Spawning a tank in the middle of downtown in GTA III is awesome!"

See? Told ya.

So, with that in mind, here's a countdown of the most amazing, game-changing cheat codes. Oh, and you don't have to feel guilty about trying these out. It's okay, the game developers want you to. It's part of the game.

10. Big Head Mode—NBA Jam

This game was a HUGE arcade hit in 1993, but the cheats didn't show up until a year later, when the arcade smash found its way to the SEGA Genesis. If you enter this code, the heads of the NBA All-Star players become three times larger. It was so popular, it seemed odd when you played the game in regular mode.

Hold UP, the turbo button, and the steal button until tip-off.

9. Spawn a Tank in GTA III, PlayStation 2

Tank spawned with a cheat code in Grand Theft Auto III © Rockstar Games

I mentioned this earlier, so you know it has to make the list. GTA, at its core, is about shooting stuff up and making a mess of the city. So why do it in a car when you can do it in a tank?

During game play, press CIRCLE six times, followed by R1, L2, L1, TRIANGLE, CIRCLE, TRIANGLE.

8. Captain Qwark in a Tutu in Ratchet & Clank: Up Your Arsenal

The Ratchet & Clank series is one of the funniest plat-formers ever, so it's no surprise that the team who built the game went through the extra time to add in a good joke. Captain Qwark is nothing short of a galactic hero, so seeing him dolled up in a pink ballerina tutu is a sight to behold. Man, I love this series. So . . . much . . . fun!

To unlock this outfit, first you have to complete the "Deja Q All Over Again" vid-comic, then enter UP, UP, DOWN, DOWN, LEFT, RIGHT, CIRCLE, SQUARE, SQUARE. He'll be in his new outfit as soon as you return to the game. Enjoy.

7. Unlocking Howard the Duck in LEGO Marvel Super Heroes

Howard the Duck in Lego Marvel Super Heroes © Traveller's Tales/Warner Bros. Interactive

He might not be the most popular Marvel character out there, but he sure is quirky. The great thing is that if you use him, he's actually ridiculously overpowered. Totally worth checking him out. And if you really want some good laughs, pair him with Deadpool. I mean, come on, you've got to try it now.

Go to the pause menu and select "Extras." Then enter the code J58RSS. He'll be available as a playable character from that point on.

6. Unlock a Second Quest in The Legend of Zelda

So, you've just beaten The Legend of Zelda. You are a champion. A prince among men. Now what to do? Well, Nintendo thought of that, too, by providing you with a secret second quest. But beware, the second quest is NOT easy.

5. Big Daddy in Age of Empires

Age of Empires is a classic real-time strategy game, where you play through ancient civilization. NO nukes or machine guns here, just warriors with swords and wooden shields. So imagine how cool you'd look showing up in a 1995 Chevrolet Camaro with a rocket launcher. This hilarious cheat totally breaks the game because with your high-tech and unstoppable car, you can wipe the game in about thirty seconds.

Press ENTER during a game and type the code BIGDADDY. Press ENTER to confirm, and, gentlemen, start your engines.

4. Turkey Assassins in Assassin's Creed III

You've made it halfway through the ultra serious Assassin's Creed game, and everyone in Davenport knows of your reputation. All you need is a dangerous-looking, "don't mess with me" sidekick to get the respect you've earned. You know, like a turkey wearing an assassin's hood. Yeah, that's right. I said a turkey. Enter this code and one will follow you around for the rest of the game. It doesn't change the game play, but it proves one thing: Ubisoft has a nice sense of humor.

After making it to sequence six or later in the game, return to Davenport Homestead. Hide around the back corner of the homestead building, then whistle. A turkey will come up to you. Then enter UP, UP, DOWN, DOWN, LEFT, RIGHT, LEFT, RIGHT, B, A, START. Look familiar? Keep reading; it will.

3. Debug Mode in Sonic the Hedgehog 2

Everybody loves this code, because it lets you pretend you're a video game level designer for a bit. Debug mode is a common cheat used by game developers that allows them to test out all kinds of things, like moving objects, adding in new music, passing through walls, becoming invincible. Basically, it allows you to mess around as much as you'd like with all the art, sounds, and characters from the game. There are a lot of games that allow you to do this now, but Sonic was the first major game to release this option to the players, and it was a big hit. Thanks, SEGA!

Go to the sound test menu, play tracks 19, 65, 09, and 17, and then return to the title screen and press Z and START. Then play tracks 01, 09, 09, 02, 01, 01, 02, and 04. Not a simple one to add, but it really is worth it.

2. The Warp Whistle in Super Mario Bros. 3

A Mario Warp Whistle does pretty much exactly what it says. It whistles, then it warps you to a new location. There are actually three in Super Mario Bros. 3, but the first is my favorite.

Go to World 1-3 until you get to the white block, then duck down for a few seconds. You'll drop behind the scenery. Don't worry; you are still there. Run all the way to the right until you reach Toad's house, where he'll award you with the first Warp Whistle. As Toad explains, "One toot on this whistle will send you to a far away land." Believe it or not, the others are even HARDER to find. Dig around; finding them is really the fun part.

And the winner . . . the undisputed champion of cheat codes . . . is:

1. The Konami Code, in various games

The amazing thing about this code is that it shows up in just about every NES-era Konami title. Fans of Konami games usually tried out the code the first time they fired the game up, just to see what it would do. It first appeared in Contra, where entering the code gave the player thirty lives, but it also appeared in everything from Tony Hawk's Pro Skater 5 (entering the Konami code on the start screen unlocks a FULLY PLAYABLE original version of Tony Hawk's Pro Skater!) to Teenage Mutant Ninja Turtles (the Konami code here gives you four continues instead of the two the game gives you without the code). So far, there have been over 100 games to use the Konami code, and more arrive on the scene every year. Yeah, you'll want to memorize this one.

UP, UP, DOWN, DOWN, LEFT, RIGHT, LEFT, RIGHT, B, A, START.

WORLD OF WARCRAFT

2004

WoWZERS!

World of Warcraft © Blizzard Entertainment

It was, and still is, massive.

It was, and still is, multiplayer.

And it was, and still is, online.

It was, and still is, World of Warcraft, the MMO game that burst on the scene in 2004 and is still as vibrant and fun today as it was a decade ago.

You can't say that about every game made in 2004, now can you? So what happened? How has World of Warcraft stood the test of time, while hundreds of other games launched during that time fizzled away? I've asked myself this question a bunch of times, because it really is one of the most amazing feats in the history of games. Sadly, as technology gets faster and games become more inventive, the old games tend to disappear—but not WoW.

Surprisingly, when WoW launched, the game was pretty basic. While the visual style and deep story were innovative in the massively multiplayer online (MMO) space, the game itself was a standard role-playing game (RPG). You go on quests, you chop up monsters, you collect gold and experience points. As a side option, you choose your class and pick a few skills to level up. Standard stuff, except for a few big differences. First, you're surrounded by tons of other players, people playing the game right along with you. And unlike your average RPG of the day, it takes a LONG time to level up. Hours, days, WEEKS. In fact,

Maybe part of it was that World of Warcraft launched in 2004 to an already invested fan base. Blizzard Entertainment had a string of hits before WoW, including Warcraft: Orcs & Humans, Warcraft II: Tides of Darkness, and Warcraft III: Reign of Chaos, set in the Warcraft universe. Fans already knew and loved the orcs, the humans, and the art style. In a way, Blizzard fans loved WoW before they even tried it.

Blizzard teased everyone with video game trailers months before the game launched. Fans gobbled them up and shared them with everyone they knew because they matched the quality of any animated movie at the time. The popularity of these game trailers became a big part of Blizzard's culture, so much so that a full-length movie, *Warcraft*, was released in 2016.

if you want to level up faster than a snail's pace, World of Warcraft becomes your full-time job.

It's worth mentioning here that while World of Warcraft was a huge breakout success, it, too, stands on the shoulders of games that came before it. In particular, EverQuest and Dark Age of Camelot. These games pioneered things like raiding parties and MMORPG leveling systems. It is just that WoW took those early concepts and, in many cases, perfected them. For example, I just said that it took a long time to level up a character in WoW, but to die-hard EverQuest players, it seemed like it was more cheetah speed than snail speed.

However, gamers didn't mind, because although the progress at first was slow, you felt like a true hero when you finally did level up. And not just because of the time involved.

Before WoW, the way you leveled up in MMO games was by repeating the same tasks over and over again, e.g., killing monster after monster to gain tiny amounts of experience points. Blizzard knew it would be much more interesting, and addicting, if they tied stories and quests to these tiny tasks. And gamers were attached to the idea in a HUGE way.

For example, you may be wandering through a new land and happen upon a campsite of loud and proud hunters. They have a pile of wolf skins stacked behind them, and they challenge you to try your hand at wolf hunting, betting that you can't bring back more than they did that day. You take off on the challenge quest to bring back more skins than the hunters, and after doing so you return to the campsite. The hunters are impressed with your efforts, but they have moved on to more dangerous prey. They brag once again about their amazing hunting skills, and once again challenge you to try to top them by collecting more dangerous bear skins this time. You go hunting again, this time bringing back a massive pile of bear skins.

When you return the third time, the hunters have accepted you as an equal, a great hunter like them. Finding you worthy, the hunters invite you to join THEM on a very dangerous hunt for a massive Kodo, a nasty lumbering reptile with a rough leather hide covered in thick, woolly hair.

Sure, in the end you're doing the same basic task over and over. You're going on hunting parties. But the story of becoming a worthy hunter and joining in with a band of great hunters adds depth to the experience and keeps WoW gamers coming back again and again.

And while this was enough to get people interested in the game, Blizzard didn't stop there. In fact, this was just the beginning.

Blizzard knew their fans would tire of their game eventually if they just let it sit there. After all, there are only so many wolves you can kill or herbs you can gather before it starts feeling repetitive. So every time there was a dip in players on the servers, Blizzard would introduce something new and exciting.

Usually, Blizzard would drop new gear, new decorations, new achievements. Occasionally, to keep things even more exciting, Blizzard would give their gamers a new area or a dungeon to raid. And just because they loved their gamers so much, Blizzard would include special holiday events so you had something to do during the holiday break at school. Finally, every few years, Blizzard would release a HUGE expansion that updated and changed the universe of the game in a big way. It was like a trail of candy leading to a cool swimming pool full of awesome on a summer day. One new goodie here and there with the promise of something great down the line.

The timing of Blizzard's releases is one major thing that keeps gamers running back, battle-ax in hand, ready to go on another adventure.

Another major innovation that the guys at Blizzard dreamed up was something called talents and talent trees. Okay, here's how talent trees work in a nutshell. It all starts with choosing a class for your character. You know, like a Druid, or a Hunter. Or maybe you want to be a Mage, or a Priest, or a Death Knight. It's totally up to you. At first, your class defines who you are in the game, with limited abilities and skills, but just like in the real world, there is always more to a person than we see on the surface. Here is where the talents come in. You earn your first talent point when you hit level ten. By then you've learned

In 2012, Democratic state senate nominee Colleen Lachowicz of Maine was teased by her opponent because she played World of Warcraft. She showed him by winning the election.

Talent trees weren't a brand-new concept. In fact, another game you might have heard of called Diablo II included them the year before WoW was first released. But it was totally cool with the developers of Diablo II if the developers of World of Warcraft stole, then built on their idea, because they were the SAME GUYS.

World of Warcraft is a subscription-based game, meaning that players not only buy the game, but in the United States they continue to pay up to fifteen dollars a month to play on the server and keep the new content rolling in. In 2005, there were 1.5 million registered players. At its peak in 2010, there were over twelve million WoW players playing and paying every month. Eleven years after its launch, in 2015, there were still 5.6 million players enjoying Blizzard's MMO masterpiece.

the game pretty well and know what you like and what you LOVE. So you get to spend your talent point to purchase a special talent that reflects how YOU like to play.

Let's say you're a Rogue who is a pretty good marksman and good in combat with feral beasts. But maybe you want to be a Druid who is a bit of a healer. Now you can use your talent point to learn a cure spell. Or maybe you've found out that you like to play as a tank, someone who dives right into the action and soaks up damage. In that case, you might use your talent point to add a bit more health or defense. The cool thing here is that it's completely up to you and there are TONS of talents to choose from.

This complex talent tree ends up allowing for a nearly unlimited amount of characters, each one an expression of the gamer who created it. As a result, the game feels totally individual and real, so even if you run into another Druid, *your* Druid is still unique.

As always, when talking about Blizzard and World of Warcraft, these innovations were just the beginning. How has World of Warcraft hung around, while hundreds of other games launched during that time have fizzled away? Because:

- **Blizzard changed the old way of just grinding to level up to something that had more meaning by inventing quest-based leveling.**

Quest list in World of Warcraft © Blizzard Entertainment

- While WoW might not have been the first MMO, it showed everyone how to add polish. The look of World of Warcraft was top-notch, and that dedication to quality showed in every feature in the game.

- Talent trees made it so gamers could change the personality and skills of their in-game avatars to match their play style.

- At a time when big blockbuster games were giving players around six to twenty hours of original, unique game play, World of Warcraft's open-world game and endless achievements and quests offered gamers literally hundreds of hours of game play.

- Frequent updates of new content kept players busy with constant goodies, as well as excited for what was to come.

- Blizzard perfected the monthly subscription model by not only charging players for the game at the cash register, but also charging a monthly fee of fifteen dollars to play online and get that constant stream of new goods. Gamers didn't mind, because they were getting hundreds of hours of entertainment, and when you compare that to the cost of a movie ticket and a box of popcorn today, it really is a pretty good deal.

- Not only did World of Warcraft allow you to choose your race, talents, and every stitch of clothing for your avatar, they also allowed players to choose the game they wanted to play. There really is no RIGHT way to play World of Warcraft. If you liked to hang out in the auction house all day and swap goods, go for it. If you wanted to go on big raids with friends and destroy hordes of monsters and search for loot, well, then WoW was your favorite game. If you hated gardening in the real world, but wanted to buy a farm and raise digital crops, WoW had a plot of land ready for you. Even if you wanted to just hang out in a popular

The first MMO, Meridian 59, showed up in 1996. But it was Ultima Online in 1997 that made the genre popular. Then EverQuest and Dark Age of Camelot came along, and the genre really took off. In fact, it's pretty fair to say that WoW owes a great deal to these early MMOs.

town area and chat with friends, there was plenty of opportunity for that as well. World of Warcraft was a true play-as-you-want game.

- WoW was the first MMO to instance dungeons. That's a fancy way of saying that you and your party could go through a dungeon on your own without worrying about running into other players doing the same thing, in the very same place.

- And if you hung out with a group often enough, or if you already had a group of friends that played World of Warcraft, then you could form a guild. A guild is simply a group of WoW players that get together often to go on raids and hang out in WoW.

All these great things added up to a pretty stunning game that not only improved upon the MMO games of the past, but was so successful that it became the blueprint for all future MMO games. In fact, it's darn near impossible to find an MMO today without all the World of Warcraft innovations in its list of features. In short, Blizzard perfected the MMO.

But the most important thing that WoW did, the thing that no other game has ever been able to quite reach, was create a culture of players that is totally unique. Die-hard WoW players often have a completely separate digital life inside the game. If you don't know what I'm talking about, try watching the web series *The Guild*, starring Internet darling Felicia Day. The show follows a guild of players that meet up to face challenges together in real life, as well as in the game, and it shows us just how awkward their daily lives are compared to how awesome they are in the digital world. Sure, the show is a comedy, and exaggerated, but sometimes it is so honest about the stereotypical World of Warcraft gamer that it kind of hurts a little.

WoW was, and still is, one of the most successful games of all time, and it isn't finished yet. The game is still going strong, and there's no stopping this train.

CREATE-A-PLAYER

This is kind of an old-school name, but I still think it really is the best description of the feature. Create-a-player is the part of a game where the gamer uses tools, sliders, and new hats to create and modify their own character. It has been called a lot of things over the years, from character creator to avatar maker, but the idea is always the same.

Changing what your character looks like is your chance to express who you are and how you like to play. While the player is usually allowed to adjust height, weight, skin tone, and head shape, the real fun comes in swapping out items like hairstyle, clothing, and costumes. The more creative a development team gets with their create-a-player options, the more freedom a gamer has in creating an in-game avatar that really expresses them.

This has been a big feature in sports games for a long time. It was Nintendo who gave us the first version, way back in 1989, in their game Baseball Stars. Before long, every sports game out there had this feature because there's nothing quite like creating a hoopster that looks just like you to start for the Cavs alongside LeBron. AmIright?

But that was just the beginning. Create-a-player or player customization has become such a huge feature in some games that gamers lose hours and hours before even starting game play.

Here is a small list of games with GREAT character creator systems that are almost as fun to tinker with as the game itself. Check them out when you get a chance, but be warned, tweaking the perfect hair color for your freckled, Mohawk-wearing, long-armed, unibrowed, green-skinned, robotic, trench-coat-wearing, one-legged cyborg can be addicting.

- NBA 2K15. You can make anything from a pudgy five-foot-three-inch superdunker to a gangly seven-foot-nine-inch skeleton man (eight foot two with the afro).

- Destiny. You start by choosing one of the three classes, Titan, Hunter, or Warlock, and from there the choices are almost limitless.

- Champions Online. This free-to-play MMO not only allows you to tweak the visual look of your superhero, but you also get to choose your character's special abilities. Everything from superspeed to stretchy arms is on the table. Oh, and don't forget the cape.

- The Elder Scrolls V: Skyrim. There are just so many races to choose from here, and you can choose just about anything from a vampire with a tiger tail to a muscle-bound elf with a lip piercing.

- WWE '13. It is so fun to create your wrestler in this game that sometimes you just create a character then forget to even play. So many options to create WILD characters that it really is worth checking out. Oh, and don't forget to choose your entrance dance, music, and lighting setup. That's part of the fun, too.

- FIFA 15. This time they put YOU in the game with Game Face. Using the camera on your Kinect, you can take a photo of yourself and map it right onto the face of your character. How cool is that?

- And I can't leave the Mii creator off the list. It just wouldn't be right. While the fine details are missing that you'd find in other character creators, it is simply amazing how this simple tool set can give you just about any look you're after.

And there are so many more out there. In fact, it's getting harder and harder to find a game that *doesn't* include this feature in one way or another. There's just nothing quite like adding yourself to your favorite game. Even if your gaming version of yourself looks like a cross between Yoda and a yeti. Or perhaps a superhero and a rainbow-tailed pony. Hey, who am I to judge?

A selection of character creation screens from The Elder Scrolls V: Skyrim © Bethesda Softworks, LLC

HALO 2

2004

ONE DOWN, FIFTY BILLION TO GO

Halo 2 © Bungie

Think of a movie. The biggest blockbuster movie you can possibly think of.

Think of the kind of movie where people dress up in costumes and sleep in tents on the sidewalk for a week to get tickets to the premiere. Now, imagine how much money that movie made on the first day, then triple it—because that is how much Halo 2 made on day one.

All right, I know what you're thinking. Why not write a chapter about the original Halo? Why jump to Halo 2? Good question, but I have my reasons. However, just to get you caught up, let me sum up Halo for you as quickly as possible.

The first time anyone heard of Halo was actually at a Macworld conference. Steve Jobs himself called Alexander Seropian and Jason Jones, both longtime Apple developers, and brought them onstage with him to show off their new game to the world. Unfortunately, they had never promised to make it a Mac exclusive, and just a few weeks later the Chicago-based developers were packing their bags, their computers, and all their toys to head to Seattle, home of Bill Gates and company.

At the time, Nintendo and Sony were the kings of the block. Ever since the PlayStation pushed out SEGA, it looked like there was only room for the two of them in the market. But Microsoft was very proud of its new high-end graphics engine, called DirectX, and they knew that, with their connections in the PC hardware world, not to mention their deep pockets, they could build an affordable, top-notch gaming system.

Taking a page from Nintendo's unwritten rulebook on how to sell consoles, Microsoft knew that they would need a huge game to be the champion for their Xbox. One look at what Seropian and Jones were doing with Halo convinced them they had a winner. And obviously they were right.

Halo was a MASSIVE hit for them. One that totally deserves its place in the Video Game Hall of Awesome for being the first really satisfying physics-based shooter, for introducing us to the iconic character Master Chief, and for telling an epic story that rivaled anything being written in sci-fi books at the time. But it was Halo 2 that stepped up to the plate and hit the home run.

Master Chief from Halo 2 © Bungie

Doing what they did best in Halo 1, Bungie started by providing a world-class story mode. Halo 2's single-player game was incredible. Picking up right where the first Halo game left off, the gamer once again assumes the role of Master Chief and leads the resistance to save the people of Earth from a gruesome demise. Everyone who played it loved the story. In fact, the only thing they didn't like was that it ended at all. But that was okay because the battle could continue online indefinitely with Xbox Live, and that's where the *real* innovations start.

To put things in perspective, it is important to remember that PC games were really doing well at the time. Especially multiplayer online games. Half-Life 2 was just announced, id Software was showing off its next version of DOOM, and EA was making a lot of noise with Battlefield 2. The competition for gamers' time was fierce, and it was easy to see that if you didn't allow players to play online, you were going to lose the race.

And while Halo was a massive hit that helped put the Xbox in the ring with the PlayStation 2 and the Game-Cube, the only way you could play with your friend in Halo was in split screen on the couch. Fun, but not ideal. So Microsoft developed Xbox Live, their version of online gaming. And Bungie, the Halo developers, had big plans on how to make sure Xbox was the best of the bunch with smart matchmaking.

The Halo universe is so compelling that Steven Spielberg is under way with a Halo TV show in partnership with Showtime. There is no release date as of yet, but keep your eyes open because with names like Halo and Spielberg involved, it should be a doozy.

Microsoft Xbox © Evan Amos

You see, until Bungie revamped online gaming with Halo 2, players had very little control of who they played against online. Imagine if it were your first time ever playing DOOM online. You log on, expecting to have a great time, only to find yourself in an online battle with seven other players who have been playing and perfecting the game for a year. You wouldn't stand a chance. Not only that, but getting smeared two seconds after you join the match, and doing it over and over, is just not fun.

Also, the opposite is true. If you've been playing a game like Battlefield 2 for six months nonstop, it can be

Back in 2004, a user named 67thRaptorBull complained about Halo 2's Class-2 Projectile Cannon, which he described as a "noob tube." The term is now used to describe weapons in lots of games, from Battlefield to Call of Duty.

In the three years it took to develop Halo 2, Bungie employees consumed more than twenty thousand pounds of pizza, twenty-four thousand gallons of soda, and more than one thousand pounds of bananas.

pretty boring to be paired up against a bunch of noobs (a gamer term for new players).

Bungie and Microsoft fixed this issue by adding a complex matchmaking system that looked at everything from your real-world location, to the number of hours you'd spent online, to the list of achievments you'd notched. Then it paired you up with the gamers that most closely matched your level. This allowed for the constant competitive and challenging game play that players craved.

And the innovations didn't stop there. Although to be honest, Halo: Combat Evolved and Halo 2 shared a lot of innovations, and it's kind of hard to mention one without the other. So I'm going to cover them both here, in descending order from five to Holy Cow—I can't believe Halo did that first.

5. **REGENERATING HEALTH BARS.** This one first appeared in Halo, but they really only tinkered with the idea. In Halo 2, however, everything Bungie did was focused on making the game more efficient and fast to play, and removing the need to search around an environment for a health pack was a big help. Here is how it worked: If a player was shot, or hit by a grenade, then obviously, the health of that player went down. But if the player could hang on and not get shot again right away, the health bar would refill and eventually restore back to full health automatically. It definitely changed the way you played, and is a feature that has been picked up by just about every FPS out there, including the popular franchises Call of Duty and Battlefield.

4. **ZOOM IN EASILY WITH THE CONTROL STICK.** The controls for Halo 2 were so smooth and well planned out that every button and stick on the controller seemed like it was created for Halo. The right stick wasn't just used for aiming; if you clicked down on

the stick, the gun zoomed in. If you had a sniper rifle, you could click again and zoom in even closer. This not only made it easier to use zooming weapons, it freed up a button on the controller for the next innovation.

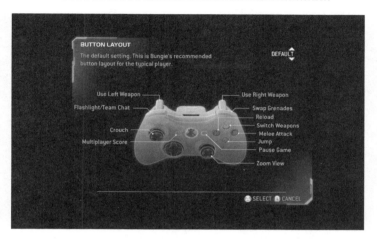

Button mapping for Halo 2 © Bungie

3. **GRENADES WITHOUT SWITCHING.** While most console shooters at the time used the left trigger to zoom in, Bungie solved that issue with the zoom-in approach mentioned above. This allowed them to map, or assign, the action of tossing a grenade to its own button. It made throwing a grenade so much easier, and more fun. Gone were the days of cycling through an inventory to find a grenade while your enemies rushed in. Just a flick of the left trigger and BOOM!

2. **THE BEAT DOWN.** Okay, this one is really big. Although other games had included melee attacks, Halo made them an essential part of the game play. Every gun had a "beat down," animation that turned it into a one-hit kill when you snuck up on an enemy from behind. Without Halo's innovative beat downs, this

action wouldn't have been featured in future games (e.g., the knives in Call of Duty).

And last but not least:

1. **HOLY COW—I CAN'T BELIEVE HALO DID THAT FIRST:** TWO WEAPONS. Before Halo, players could pack around a huge number of weapons in most FPS games. In fact, when the franchise launched in 2001, the idea that Master Chief could carry only two weapons at once was seen as a bit of a disadvantage. After all, James Bond could carry and switch among ten different weapons in most of his popular games, including rocket launchers and a trunk full of machine guns. But as people played Halo, they came to realize that the limitation completely changes the player's strategies and choices. All of a sudden, choosing what gun to pick up was just as important as how good you were at shooting it. It was a revelation for game developers and the FPS genre.

Add these stunning game-play innovations to Xbox Live, and you get a hit like no other. In November 2004, Bungie released Halo 2, and it was the biggest media release of all time. In the first twenty-four hours, Halo 2 stuffed 125 million dollars in the bank. That's 2.3 million copies of the game floating out there on the first day. And not only that, but over one million players had logged on to Xbox Live in that first day as well, nearly bringing the servers to their knees.

Halo 2 had not only delighted both single-player and online shooter fans, the game also set the stage for a three-way epic battle down the line: Xbox vs. Nintendo vs. PlayStation. It's a battle that is still raging today, but without Halo 2 and Xbox Live, there's a good chance the Xbox would never have left the ground.

PREPARE TO BE SORTED

· · · · · · · · · · · · · · · · ·

Designing video games is hard. I know, I've probably said that before, but let me say it again just so you don't forget it.

DESIGNING VIDEO GAMES IS HARD!

It isn't just coming up with a new idea, or taking a new spin on an old genre. There is SO much more to it that lives under the surface. But I'm going to let you in on a little secret. Ready . . .

It's not about the game. It's about the gamers.

No. Really. And if you get how gamers work, designing a game that appeals to ALL of them can really make you a champion game designer. So here it is. The four types of gamers, and what makes them tick.

Gamer Type 1: The Achiever

These players will spend countless hours trying to complete games and try over and over for impossible achievements. For the Achiever, accomplishing difficult tasks and guided challenges is what makes them tick, but they also LOVE to share their accomplishments. They love to tell their friends and fellow gamers about their amazing gaming adventures. Whether it be online, in-game, and even while standing in line for lunch at school, these gamers love to show off. So, what do Achievers want? Badges, goals, and impossible tasks, and then they want to tell the world they have, well, *achieved* them.

Gamer Type 2: The Explorer

These gamers are creators and finders, and they tend to like single-player or solo games the most. Like their name implies, they like to go over the next hill, look behind the closed door, check out what's on top of the tallest building. They love to find secrets and Easter eggs, and they are the kids at school that start their sentences with, "Guess what I found last night in Far Cry?" To make these gamers happy you need to hide a few secrets, plant Easter eggs and inside jokes, even leave a fun glitch or two lying around. Don't worry, they'll find it, and they will probably take your game apart in the process. And chances are, they'll even build it back up for you. That's how they roll.

Gamer Type 3: The Socializer

Socializers tend to get along with everyone, so if you want your game to have a good community, you're going to need these gamers. They are the ones that tell you "Nice shot" after you score a goal in FIFA, and the great thing is, they mean it. Socializers LOVE chat and voice in games, and they dig building long, deep lists of gamer friends. To get these guys and gals involved with your game, build enough downtime during the game it-self for them to get a little chatty. Or at the very least, make it easy to give a digital high five to other players while in game. If you do, they will love you for it, and the best thing is that their social style doesn't stop in the gaming world. They will tell their real friends about your game, and that means more people who will want to check your game out.

Gamer Type 4: The Destroyer

Their name says it all. These gamers like to smash, dominate, destroy. Destroyers LOVE competition. They love to beat you, then give you a chance to play again, just so they can beat you even harder the second time. Sometimes these gamers are called Griefers, because part of the fun for them is ruining your gaming experience. They are the players that sneak into your Minecraft building, fill it full of TNT, and then stand there with flint and steel, waiting for you to notice them before they will strike and run away laughing. You know the type. Appealing to these gamers is the easiest of the bunch. Just give them opportunities to smash and dash, and they will come running.

So . . . what do you think? Think you could design a game that appeals to all four types of gamers? Does your favorite game appeal to all of them? Or, if you're ready to be honest with yourself, where do you fit in? What kind of gamer are you?

If you need me, I'll be looking over the next hill, digging for something special that nobody has ever seen before. All by myself, thank you very much.

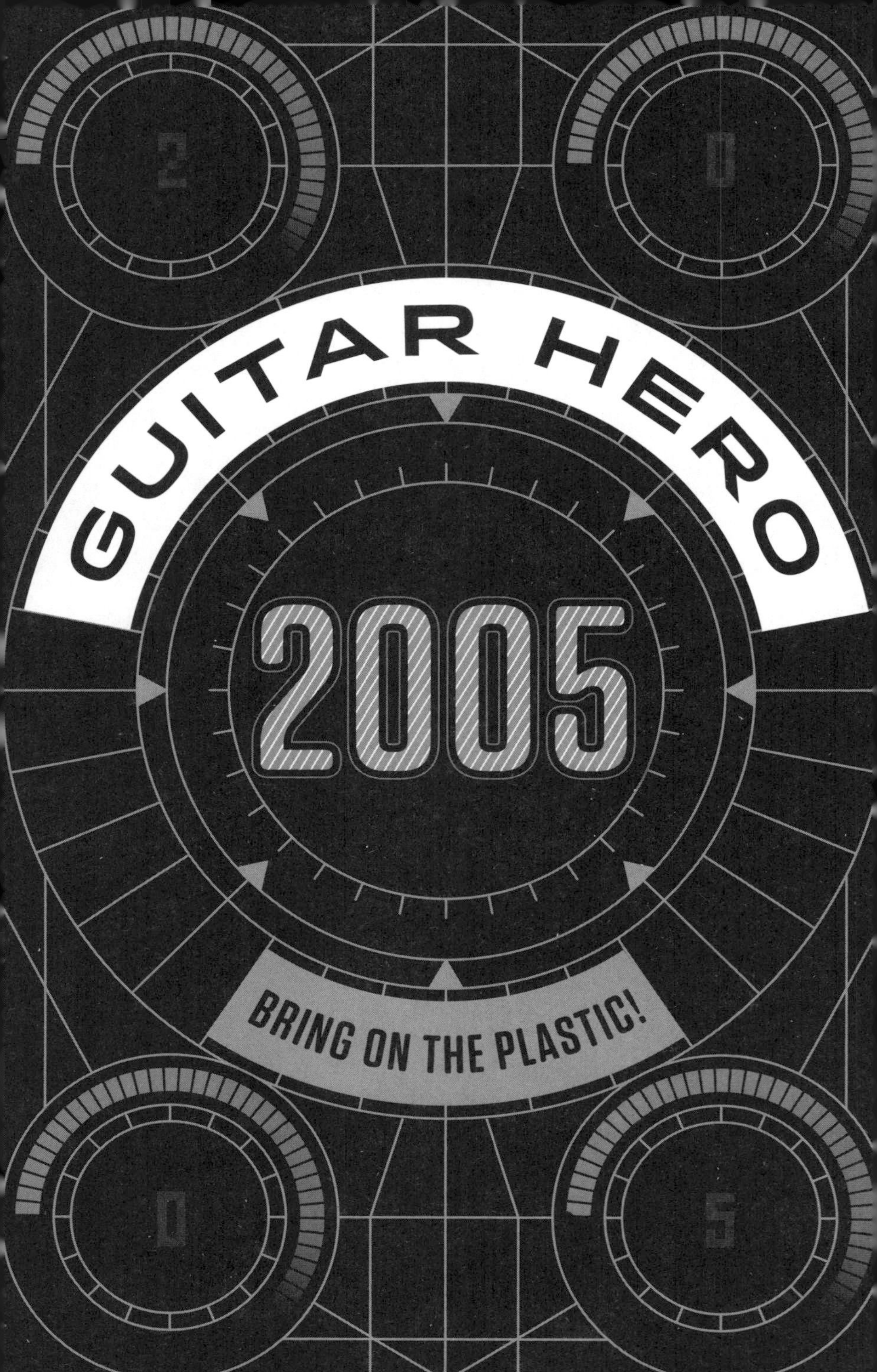
GUITAR HERO
2005
BRING ON THE PLASTIC!

Guitar Hero © Activision Publishing, Inc.

So, when I was a kid, which was a pretty long time ago, I remember my mom getting after me to tuck my video game stuff away.

I mean, there was no such thing as a wireless control-ler back then, so there was always a rat's nest of cords winding out from under the TV, and then there were all those cartridges.

Oh, and that's not all. Back in the day, there was no GameStop. You didn't turn in your old games for new ones, so every gamer nerd back then had quite a collection of old games lying around. Kind of a graveyard of games you really didn't want to play anymore. When you think of it, those Atari 2600, TI99/4A, and NES cartridges even look like little tombstones.

And then there were all those peripherals. You know, like the Nintendo Light Gun and Power Glove. Those took up even more room on your living room floor. And to make it worse, most people had only one TV. I know we did. So my "video game stuff" was a pretty big issue.

In 2000, Babbage's Etc., a book, movie, and video game retail store, was purchased by a company called Funco, the publisher of the hit video game magazine *Game Informer*. It didn't take long for Funco to realize there was big business in selling video games, new or used, so in late 2000 they changed their name to GameStop. GameStop chains opened across the country, and within two years it was the world's biggest seller of used video games.

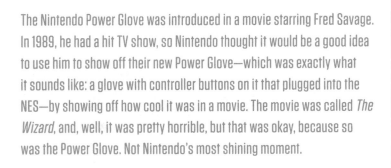

The Nintendo Power Glove was introduced in a movie starring Fred Savage. In 1989, he had a hit TV show, so Nintendo thought it would be a good idea to use him to show off their new Power Glove—which was exactly what it sounds like: a glove with controller buttons on it that plugged into the NES—by showing off how cool it was in a movie. The movie was called *The Wizard*, and, well, it was pretty horrible, but that was okay, because so was the Power Glove. Not Nintendo's most shining moment.

Before Harmonix released Guitar Hero, they had already made a very nice reputation with rhythm/music gamers with their cult classic games Amplitude and Frequency. They followed this up with Karaoke Revolution, where gamers plugged a microphone into their PlayStation 2, and the console judged their singing ability based on how close they came to the original version of the song.

But can you imagine what kind of mess I would have left behind if I'd had an entire rock band in my living room? Well, in 2005, that was exactly where we were heading with RedOctane and Harmonix's new megahit, Guitar Hero.

It was 2005. *Star Wars Episode III: Revenge of the Sith* hit the theaters, and we thought the series was all wrapped up. (Luckily, we were wrong on that one.) Carrie Underwood won *American Idol*, and she cried real tears. Destiny's Child broke up, and we all cried real tears. YouTube was launched, so cats and skateboard fail videos finally had a place to live online, but most of all, the world was in search of a hero. A GUITAR hero.

By now you've probably noticed a pattern. It's not always the first person to the party who ends up with all the nachos. In fact, more often than not the games that win our hearts are those that come late to the party but do it with style. Guitar Hero is no exception; despite what many people think, it wasn't the first guitar-based music game. In fact, the Japanese company Konami had already made an arcade game called Guitar Freaks that played an awful lot like Guitar Hero. It even had a plastic guitar with buttons and a strum bar.

A few people in the US noticed, but not enough for it to take off the way DDR did. Not until RedOctane and Harmonix got together. Harmonix was doing some cool things with their singing game, Karaoke Revolution, and they totally got music games. RedOctane was doing some cool things building dance pads for Dance Dance Revolution, and they totally got big plastic peripherals.

It was a match made in gamer heaven. A real "peanut butter in my chocolate" type of matchup. Before long, RedOctane was in the plastic guitar business, and Harmonix was in the hero-making business.

Harmonix actually started working on the game using the Guitar Freak controller until RedOctane had time to build them a prototype. By that time, Harmonix had decided on three features that would set the game apart from anything anyone had seen before.

1. They wanted the notes to slide down a fret board (the neck of the guitar), and hitting notes accurately would be key to making players feel in control.

2. They knew that adding a whammy bar would make gamers feel like true rockers. A whammy bar is the silver handle below where you strum the guitar. You know, that thing you crank that makes the guitar moan and scream. And . . .

3. Tilting the guitar in the air at just the right moment had to make the gamer feel like a true Guitar Hero. They called this move Star Power, and it was seriously AWESOME!

RedOctane made sure these features were jammed into the controller, and when the team got a chance to try out their new ax with their new game, they knew they were on to something big.

All they needed now were songs, and they needed a LOT of them. They built a wish list of 100 tunes that they thought would melt gamers' faces, and started working on licensing them. In the end they landed with forty-seven tracks: thirty monster guitar rock classics and seventeen bonus indie songs made up from local New England-area bands.

However, one thing most people don't know is that every one of the thirty hit songs was recorded specifically

A lot of investors backed away from RedOctane after hearing their "crazy" idea to make a guitar-shaped video game controller. Greg Fischbach, one of the founders of Acclaim Entertainment, said a few years later that they regretfully passed on RedOctane's idea because, in his words, "Who's going to buy a peripheral like that?" Turns out, everyone but you wanted one, Mr. Fischbach.

The bonus songs can be unlocked with money you earn playing the game. Many of these songs featured bands that some of the Harmonix employees actually played in.

for Guitar Hero by a cover band. For example, when you think you're hearing the bearded band ZZ Top cranking out "Sharp Dressed Man," you're actually playing along with WaveGroup. In fact, WaveGroup created most of the tracks for the entire Guitar Hero franchise. Studio musician and true guitar wizard Marcus Henderson is the guy laying down most of the guitar solos you hear.

WaveGroup went to great lengths to match the original sound of the tracks to keep them feeling real. Voice impersonators were hired, and when that didn't work they even went further. For example, for Black Sabbath's "Iron Man" track, the guys at WaveGroup found out that the vocal effects in the original song were created by lead vocalist Ozzy Osbourne singing from behind a metal fan. They tried out a few fans, but the sound was never quite right. Eventually, they ended up going on Craigslist and finding a fan from the 1970s exactly like the one Black Sabbath used. The results were spot-on—and totally worth the effort.

Guitar Hero controller © Masem

It took time, and a great deal of passion, but in 2005 every gamer who ever dreamed of being a rock star had a way to get there, and that way was through the PlayStation 2. The game shipped with a guitar shaped like a Gibson SG, a true American classic.

Game critics got their groove on, too, and great reviews poured in from just about everywhere, from IGN to GameSpot. They loved the sound track, and the guitar controller felt great, but it was the fantasy of lighting up a room full of crazed rock and roll fans that kept you playing again and again.

In 2009, a fourteen-year-old boy, Danny Johnson, became the undisputed champion of Guitar Hero. Not only is he ranked number one online on just about every song, he rocked his way into the *Guinness Book of World Records* by playing the game's hardest song, "Through the Fire and Flames," at a 99 percent accuracy. Dude. I mean . . . DUUUUDE!

Guitar Hero shipped just in time for kids to beg their parents to jam the plastic guitar under the Christmas tree, and before we said good-bye to 2005, Guitar Hero had sold over forty-five million dollars' worth of games and guitars, becoming PlayStation 2's second-best-selling game that year in less than two months. In response, RedOctane and Harmonix, the codevelopers, jumped in on a sequel as fast as they could. And, as it turns out, it was pretty fast.

Almost a year from the day Guitar Hero shipped, RedOctane and Harmonix were ready for their second world tour. Guitar Hero II's opening show was on November 6, 2006, and it only built on the amazing sales of Guitar Hero. It had better multiplayer, so you could go head-to-head with your friends; better note recognition; and if you wanted to (and everyone did), you could now buy a second Gibson SG controller, only this time instead of black-and-white, it was bright cherry red.

Nothing felt quite as cool as standing next to your best friend, two shiny guitars strapped around your necks, as you ripped into one of the sixty-four new tracks, the wind machine blowing your long digital hair as you shredded out some sweet tunes to the screaming fans.

The plastic instrument craze only lasted for six years, but it was enough to start a massive movement in gaming: the era of wacky accessories and basement entertainment rooms filled with everything from drum kits and guitar racks to light rigs and cameras, so you could record your skillz and put them up on YouTube.

The video game world had popped right out of the consoles and cartridges and landed in the middle of the living room floor.

Sorry about the mess, moms, but you just can't stop the rock and roll!

In 2008, American rock band Aerosmith joined with Activision to release Guitar Hero: Aerosmith. And it was a very smart decision, because the band earned more from the game than they had from any other single album in their entire career.

Even though the series lasted for only a half-dozen years, it released nineteen games and brought in over two billion dollars.

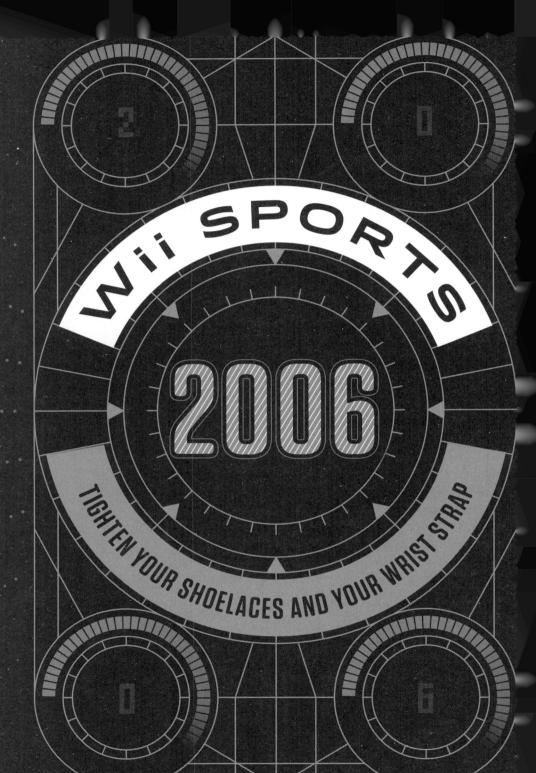

Baseball in Wii Sports © Nintendo

You know what feels really great? Lining up the perfect shot on a golf course. The sun shining down on your shoulders, the birds chirping in the trees. You check the wind, then swing back the club before bringing it around, ripping the ball off the tee with a perfect *zzzWHACK!*

Ooh, and how about holding a twelve-pound bowling ball behind you, walking up to the line, and letting it rip down the lane? It rumbles down toward the pins then crushes them for a perfect strike.

Wait, I have another. And this one is a doozy. Can you imagine how cool it would be to climb through the ropes in a boxing ring, the crowd going wild and chanting your name? You dodge, you weave, you float like a butterfly, then *POW*, you sting like a bee. Jab, jab, LEFT HOOK, and your opponent thumps to the mat.

Now can you imagine doing all of this without leaving your house? Amazing, right? Well, hold that thought and

245

Top console and handheld games of 2005:

1. Madden NFL 06 (PS2), Electronic Arts, over 2.9 million sold

2. Pokémon Emerald (GBA), Nintendo of America, over 1.7 million sold

3. Gran Turismo 4 (PS2), Sony Interactive Entertainment, over 1.5 million sold

4. Madden NFL 06 (Xbox), Electronic Arts, over 1.2 million sold

5. NCAA Football 06 (PS2), Electronic Arts, over 1.1 million sold

6. Star Wars: Battlefront II (PS2), LucasArts, over 1 million sold

7. MVP Baseball 2005 (PS2), Electronic Arts, over 970,000 sold

8. Star Wars Episode III: Revenge of the Sith (PS2), LucasArts, over 930,000 sold

9. NBA Live 06 (PS2), Electronic Arts, over 820,000 sold

10. LEGO Star Wars (PS2), Eidos, over 800,000 sold

we'll get back to it, because if you think these sound fun, you are not alone.

2005 was a banner year for video games, topping over 10.5 billion dollars spent on consoles, games, and accessories like the DDR dance pad. That's a big pile of cash. And much of that money went to EA as their sports games were dominating the sales chart. But all of their big sellers were on the Xbox and the PS2. In fact, of the top ten bestselling games, only one title belonged to Nintendo, and it was on the Game Boy Advance.

So far the new century hadn't been all that kind to Nintendo. There was no doubt that Nintendo was falling behind Sony and Microsoft, but they weren't ready to give up just yet. They had a plan. A very clever, very unusual, very NINTENDO plan.

They were going to make games for everyone.

Now, I know what you're thinking. You're asking yourself, "Don't Sony and Microsoft make games for everyone?"

And I'd have to reply, "Well, today they do. But in 2005, not so much."

You see, back in the mid-2000s, games were getting more and more realistic. Gamers loved seeing the wrinkles on the Madden NFL jerseys. They loved seeing burned rubber left behind on the roads in Gran Turismo 4, and glowing lightsabers cutting through locked steel doors, dripping sparks to the floor, where they reflected off the shiny surface. I mean—who doesn't want to see that?

But there was something else going on, too. Not only were the visuals of the games getting more complicated, the rules and the controls for the games were getting more advanced as well. Which isn't a bad thing—not at all. It adds to the competition and realism of the game, but it also makes it harder for new gamers to jump in. Nintendo looked at what the "other guys" were doing and went in the opposite direction. Instead of detailed button-press recognition, HD graphics, and fine-tuned controls, Nintendo wanted to make a magic wand that would recognize when you waved your hand in the air.

While Sony and Microsoft were fighting for who was the top dog in the console war, Nintendo research and development, headed up by none other than Shigeru Miyamoto, started working on the Wii. Instead of focusing on building the most high-tech system with the best graphics, Nintendo focused on motion. Not controls so much, but motion.

The difference I'm trying to describe here is that in the past, button mapping and timing were the best tools you had to make the controls feel just right. For example, in Nintendo's Mike Tyson's Punch-Out!! for the NES, you would push the correct button at the perfect time to swing a left hook. Choosing a button that made sense and the exact timing is an example of getting the controls just right. But what Nintendo wanted to do with their Wii and the Wiimote was to get the MOTION right. So if you wanted to land a left hook, you had to throw a left hook.

The answer was the Wiimote, and while it appears simple, it was actually quite a sophisticated device.

When gamers started hearing about the Wiimote, they pretty much laughed it off, and so did Microsoft and Sony. In fact, a few years before the inventor of the guts inside the Wiimote, Tom Quinn, showed his invention to Nintendo, he showed it to Sony and Microsoft. Sony passed because they were only interested if they could add the technology to their controllers for under fifty cents, which was impossible, but the guys at Xbox weren't so nice. The story goes that Microsoft's head honcho and CEO at the time, Steve Ballmer, liked the idea and introduced Quinn to the Xbox team. The Xbox development group thought it was a joke. They were so rude that an unnamed Microsoft executive followed up with Quinn later on and personally apologized.

Nintendo Wii © Evan Amos

Boxing in Wii Sports © Nintendo

Golfing in Wii Sports © Nintendo

Nintendo tested their Wiimote until it could tell the difference between a big golf swing and a tiny twist of your wrist to put backspin on a tennis ball. When things felt just right, they did something that surprised even them: They asked Mario to sit this one out.

I know, right?

For years, decades even, Mario had been the star of every Nintendo launch. Who could replace a guy like Mario?

Well, the answer is—you.

Miyamoto was at the helm again, driving the vision and design of Nintendo's new game and new console. And this time he wanted the game to reach everyone. Young boys and girls, teens with braces, dads with handlebar mustaches and potbellies, moms who had no idea they would fall in love with games, and even grandparents. What better way to do that than to put them all into the game? Introducing the Miis, a create-a-player system that allowed Wiigamers (I made that word up) to create just about any character they could dream up.

Nintendo was doing everything different with the Wii:

- While everyone else was focused on precision timing and complicated button mapping, Nintendo created the first motion controller with the Wiimote, which gave us simple, intuitive motion controls.

- While Sony and Microsoft were spending millions developing new, realistic-looking characters for their systems, Nintendo introduced the Mii, a nonthreatening, toylike character that appealed to everyone.

- While their competitors were focusing on uber-realistic, detailed graphics and expensive hardware, Nintendo kept the Wii's graphics simple and basic to make an affordable console.

- While everyone else was going hard after teen boys and experienced gamers, Nintendo wanted ANYONE to be able to pick up a Wiimote and have fun.

The PlayStation 3 shipped on November 11, 2006, and eight days later, Nintendo rolled out their new Wii. Inside every box was a host of Miis waiting to be shaped into gamers' likenesses, and a copy of Wii Sports, the game that tied all the new features of the Wiimote together in one superfun and engaging little package.

Wii Sports was a collection of five well-known and easy-to-imagine sports games that didn't require any instructions. All you had to do was pick up a controller, pretend it was a tennis racquet, and swing. That's it. Want to go bowling? Go ahead and make a bowling motion. Boxing? Throw a few punches. Golf? Well, you get the idea.

On opening weekend it was nearly impossible to get a Wii. It launched for 250 bucks and it included a game, while the Xbox 360, which had been out for a year, was still hovering around $400 without a game. The PS3 cost either five or six hundred bucks, depending on which model you were after, and it also didn't come with a game. The pricing was definitely a factor that first month, but it wasn't the only one. Everyone had seen the TV commercials of people playing virtual bowling in their living room, and the idea of the odd controller was so new, and the game looked so easy that everyone wanted to give it a try.

Bowling in Wii Sports © Nintendo

The game was simple, good fun. If you were lucky enough to get a Wii that first month, you were probably going to throw a party and invite friends over to gather around the TV for a game of tennis. Word of mouth became the best tool in Nintendo's marketing bag, and right out of the gate they were outselling the higher-powered Play-Station 3.

Nintendo didn't totally ignore the hard-core gamers. In fact, their launch titles for the Wii contained some of the same games as the PS3, including Call of Duty 3, Madden NFL 07, and Need for Speed: Carbon. However, they led with their more family-friendly games, like The Legend of Zelda: Twilight Princess, Disney's Cars, Rayman Raving Rabbids, and of course, Wii Sports.

The early part of the decade had been a little rough on Nintendo as they watched their two competitors edge them out, but by the time the Wii, PS3, and Xbox 360 had run their course, Nintendo found themselves back on top. To date, the Wii has sold over 101 million copies, while the PS3 and Xbox 360 sold nearly eighty-four million copies each. And that simple sports game that you just had to try? Well, it ended up being the number one–selling console game of all time, raking in a grand total of 82.69 million units. And it did it on a single system. That's going to be a tough number to beat. But I have a feeling a mustached guy in a little red hat will figure out a way to beat it someday.

If we've learned anything from watching Nintendo over the years, it is that they love to set records. Almost as much as they love to break them.

Tennis in Wii Sports © Nintendo

PORTAL

2007

THE CAKE IS A LIE

Portal © Valve Corporation

Probably at no time in history has a game started out as an independent student project and ended up as such a massive mainstream hit.

Portal's rise to success has been legendary, but as with all stories, there is more than what we see on the surface. Or perhaps, more *behind* the surface, but we'll get to that in a minute.

First I want to talk about something really cool. Did you know you could go to college to become a game developer? Yeah, that's true. You can actually get a college degree in video games. There are colleges all over the world that are teaching courses in video game development, and launching enthusiastic students on to promising careers in the game industry, a great path filled with challenges that will keep them learning for their entire lives. You can study everything from video game design, to audio and music production, to software engineering, to art and animation. You can even study project management, marketing, and video game finance.

It's an industry that is growing incredibly fast, and for most people, starting off at the right college is the best first step. It certainly was for a group of students at DigiPen Institute of Technology, who were working together on a project called Narbacular Drop. Here's how it all began.

The year was 2005, and Paul Graham, Realm Lovejoy, Scott Klintworth, Jeep Barnett, Dave Kircher, Garret Rickey, and genius designer Kim Swift had dreamed up and developed a game that featured a 3D world that looked an awful lot like Quake at the time. But unlike Quake, the game wasn't a shooter. It was a puzzle game featuring a character that couldn't jump. If that wasn't difficult enough, the students, who called themselves Nuclear Monkey Software at the time, added a unique portal feature that made the game totally unconventional. The player opened a single pair of interconnected portals at a time, each styled as a huge face with flaming eyes. You entered through the portal with orange eyes, and you exited through the portal with blue eyes. Nobody had ever thought of, let alone seen, anything like it.

The game was simple, yet complicated at the same time. A combination guaranteed to drive gamers nuts, in all the right ways. After getting high marks and praise from their classmates, the team at Nuclear Monkey Software entered the game into the school's annual career fair, where DigiPen invites video game developers to visit their school and interview graduating students.

Robin Walker, a longtime Valve employee attending the career fair, fell in love with the game at once. So, Robin invited THE ENTIRE TEAM to the Valve studio to meet with the owner, Gabe Newell.

Filled with excitement, the students made the trip right away, and after getting his hands on the game, Gabe Newell offered THE ENTIRE TEAM jobs at Valve.

Yup. You read that right. Valve hired every last student from the Nuclear Monkey Software team on the spot, and the Portal team was born.

But even before making the trip to Valve, the game made its way to the top of the list in the award circuit. Just check out this list of awards Narbacular Drop collected in 2006:

- IGF (Independent Games Festival) Student Showcase, winner

- Slamdance Guerrilla Gamemaker Competition, finalist

- GameShadow Innovation in Games Festival and Awards, nomination

- *Game Informer* Top Ten Games You've Never Heard Of

- *Edge* Internet Game of the Month (March 2006)

- Gamasutra Quantum Leap Awards: Most Important Games, honorable mention winner

Yet, despite all these honors, once at Valve, the team started the entire game over from scratch. It seems to be something Valve is good at.

Part of the advantage of being hired by Valve was that the group now had access to the creators of some of the most legendary FPS games of all time. Part of the disadvantage of being a young team hired right out of college was that they didn't have the experience yet to warrant a massive budget of their own. That would have to be earned. So, surrounded by fantastic game developers, and short of money, the decision was made to set the new Portal game in the Half-Life 2 universe.

The Portal team worked with Half-Life series writer Marc Laidlaw to fit their new game into the plot. Set in the futuristic Aperture Science, Easter eggs and hints were sprinkled throughout the series to tie the two games together. The concept of a computer AI guiding the player through experimental facilities to test the portal gun was decided on pretty early in the writing process. The team quickly began working on dialogue, drafting early lines for the AI computer, and after a few rounds of back-and-forth, they decided that the AI computer needed to be polite, witty, and perhaps a tad dishonest.

The more they experimented with the writing for the AI guide, the more they fell in love with the voice, and

The decision to build Portal using art and tools the Valve team used to build Half-Life 2 not only saved them a lot of time and development money, it also gave the game a consistent feel that helped extend the life of Half-Life 2. Fans were hungry for this new content, which helped Portal become a massive success at launch.

GLaDOS, the AI computer guide in Portal, stands for *genetic lifeform and disk operating system*. Makes you wonder if Gabe Newell's previous days working on Microsoft's famous operating system had any influence here, doesn't it?

The Orange Box included Half-Life 2, Half-Life 2: Episode One, Half-Life 2: Episode Two, Portal, and Team Fortress 2. Quite a good deal, being that the entire collection cost less than Half-Life 2 when it was originally launched.

eventually GLaDOS was born. She quickly became central to the game's story. They designed a clear beginning, middle, and end, and GLaDOS figured into every part of it. But they didn't want GLaDOS to be boring, so along with her humorous tone and dry wit, the writers for Portal planned a change in her personality as the game progressed.

Within the game—pretty early on, actually—GLaDOS asks you to help test out the new, experimental portal gun. She explains how to do it: Simply shoot a wall and an orange portal will open up. Then shoot another wall, and a blue portal will open. Climb through the orange portal, and you will come out the blue portal. Sounds easy. And it is, in theory, but boy, do the puzzles and challenges get difficult in a hurry. Add a barrage of flying bullets all around, and you'll need more than just a funny robot voice telling you what to do. You'll need motivation. And what better motivation than CAKE?

GLaDOS promises you a great reward of perfectly decorated, scrumptious cake, and it's just enough to push you on toward the end. That and the fact that the game is simply amazing, fun to play, with a story so good, you have to finish just to see how it ends.

It took two years for the small team of ten Valve developers to perfect Portal. That sounds like a long time, but it's actually a remarkable feat, considering the quality and game-play innovation involved with the game. When it was ready to launch, Valve included it in something they called the Orange Box.

The Orange Box compilation contained FIVE great Valve games, and it launched to the public on October 9, 2007, but if you were one of the early-adopter types, and had a Steam account, you could get the game a day early through direct download. It doesn't sound like much now, but back then it was HUGE news. It was one of the first major releases to really promote buying the game directly through a digital store, rather than heading off to your local video game store in the mall for a copy.

While fans around the world were excited for the Orange Box, the big surprise hit of the game was Valve's little experimental student project, Portal. Fans were delighted by the game's refreshing mechanics, fun story, and familiar setting, and before long the game had become a classic.

It's hard to list any specific innovations for Portal, because really, the gameplay itself IS the innovation. Jumping from portal to portal as you navigate through Aperture is impressive from the moment you pull the trigger on your first portal gun to the very last time you solve a complicated portal puzzle. Honestly, the only way to really understand Portal and its impact is to play the game. You really should give it a shot. It will make your mind a little scrambly at first, but you'll catch on quickly and fall in love with the game mechanics.

And, oh boy, if you thought Portal's predecessor, Narbacular Drop, cleaned up at the awards, check out the list of game awards Portal picked up.

- At the 2008 Game Developers Choice Awards, Portal won Game of the Year, along with the Innovation Award and Best Game Design.

- IGN honored Portal with several awards: Best Puzzle Game for PC and Xbox 360, Most Innovative Design for PC, and Best End Credit Song (for "Still Alive") for Xbox 360. IGN also placed GLaDOS (from Portal) as the number one video game villain on its Top 100 Villains list.

- In its Best of 2007, GameSpot honored the Orange Box with four awards in recognition of Portal, giving out honors for Best Puzzle Game, Best New Character (for GLaDOS), Funniest Game, and Best Original Game Mechanic (for the portal gun).

- Portal was awarded Game of the Year (PC), Best Narrative (PC), and Best Innovation (PC and console) honors by 1UP.com in its 2007 editorial awards.

- GamePro honored the game for Most Memorable Villain (for GLaDOS) in its Editors' Choice 2007 Awards.

Portal 2's Space Sphere, a charming orb-shaped robot, actually made it to SPACE! An anonymous tech at NASA got away with laser engraving an image of the little guy, along with the quote "IN SPAAAAAACE!" to an unidentified part of a Japanese supply craft rocket that went on a mission to restock the ISS in 2012. Now, THAT is out of this world.

- Portal was named the Game of the Year in 2007 by Joystiq, Good Game, and Shacknews.

- In *Official Xbox Magazine*'s 2007 Game of the Year Awards, Portal won Best New Character (for GLaDOS), Best Original Song (for "Still Alive"), and Innovation of the Year.

- In GameSpy's 2007 Game of the Year Awards, Portal was recognized for Best Puzzle Game, Best Character (for GLaDOS), and Best Sidekick (for the Weighted Companion Cube).

- The web comic Penny Arcade awarded Portal Best Sound Track, Best Writing, and Best New Game Mechanic in its satirical 2007 We're Right Awards.

- Eurogamer gave Portal first place in its Top 50 Games of 2007 rankings.

- GamesRadar named it the best game of all time.

- In November 2012, *TIME* named it one of the 100 greatest video games of all time.

- *WIRED* considered Portal to be one of the most influential games of the first decade of the twenty-first century, believing it to be the prime example of quality over quantity for video games.

There's just something about zapping a hole in a floor and burning through into another dimension, only to spin forty-five degrees into a clean white room, totally dizzy and confused, with the voice of GLaDOS calmly telling me that everything is NOT okay that I will NEVER forget. And if you'll allow me a moment here, I'll just add that Portal is one of my all-time favorite games.

So far, at least.

COME ON, JUST ONE MORE TRY

H ow do they do it? How do game designers make games so darned addictive? What is it that makes me go nuts when I lose a game, that makes me want to get right back on it and play again and again? And AGAIN!!!

Creating a video game isn't just luck. A lot of it has to do with science. Games are designed to be just hard enough to be truly challenging, while allowing us game players just enough success, or hope, that we feel like with one more try we can do it.

It would take an entire book—heck, maybe even a series of books—to cover all the details, science, and psychology of what makes a game addictive, but we have time to glance at a few broad categories here. See if you recognize any of these techniques in your favorite games.

The High Score

Whether you're trying to get a perfect score in Candy Crush, or moving Pac-Man through a maze, the high score is one of the most addictive things on the screen. Nothing beats tapping in your initials when you beat the high score, and nothing is more frustrating than missing it by just a few points.

Beating the Game

A good game writer can build a story that you just NEED to see to the end. A lot of games fit this category, and if you are a storyteller at heart, this is probably one that drives you back time and again. Not knowing how a story ends is a great way to keep players coming back to finish the game.

Role-Playing

Some people spend hundreds of hours creating and shaping a character in a game. Over time these characters become very important to gamers. And when a character that feels like family leaves on an adventure, we want to make sure they are safe. Oh, and we want them to get all the loot and win all the battles, too. That way, you can improve your character even more, and the cycle continues. Don't believe me? Ask a 999-ranked Monster Hunter player about their character. They'll let you know what I'm talking about.

Discovery

Exploration is usually connected to role-playing games, but lately it has shown up in just about every genre. Whether it's unlocking a new area to race around in Need for Speed, or opening up a new section in Far Cry 4, the tease of something new just out of reach is one that most gamers just can't resist.

Relationships

Playing online games with friends can build a community that keeps players coming back again and again. For some players, this can be a place where they can really be themselves. Perhaps even the only place, so returning for more just feels right. Ya know?

Competition

A goal being scored in Rocket League © Psyonix, Inc.

Winning. Yeah, I'll admit, this is me. Getting beaten by a last-second goal in Rocket League is a guaranteed way for me to want a rematch! I hate losing. There, I said it. So, if I have a chance to get back in and win, you'd better believe I'm going to jump in.

Creativity

There's just something great about building a world that has never been built before in Minecraft. Saving the world, opening it up for friends to help, and sharing it online or through a YouTube video only makes this experience better.

And there are many more. What is it that makes you come back to a game time and again?

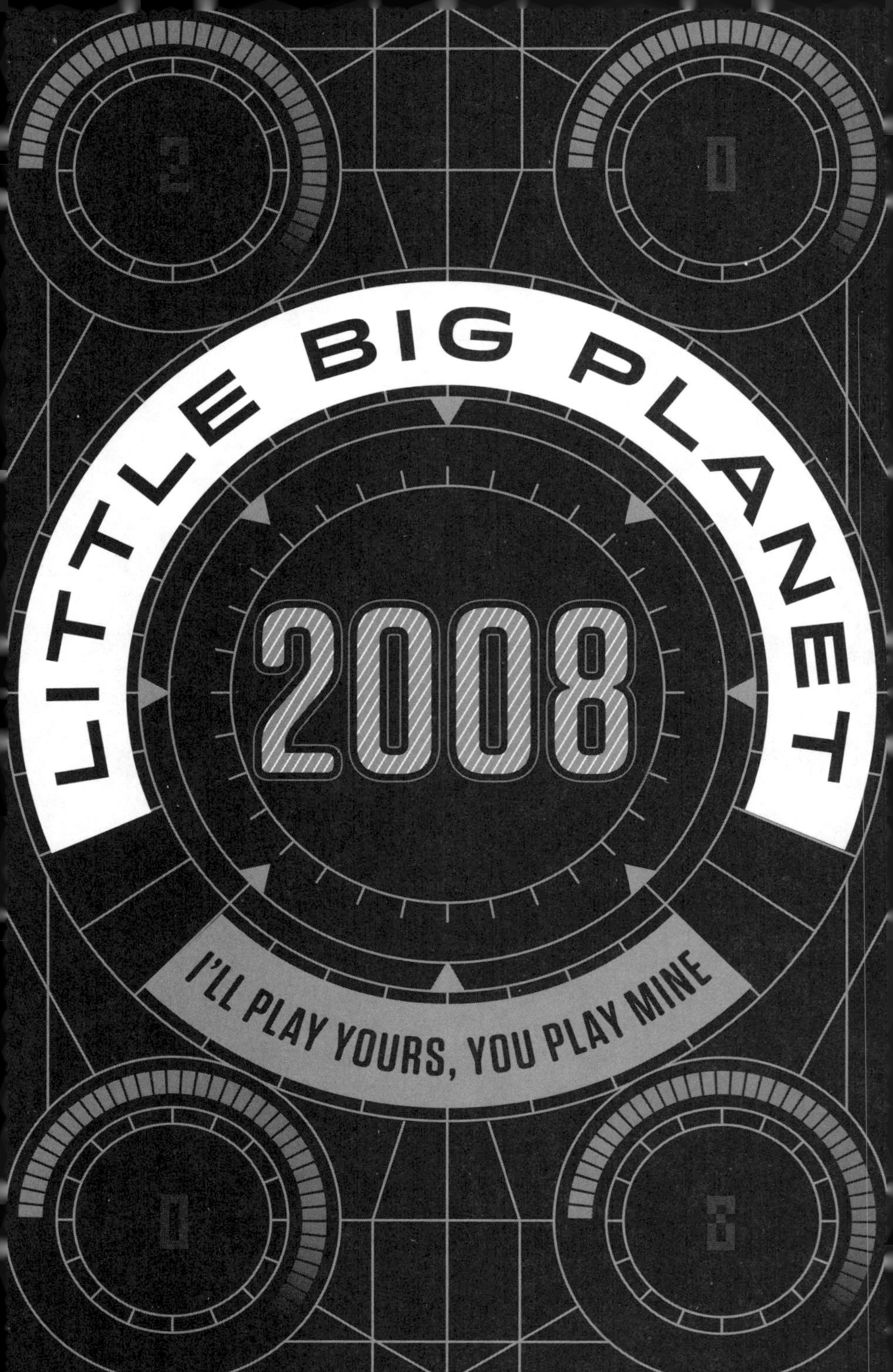
LITTLE BIG PLANET
2008
I'LL PLAY YOURS, YOU PLAY MINE

Little Big Planet © Media Molecule/Sony Computer Entertainment, Inc.

By 2008, there were gamers in all walks of life.

You didn't need to be a geeky teen boy who stayed up all night playing shooters in your basement to be a gamer; you could just as believably be a thirty-year-old mom playing Final Fantasy after you dropped your kids off at school.

The gaming industry was growing up and getting more diverse, which was exactly what it needed. Games were now commonplace.

Which led to something very interesting: Gamers wanted to make games themselves. While building games like The Sims was popular, and creating your own avatars in World of Warcraft and Madden was fun, gamers everywhere were itching to try their hands, and minds, at making totally original games to show off their passion.

Luckily for them, a small company in the United Kingdom felt the same way, and they were about to scratch their creative itch on the PlayStation 3, with Little Big Planet.

It started a couple of years earlier, when longtime game developers Mark Healey and David Smith, who were working at Lionhead Studios at the time, started thinking about puppets, creation, and user-created content. These were lofty topics, the type of thing that game developers dream of creating. They wanted to make a game that would not only provide hours of fun as a gamer, but that would allow gamers to make their own levels. Decorate and change their own environments. Alter their character's appearance, how he moved, what she sounded like, how they lived and died.

What Healey and Smith had in their minds was, well, pretty much impossible, and they knew it. I mean, they were just two guys who broke off from a gaming studio to build their own independent game. A game that they knew would have to be really big in order for it to work.

But they had the passion. They had the skills to get it started. They even had a few friends who promised to help. What Healey and Smith didn't have was a champion—someone to have their backs, and trust that their massive vision for a game made by gamers for gamers to make games was possible.

Enter Phil Harrison, head of development for Sony Computer Entertainment's Worldwide Studios.

You know, one thing that always strikes me as amazing is how the game industry is both HUGE and very small at the same time. There are thousands upon thousands of people making video games, but somehow everyone seems to know someone who knows someone special in the game biz. It's like a one-step-removed thing. I mean, I worked with a guy who made a game with Miyamoto. Does that mean I know Miyamoto? Well, no, but my friend does, and who knows? This connection might someday put me in touch with one of the most if not THE most influential minds in the history of games. And that's kind of what happened here. Somehow, through their network of connections, Healey and Smith arranged a presentation meeting with Phil Harrison, and they knew this was their big shot. They were NOT going to mess it up.

Instead of presenting a slick, noninteractive slide show filled with boring text and impossible promises, Healey and Smith built a working prototype of their new idea. They called it Craftworld, and at the time, it starred a yellow-cube-headed man with a pink body named Mr. Yellowhead. They focused on game play, not their really big creation mechanics, because they felt a game based on creation was too risky, too strange to put in front of Sony's biggest executive. In the prototype you used the right analog stick on the PlayStation 2 controller to move Mr. Yellowhead's arms, and the left analog stick to move his legs. The object of the prototype was to guide Mr. Yellowhead past a bunch of geometric-shaped objects by grabbing on to them and pushing or rolling them around. If you've played LBP, you'll recognize that some of those original prototype concepts made their way into the actual game a couple of years later.

However, Healey and Smith's attempts to hide the creative aspect of the game in order to not "weird out" Harrison didn't really work. Harrison immediately saw through the cool prototype, and noticed that what the game really offered was a massive digital sandbox that players could use to create their own experiences. In other words, Harrison's vision for what the Craftworld prototype could become matched Healey and Smith's perfectly.

What was supposed to be a forty-five-minute introduction meeting ended up lasting three hours, and before it was over Harrison had committed to funding Healey and Smith's new game studio, Media Molecule, for six months so they could develop their new concept further.

The prototype of Craftworld was scrapped, and out of the scraps that fell on the floor, Little Big Planet was born.

The team at Media Molecule got rolling on the official game early in 2006, but even with Sony's backing they still struggled with exactly what direction they needed to take the game. They believed in their create-first mentality, and they also loved their grippy little puppet-based hero character, who was now called Sackbot. But they still worried that people would have a hard time understanding their game. I mean, there had never been anything quite like it before.

In spring 2007, Sony informed Media Molecule that they wanted them to showcase their project at GDC—the Game Developers Conference. Media Molecule knew that this was a pretty big opportunity, so they hurried to polish the artwork, which now looked like a game made up of beautiful, rich swaths of fabric, natural sponges, and

The puppet controls didn't end with the arms. You could also control Sackbot's emotions and expressions in-game by pushing UP (smile), DOWN (frown), RIGHT (angry), or LEFT (happy). Also, the DualShock 3 Controller had this cool new feature: It recognized when you tilted the controller, so Media Molecule made it apparent by mapping the head tilt to the angle you held the controller. If you tilted up, Sackbot looked into the sky; if you tilted down, he looked at his feet. The whole thing added up to one very fun, silly, and expressive character.

brightly colored stickers. It looked like what might have happened if the movie *Toy Story* broke out in a sewing room, only with more mischief. The look and feel of the game was amazing, but the guys knew they needed one more feature to really show off their game. The SLAP!

The "slap" feature was pure silliness, but it showed off their puppet concept better than anything. They already had grabbing, pushing, and pulling down, but Media Molecule wanted to show gamers exactly how to use PlayStation 3's new DualShock 3 Controller. They mapped, or assigned, the analog sticks to control the characters' arms, and if you moved your character next to your friend's, you could WHIP the analog stick around and fling your arm into your friend's Sackbot. It would send him flying across the screen, leaving you standing there with a smile on your face.

They were ready. They had a cool new game level built to show off their new game, Little Big Planet. They had it primed for a four-player experience. They had stickers and funny costumes and a big skateboard, just ready for four Sackbots to jump on and ride down a big hill. They were ready to show their game to gamers, four at a time, in a booth at GDC. But Sony and Phil Harrison had a much bigger idea in mind. Unbeknownst to the team at Media Molecule, Harrison had decided he wanted them to join him onstage to show their new game to the world, going from four gamers to 1.8 MILLION people at a time.

Phil Harrison was the keynote speaker for the Sony presentation at GDC that year, and he was so proud of the team at Media Molecule that he couldn't wait to show the world. So, in 2007, about a year before the game launched to the world, he brought Healey and Smith onstage, and they showed LBP on a screen over fifty feet tall on a stage filled with rabid gamers. The PlayStation 3 was only a few months old at the time, and people were still blown away with the high-end graphics, complex physics, and smooth video the new console offered, and the colorful, cloth-based world of Little Big Planet showed off the system perfectly. Not only was the game shown onstage, but the presentation was broadcast live to almost two million fans who'd tuned in to see what was new for the new gaming console.

Sony PlayStation 3 © Evan Amos

And the reaction was far better than the team at Media Molecule could have hoped for. People cheered in their seats when the Sackbots rode the big skateboard down a hill at the end of the level, and laughed like crazy when Sackbots got into a slap fight during the celebration sequence at the end. But when Healey and Smith explained that the level they'd just shown the world was actually built inside the game with tools they planned on shipping in the final project, gamers went totally bonkers.

The game was a media favorite before it even launched, as players craved the new, unique experience. By the time LBP launched, Sony had helped build up a frenzy for the game, and it was a massive success from day one.

The game shipped with a handful of fun, platformer-style levels for both single-and multiplayer experiences. The levels were creative and beautiful and really showed off Media Molecule's ability to not only build a great game, but also to design fun levels themselves. But within a few days, new, challenging levels started popping up all around the world as gamers learned how to build levels of their own.

Players voted on levels they liked best, left comments, shared favorites, and posted articles on the LBP forums. In no time at all, Media Molecule's vision was achieved, as gamers flocked to the game to make games of their own. By 2011, over five million unique levels had been built and shared within the game, and the fan base only increased when new features were added as downloadable content.

Everyone was loving the game, and longtime gaming icons like Peter Molyneux claimed that Little Big Planet was the most important creative innovation in 2008. With a list of innovations like this, you have to admit he had a point.

Swinging on a sponge in Little Big Planet © Media Molecule/Sony Computer Entertainment, Inc.

- **While platformers had existed for decades by this point, Little Big Planet's real-time physics added a new level of depth and exploration to platforming. By this I mean, if an object looked top-heavy, it would probably fall over if you pushed it. If you saw a hard object that looked heavy, like a chunk of lead, it was a safe bet that you would be unable to move it, and if you saw a chunk of foamy sponge hanging from a string, you knew you could swing around on it. Little Big Planet was a what-you-see-is-what-you-get-type game, where they encouraged physical play and** exploration in order to complete their well-designed single-player levels.

- While we've discussed create mode up above as a feature of the game, it really does deserve a mention in the best innovation section as well. It was a pure imagination playground, where you could do everything from sculpting a cardboard cat to rewiring Sackbot's controls. Nothing was out of bounds in create mode, and it inspired millions of would-be game designers to try their hand at making games.

- For the first time ever, players were allowed to change the mood and expression of their character with the innovative puppet controls.

- Media Molecule not only loved their game, they loved their gaming community. They proved this by being very active in the forums. In fact, shortly after the game launched, Media Molecule started handing out things they called *MM picks* to particularly creative gamers. These awards were not just pats on the back; they were handed out as a crown you could put on your Sackbot in-game. They became the ultimate bragging rights for dedicated gamers and level creators.

- Not only did Media Molecule create some amazing tools for making content for their game, but they used the tool to find some fantastic employees. One user named Steve_Big_Guns parlayed his passion for building games in Little Big Planet into a full-time position at Media Molecule. Very clever, Media Molecule; very clever.

The creative focus of Little Big Planet went on to become the defining factor for Media Molecule games. Every game they make has this same create-first DNA, and you'd better believe they are dreaming up something innovative for the future.

A year after its release, Media Molecule released a second version of the game, the Game of the Year Edition. This edition featured not only the original game, but also eighteen exclusive levels designed by players in the Little Big Planet community.

FarmVille © Zynga

While the Wii taught us that ANYONE can be a gamer, in 2009 there still seemed to be a great divide between traditional, or hard-core, gamers and the new casual gamers.

But in reality there was more crossover than meets the eye, and the perfect way to illustrate this is to take a peek inside the barn and examine Zynga's breakout game that had just about everyone on the planet talking about tomatoes. That's right, FarmVille.

But before we talk about digital produce, we need to talk about people. Lots of them. Millions of them, actually, and before they were shearing digital sheep, these people were sharing pictures of cats and talking about their diet goals online. And they were doing all of this on a not-so-little website called Facebook. The story of Facebook is an interesting one for sure, but since this book is about gaming, I'll leave the telling of it to *The Social Network*, the movie made about its creator, Mark Zuckerberg. However, it *is* important to point out that what started out as a way for Zuckerberg and his friends to connect on the Harvard University campus ended up being one of the fastest-growing sites in the world. Facebook launched quietly in 2005, and believe it or not, it took a few *years* before there were any games at all on the popular social site.

And it wasn't Facebook's founder, Zuckerberg, who started the gaming craze—it was financial wizard and

Before founding Zynga, Mark Pincus was a founding investor in Napster, Facebook, Friendster, and Twitter. To say that this guy knows social media is a huge understatement.

investment entrepreneur Mark Pincus who made the big leap. Nobody would have pegged Pincus as a gaming tycoon. Before he became an entrepreneur, he worked for massive investment companies, attended Harvard Business School, and worked for Columbia Capital, where he learned about and invested in software start-up companies.

After playing the role of investor, Pincus launched a few start-ups of his own. He was very interested in social software, and before Facebook came onto the scene, he was already dabbling with building social media sites of his own.

His early entrepreneurial adventures didn't turn out so well. In fact, they all failed, but Pincus took his failures and learned from them when starting Zynga. Instead of trying to build the social media platform from the ground up, Zynga's goal was to take advantage of social media sites already out there and add Zynga's games to them.

Zynga is actually named after Mark Pincus's pet bulldog. The happy pooch is still the company's mascot today.

But in 2009, something new cropped up. Zynga launched FarmVille in June, peak farming season, and they gave the game the best head start possible. They introduced Farm-Ville to forty million gamers on the same day. Talk about an announcement. Within days, office computers around the globe were sharing their desktops with little farmers.

How did they do this, you might ask? Well, they did it in much the same way a farmer plants his crops.

1. **THEY PLANTED SEEDS. Two years before they launched FarmVille, Zynga launched a digital poker game on Facebook, Texas Holdem Poker, or Zynga Poker. It was one of the first games on Facebook to have actual graphics, and it had a TON of gamers checking in and playing every day.**

2. **THEY BOUGHT SOME GREAT FERTILIZER.** One year before FarmVille, Zynga bought a game called YoVille from a competitor. The funny thing is, they didn't really do much with the game. What they really wanted was access to the millions of gamers playing YoVille every day.

3. **THEY WATERED THEIR CROPS.** Zynga didn't just make a game and let it rot on the vine—they kept feeding gamers with new content and teasing that new, great things were coming soon.

4. **THEY WAITED UNTIL THE CROPS WERE READY BEFORE THEY HARVESTED.** On the day FarmVille was ready to launch, Zynga sent HUGE incentives to the forty million players on Zynga Poker and YoVille to jump over and start a farm.

The game was easy to play. You click on a square, pick the right seed to plant, click it again to plant the seed, click a couple more times to water it, and then remember to come back and click it again to harvest it before it wilts. It sounded easy, and it was. But it was based on timing, and that was where things got complicated. Follow me for a minute.

Okay, let's say you plant ten strawberry plants. Those strawberries will cost you 100 coins to plant, and they will take two hours to grow. If you don't return within another hour after they are ripe, then your new strawberries will wilt and die. That means, if you planted your ten strawberries for 100 coins at noon, they would be worth 450 coins by 2:00, and a big fat ZERO coins by 3:00. They called this appointment gaming, and it drove people CRAZY! Both in good and bad ways.

Zynga hired a full-time behavioral psychologist to help figure out what made gamers tick. This new scientific approach to game design had a big influence on games back then, and it still does today.

FarmVille farmers outnumber actual farmers in America at a rate of eighty to one.

This game mechanic earned the name *wither mechanic* in the game industry, and while it was successful for Zynga at the time, it is now frowned upon because it punishes players for not showing up on time. Most games nowadays, FarmVille included, have removed the wither mechanic altogether, making the games more friendly for the casual audience.

The result of having psychologists on staff was something called the *core loop*. A core loop is a repeatable step that goes on and on forever, and always ends in rewards. Psychologists have been studying these for decades, but Zynga was the first company to put it so plainly in your face in a game. Buy seeds, plant seeds, harvest plants, sell plants, repeat. It worked great and kept players addicted.

It didn't take long before FarmVille was the most popular game on Facebook. The plan had worked, and now all Zynga had to do was keep making new content for their game and keep finding new people.

This is where the true innovation came in, because not only was Zynga really good at making games for this new platform, they were geniuses at remembering that Facebook is first and foremost a hangout for friends. So Zynga asked their gamers to find new players for them.

Players wanted to build and design beautiful farms, sure, but they also wanted to show them to their friends. Knowing this, Zynga designed some of the most attractive and useful items in the game—the barn, for instance—in a way that would force you to ask people in your Facebook friends list for help. And boy, did it work.

One of the early big moneymakers for FarmVille was gas. Yeah, that's right. Zynga let you buy a tractor using money earned playing the game, a term gamers call *grinding*. And the tractor was AMAZING because it could harvest entire fields automatically. Unfortunately, it used gas, and gas could only be purchased with real money. Talk about a gas crisis!

John Deere sells approximately five thousand tractors a year. When it was really rolling, FarmVille sold roughly five hundred thousand tractors a DAY!

If you started building a barn, you'd soon run into a problem you couldn't solve on your own. You needed nails to keep building. Then FarmVille would pop up a screen telling you to go to your friends for help. As soon as you clicked "okay," a message would be posted to your Facebook friends' walls asking them to stop on by and lend a hand.

FarmVille grew in popularity so fast, and the game itself was so complex, that hundreds of sites covering strategies, crop index charts, and hints on how to make your farm productive can be found on the web.

Pop-up friend request in FarmVille © Zynga

Then when your friends clicked to help out their buddy, like a good friend would do, FarmVille would launch right there in their browser. If they already had a farm of their own, they'd be ready to go, but if not, Zynga was more than happy to sign them right up. And just like that, they'd be hooked, too! They couldn't help it. I mean, there were tomatoes to grow! Who doesn't like digital tomatoes?

Facebook exploded. And as Facebook grew, so did Farm-Ville. In fact, FarmVille grew so fast that by 2010, one in five Facebook users had launched their own farms. That meant that as you scrolled down your Facebook feed, it was impossible to NOT get an invite from someone.

In its heyday, FarmVille had eighty million users and about one-quarter of them checked in at least once a day. Most of those gamers checked in multiple times a day, and some people checked in more than 100 times a day. Seriously! It was hard not to because if the game wasn't reminding you it was time to harvest your strawberries, your friends were asking you for nails.

Social games were here to stay, and the price was right. It was free. Well, it was free unless you decided you wanted the super special items and a few tanks of gas for your digital tractor. Everyone was going green on their computers, and the definition of *gamer*, and *farmer*, had changed forever.

It only took Zynga FIVE weeks of development before they went live with FarmVille. That is a crazy-short amount of time for a game to be created. Of course, games like FarmVille are what we call live service games. The more people play them, the more the developers put into the new game. The games live on a server, something we call "in the cloud" nowadays, so the games are constantly updated. I guess you could say that a game like FarmVille is never finished.

In 2010, over one billion dollars were spent on virtual goodies for FarmVille and other social media games.

MAKING IT MOBILE

• • • • • • • • • • • • • • • •

O kay, let's try something new. Let's make a game, you and I.

I'm sure you have a much better idea for a game, but for the sake of this exercise, let's say we're making an underwater zombie golf/racing game. Sound good? Sound AWESOME? Yeah, I think so, too.

Now that we have a design, we need to build the thing. But before we start, we should probably know what platform we're building the game for. What system, what console, and who do we want to play our new game? It's a big question, but let's say that there are only you and me and a few friends making it, and we don't have an unlimited budget. I'm also thinking that everyone would like an underwater zombie golf/racing game, so let's say that this is a casual game for everyone.

So, small development team, small budget, should appeal to everyone—oh, and let's say we want it done in six months.

With all that info, I'm going to suggest we make a mobile game. Just about everyone I know has an iPhone, or an Android phone. Sounds like a good plan.

But there are complications here, too. There are actually a few different iPhones, and they don't all have the same tech. Which iPhones should we support? Just the newest one? What about all the people who haven't upgraded? And then there are the Android phones. Wow, there are a LOT of different Android phones, with all kinds of different screens.

Man, this is getting complicated.

But, if you think this is rough, just imagine how it was before the iPhone. Back in the caveman times of flip phones and brick phones (ask your parents; they'll know what I'm talking about), there were literally hundreds of different phones out there.

Let's say we just want to make the game for the ten top-selling phones. But if we do that, we'll have to make ten versions of our imaginary underwater zombie golf/racing game from scratch to match the specs of the phones.

Oh, and that's not all. Now we have to figure out how to control the game. Some phones have tiny joystick-style buttons. Some have number keypads. Some even have arrow keys so small you'd think they were made for elves and mice.

And if your head's not hurting yet, just wait, there's MORE!

Next we have to test the game on every phone, in every language, because we know that our underwater zombie golf/racing game will be an international hit. Then after that mess is wrapped up, we have to get the game published. Each phone carrier (you know, like Verizon or T-Mobile) has its own guidelines on how to publish for its phones.

Basically, back then it was easier to push a herd of wet kittens up a snake-covered hill than it was to publish games for mobile phones. It's easier now because the iPhone touch screens caught on, and now you have things like iTunes and Google Play to help you publish your games, but there are still all kinds of unique challenges. However, no matter how challenging it is, it is still worth it. After all, how many other jobs out there allow us to make our dream underwater zombie golf/racing game?

Angry Birds © Rovio Entertainment

All right, without looking at the title of this chapter ... Oh man, you looked. Didn't you?

Okay, pretend like you don't know the answer to this question, or better yet, read the question to someone else and see if they can get it right. Here's the question. It's multiple choice.

Which breakout hit game created in 2009 sold the most units?

A. Uncharted 2
B. Assassin's Creed 2
C. Halo 3: ODST
D. New Super Mario Bros. Wii
E. Angry Birds
F. Modern Warfare 2

The answer, and it isn't even close, is—you guessed it—Angry Birds. In fact, if you go by total downloads to date, Angry Birds has sold more units than all of them combined.

It had been three years since Nintendo showed the world that gaming wasn't just for teens and hard-core video game addicts. They gave us a less expensive console, with a controller that just begged to be swung like a golf club, and just about everyone became a gamer overnight.

If you count all the Angry Birds games together, that number doubles to two billion downloads. And while downloads don't tell the whole story of how many people actually play the game, this does. In January 2014, over two hundred million people were still logging in and flicking birds at pigs every day. That's roughly the size of the entire Twitter audience.

Next, Zynga followed up by showing us that you didn't even need a console to be a gamer. All you needed was access to the Internet, a desire to harvest tomatoes at all hours of the night, and a Facebook account. Now you could play any time you wanted—you could even sneak in a little digital gardening at the library or at work.

But Rovio wanted to take it a step further. Not only did they want you playing games at home, or at school, or at work, they wanted you to play games everywhere you went. They wanted to fill your pocket full of games, and they wanted to use smartphones to make that happen. Along came Angry Birds, and phones would never be looked at the same way again.

So, what is it? What makes these feathery little grumps so irresistible? I mean, look at them. They are barely even birds. They don't have legs; the only way they can fly is if you fling them out of a slingshot, and they are ALWAYS in a bad mood. What gives?

Well, first off, it's pretty hard to ignore the fact that they are just so darned cute. And funny. Don't forget funny. And, of course, you don't want to overlook the Green Piggies, because they played a part, too.

iPhone © Daniel Zanetti

But the biggest contributor was probably the release of the iPhone in 2007, and the App Store in 2008. When the iPhone was announced—well, you've heard the stories. You've probably even seen the long lines at the Apple store in the mall that come with every new phone. Let's just say people went a little bananas, because not only did Apple's new phone look cool, but it became a replacement for your camera, your iPod, your watch, your video camera, your planner, your GPS, your . . . you get the picture. The iPhone promised to be the end-all device of its time, and it delivered. But it wasn't until a year later, on July 10, 2008, that the App Store launched, and back then there weren't too many apps up there. But there were enough that it made a small mobile game developer in Finland named Rovio pay attention.

At the time, Rovio wasn't doing all that hot. They'd released a bunch of mobile games—almost fifty of them, actually—but none of them were really setting the world on fire. Just days before the App Store launched, Rovio challenged its talented and creative team to come up with the next big thing to build for the new iPhone. The team responded. There were tons of interesting new ideas, but one little drawing by an artist named Jaakko Iisalo kind of stopped the conversation. It was an illustration of a bunch of cross-eyed, legless birds storming a castle. There was no game play. No story. The illustration didn't really even look like a game at the time, but something about those primitively shaped birds with their angry eyebrows made people want to know more.

So Rovio pinned the illustration on the wall, and Iisalo and the other designers started dreaming up what the game was about, and how it might be played.

A few ideas were starting to bubble up, but things really started taking shape when they discovered the sworn enemy of the birds: Green Piggies. Lots of them. Green Piggies in helmets. Green Piggies with goofy smiles. Green Piggies with wide-set eyes and push-broom mustaches. There were Green Piggies everywhere, and after they stole the eggs from the birds, the fight was on. And it was going to be A BATTLE TO THE DEATH!

All of a sudden, the birds started getting names and characters. There was Red, the leader of the flock; he is

One of the few games ready on the App Store at launch was SEGA's Super Monkey Ball. It had more than 100 brightly colored stages that you would roll your monkey through, taking advantage of the iPhone's tilt controls. You have to really dig, but you can still find the game today.

round, grumpy, and packs a punch. There was Bomb, a black bird with a feather poking out of his head that looks like a fuse. Fling him, then tap the screen again, and he'll blow up. Chuck was a yellow triangle-shaped bird; believe it or not, he was the happiest of the bunch, even though he tore through wood like a buzz saw. Then there were the Blues, a trio of tiny little bluebirds that launched as one, then split up to give you a shotgun approach at the Green Piggies. And then there was Matilda, a white, chicken-ish critter that plopped out an egg that caused all kinds of damage as she flew by.

Angry Birds © Rovio Entertainment

There were hundreds of levels, physics puzzle challenges that tested your skills as a bird flicker, and challenged you to find the right strategy to defeat all the Green Piggies in each puzzle. Each of the Angry Birds played their part, and as a payoff, when you cleared out an area, you were treated to a funny animation starring the quirky cast of birds and pigs.

The Green Piggies were inspired by a massive outbreak of swine flu that was all over the news.

In 2009, Angry Birds was flicked into the new App Store, and in no time at all the game was flying up the charts. I am not exaggerating. Within the first day of launching their app, Rovio was number one. Now they had the fastest-growing game on the fastest-growing mobile device on the planet, and it was only going to get better.

It launched on the iPad the minute it arrived on scene, instantly becoming the most installed app on iPad. Within one day of Angry Birds launching for Android, it racked up over one million installs.

The game has seen many one-million-download days, and on Christmas Day in 2012, the game saw its biggest download day ever. Eight million new users grabbed Angry Birds that day, mostly due to new mobile devices being handed out as holiday presents.

There was just no stopping Angry Birds. It's hard to get numbers on a game that is still rolling right along, but at the time this book was put together there were over two billion downloads of Angry Birds games. Okay, ready for some mind-blowing numbers? There have been more downloads of Angry Birds games than there are people in Africa, Oceania, and Europe . . . COMBINED!

If you've wanted to hang out with these Angry Birds in person—and let's face it, who hasn't?—the best place to do this would be at Angry Birds Land in Tampere, Finland. It's a full-blown Angry Birds park. Unfortunately, no Green Piggies are allowed.

You see, when you create something new that everyone loves, it becomes a craze. People already had Angry Birds on their phones, and they wanted more. They wanted to wear Angry Birds T-shirts. They wanted Green Piggies bandages. They wanted Angry Birds fruit snacks, notebooks, and backpacks. Within a couple of years it seemed like the world had gone bonkers, and you couldn't go anywhere without seeing those angry cross-eyed birds and their enemies, the Green Piggies.

Angry Birds was doing something very few games had ever achieved, and it did it in record time. Not only had it dominated the mobile phone game, it was moving on to

Angry Birds has its share of famous fans. Conan O'Brien, Anna Kendrick, Vice President Joe Biden, UK Prime Minister David Cameron, and Justin Bieber have all claimed to be Angry Birds addicts.

become a part of pop culture. The Angry Birds craze was exploding, and the colorful little birds and their nemeses, the Green Piggies, were showing up everywhere.

- In season twenty-three of *The Simpsons*, there's a parody of Angry Birds called Furious Fliers.

- Red, the leading character in the Angry Birds franchise, makes a cameo appearance in the *Sonic Universe* comics—issue thirty-two, if you want to dig it up.

- Angry Birds toys became big news in 2011, when Rovio signed a deal with Hasbro to manufacture Angry Birds figurines that would interact with mobile games on the iPad and iPhone.

- Angry Birds became retail darlings with the release of stuffed, plush Angry Birds and Piggies toys.

- Angry Birds T-shirts, bandages, lunch boxes, and even candy and fruit snacks were all big hits with Angry Birds fans around the world.

- And let's not forget *The Angry Birds Movie*. Sure, they might have added legs and arms to the little birds, but that didn't change their attitudes. These angry yet lovable feathered friends faced off against the Green Piggies on the big screen in May 2016.

The Finnish developer branched out a bit afterward, but it always put its adorable characters right in the middle of everything it did. I remember reading an article where Rovio CEO Mikael Hed said they had a goal to be bigger than Mickey Mouse. I will admit, I shrugged it off at the time. But, you know, time will tell, and if the success of Angry Birds is any indication of the future of Rovio, I wouldn't count them out just yet.

ALL KINDS AND SIZES

● ● ● ● ● ● ● ● ● ● ● ● ● ● ● ●

People have a tendency to divide all game developers into two piles: indie developers and mainstream developers. And while there *is* some overlap, it can be a useful distinction. Let's break down the big differences, shall we?

Mainstream Budgets

Mainstream developers are usually larger companies who either have some investors backing their work or, if they are successful enough, are able to pay for their own game development—companies like EA, Activision, Bungie, Ubisoft, and Valve. You've heard of them and probably played a handful of their games. These big boys hire hundreds, if not thousands, of game creators across the globe. Many of them operate in multiple countries, have projects that run in the tens of millions of dollars, and keep their employees happy by offering them health benefits, a constant paycheck, launch/office parties, and visits to the big trade shows, like E3.

Another advantage to working for a mainstream video game developer is the office space. EA's office in Redwood Shores, California, has two restaurants, a massive gym, indoor volleyball and basketball courts, a huge grass courtyard that often doubles as a soccer pitch, its own Starbucks, and even a company store.

Indie Budgets

Generally, indie developers are, well, independent. They are not funded or backed by multimillion-dollar companies. They usually fund the games out of their own pockets, or through crowdsource sites like Kickstarter or Indiegogo. Indies often don't take a paycheck until the game has shipped. And even then, only a few of them ever see anything in return. As a rule, indies usually work out of their own homes. No fancy offices, unless their parents happen to have a fancy basement.

Mainstream Teams

Mainstream developers can have anywhere from ten to three hundred people on a game team. Generally, people on the team will each have a very defined role: a texture artist specializing in terrain, an audio specialist who is the go-to guy for ambient bird noises, a marketing guy who is in charge of social media coverage, and so on.

Indie Teams

Indie games are generally made by really small teams, and sometimes the "team" is only one developer. Especially at first. Most indie developers often have to play many roles on one project. It isn't out of the question for an engineer to create some art for the game, or for an artist to be writing the music score in his spare time.

Mainstream Developers Love Franchises

If a game is a hit, why not make it again? And again. Mainstream developers love franchises because dedicated fans love to return and visit worlds and characters they had a good experience with. It lowers the risk for the developer, which is a big advantage.

Indie Developers Love to Reimagine

If a game is a hit, why not make something totally new? In general, indies love making innovative, unique titles. Sure, the risk is higher, but so is the fun in trying something new and exciting. Experimental game development is a huge influence for indie developers.

Mainstream Security

Mainstream developers are very careful about what they share with the world, and the timing with which they share it. Most employees of a mainstream developer are under contracts that make sure they don't share company secrets. They are supercompetitive, and leaking information about a game or a feature before it's ready could cost them a lot of money. Security is key.

Indie Sharing

In contrast, indie developers are known for sharing everything from concept to code on indie developer forums. It isn't uncommon for two indie developers to swap games for a while, to help each other out with areas of the game that might not be their specialty. Because they are small, indies benefit from learning from one another, and for an indie, sharing is key.

As you can see, there are a lot of differences, but they do have one thing in common: They both love making games.

Minecraft © Mojang AB/Microsoft Corporation

So, what did you do last week? Create the bestselling PC game of all time? Build the first version of a game that would end up on Xboxes, PlayStations, iPhones, and Androids around the world? Start a company that would make a bunch of your closest friends into millionaires? No? Me, either.

But one week was all it took for Swedish programmer and designer Markus Persson, better known to gamers around the world as "Notch," to build the first version of Minecraft.

Yup. Six days. That's it. Less than a week from the time Markus Persson had the idea in his head, until it was in front of live players. Crazy.

In 2009, Notch set out to create a sandbox game for his new company, Mojang AB. He started working on the game on May 10, and on May 16, the alpha version made its public debut.

An alpha version of a game is a really rough, but still playable version of the game that developers use to test if a concept is working. Generally, an alpha version will have just enough running smoothly for a gamer to know if he or she likes the game or not. Basically, it's a good example of what's to come, but nowhere near the finished game.

Six days.

Notch was simply sharing his new game, which he called Cave Game, on the indie game forum TIGSource to get feedback. TIGSource was a pretty popular place for indie game developers to test out their new ideas. Most games get a couple of views and a few comments from dedicated developers, but once in a while a game really gets noticed.

Cave Game was one of them, and it happened fast. In fact, the first user-created screenshot was shared just forty-three minutes after Notch uploaded his game to the world, and users have been creating and sharing ever since.

The game was called Cave Game for only a short time, because another indie game developer, not Notch himself, suggested the title Minecraft for his new game. The name made sense, Notch embraced it, and so it stuck.

The game was already on its way to success, but even from this earliest version, there was one question: What made Minecraft fun? I mean, it didn't have levels or bosses. It didn't have a story, or even a way to win.

And that right there, that lack of rules or instructions, might have been the reason for Minecraft's success.

Minecraft has been called the ultimate sandbox. You remember playing in a sandbox, don't you? You could trench out rivers and fill them with water. Build a castle with sticks and rocks, then fill in the cracks with sand. You could pick grass and stick it in the ground like little trees, then you could stand up and play DESTROYER by stomping on everything and starting over again. Mix in a few LEGOs and a big blue sky that shifts from day to night, and you pretty much have Minecraft.

Except for one thing: When you're done you don't have to shake the sand out of your socks or clean up all the little blocks from your bedroom floor. Maybe that's it. Minecraft is pure LEGO/sandbox play without all the cleanup.

The game was such a massive hit that there's a darn good chance you've already played the game, but if you haven't, here's how it works. Minecraft allows gamers to destroy and place one-by-one cube blocks in an open world. There are different materials that do slightly different

Before Notch shared a playable version of Minecraft on TIGSource, he uploaded a video of himself playing the game to YouTube. The video is still there, and it has nearly nine million views! YouTube would later become a major contributor to Minecraft's success, as users started uploading, and watching, millions of user-created videos.

things, but in creative mode you pretty much just use them for decoration. You can build anything from a roller coaster to a statue of your favorite author, and the only limitation is your imagination.

But creating isn't your only option. When Minecraft launched in 2009, it also came with survival mode. And this mode is what gave the game its name. Although the game is most often described as a game without goals, survival mode does have a bit of structure. First of all, you must "mine" for various items and resources. You really want to do this during the day, and at first you want to do it as fast as you can. You then use those items to build a quick shelter before it gets dark and the zombies, skeletons, and creepers come out and chase you down.

A creeper from Minecraft © Mojang AB/Microsoft Corporation

The creeper started out as a coding mistake. It was actually based on a pig model gone horribly wrong. The torso rotated up ninety degrees, and it had these four little legs poking out from the bottom of its long piggy body. Notch swapped the color palette for something green and spooky, and just like that, creepers were born.

After a bit more mining, you can combine the resources you gather into more complex tools and items. This part

When the game first launched, things were sure different. For example, crafting wasn't introduced in the game until January 2010. But that wasn't as important as the next "fix." Before March 2010, if you died in Minecraft, you were unable to respawn. That's right—before that date, if you died in Minecraft, it was GAME OVER.

There are many books written about Minecraft. There are how-to books that teach users new building techniques and how to use redstone to make cool gadgets. There are history books, covering the detailed history of this amazing game, and there are more Minecraft fiction books than you could read in a year.

of the game is called "crafting." So you see, the two basic rules of the game are included in its title. Mine(then)craft.

Notch's brainchild inspired gamers to build and share their creations like no other game had before. Remember, this was 2009, and YouTube had just celebrated its fifth birthday. YouTube celebrities were becoming a thing, and "let's play" videos were one of the most-watched categories in the massive streaming video storage locker. In no time at all, gamers were showing off creations that blew minds, and teams of very talented Minecrafters became popular as fans would spend hours watching them build cities in prerecorded YouTube videos.

And that's not all. Some YouTube sensations, like Sky, didn't just build cool creations, they used Minecraft as a storytelling tool. Sky's videos had clever stories, voice-overs, and funny effects. All of this added up to Sky having over ELEVEN MILLION YouTube subscribers by 2013, which allowed him to become a professional Minecraft player/ YouTuber. How cool is that?

Sky from "New World" video © Sky Does Minecraft

Which is really interesting, because when Notch set out to build Minecraft, he had zero intention of it being a story-driven game. Yet the game really is a tool that inspires creativity, and when you're a storyteller, creative tools help you tell stories.

And because Minecraft was an indie game, Notch made it really easy for people to alter his game and share these modifications with the larger gaming community. These mods of Minecraft popped up all over the place as designers and programmers hacked away at Notch's code, adding new elements and changing the way it looked and played. They created everything from a Hunger Games mod, which allows you to play as a tribute and fight to the death, inspired by the world-famous *Hunger Games* books by Suzanne Collins, to Twilight Forest, an adventure mod set in a magic forest full of portals, dangerous monsters, and treasures. They basically created everything. . . .

Many tech-savvy parents have purchased Minecraft for their kids in hopes of inspiring them to learn more about modding or coding themselves.

All this positive new support for Minecraft caught the eyes of educators around the globe. Smart teachers were taking notice, saw that their students loved the game, and these brilliant teachers decided to use Minecraft as a teaching tool, rather than just a free-time distraction.

Some teachers, for example, are using Minecraft to prebuild virtual ancient worlds and then assigning students to work in groups to complete quests, such as fortifying a village against marauders. Not only do the kids learn to work together and problem-solve, they also pick up a few history lessons about ancient urban planning and warfare along the way without even realizing it.

Other teachers are downloading Minecraft teaching mods to set up experiments teaching students about gravity, velocity, and other forms of physics. Still others have created giant models of animal cells to teach biology.

The game was unique from the start, and packed with innovations in the sandbox gaming world. But one of the most fun things about Minecraft is finding all the hidden secrets that Notch and his team snuck into the game. The great thing is that the team at Mojang rarely tell anyone about these secrets, they just let players find them and then let the Minecraft community spread the word. Here are a few things you might not know about Minecraft, but after this, I'll bet you'll try them out.

In Sweden, playing Minecraft is required in school. In 2013, Minecraft was added to the core curriculum in Sweden. They found that learning Minecraft builds imagination, teaches schoolkids about environmental issues, and makes them better problem solvers. I think they are onto something and we should implement the same thing in schools everywhere. You with me?

- **DOG COLLARS COME IN MANY COLORS.** If you hold dye in your hand, then left-click on a dog, the collar will be dyed to that color.

- **INVISIBLE ANIMAL FENCES.** If you place a normal fence next to a nether fence, they won't connect, and you can walk through them, but animals can't.

- **THANK YOU, PUMPKIN!** If you wear a pumpkin on your head, you are totally invisible to endermen.

- **UPSIDE-DOWN MOBS.** You can make any moving creature in the game, called mobs (short for *mobile*), flip upside down. This one takes a few steps, but it's worth it. Get an egg and an anvil. Place the egg in the first slot of the anvil. Name the egg "Dinnerbone" or "Grumm," then go ahead and hatch the egg. When the mob, or animal, spawns, it will be upside down.

Upside-down cow in Minecraft © Mojang AB/Microsoft Corporation

- **DISCO SHEEP.** Get a name tag and an anvil. Place the name tag in the first slot of the Anvil, and name the tag Jeb_. Then spawn a sheep and right-click on the sheep. The sheep's wool will rotate through every color of the rainbow. Totally fun.

- **MINECECRAFT.** There's a 0.1 percent chance that when you launch the game, instead of the main menu logo saying Minecraft, it will say Mincecraft.

While little things like this don't really change the way the game is played, they are fun to goof around with and very popular with die-hard Minecraft gamers.

What started out as a one-week experiment went on to be one of the most important games of our time. And in true indie fashion, Notch, who never intended to run a multibillion-dollar, multinational corporation, decided in 2015 to step away from Mojang, the company he started.

Notch sold Mojang and the rights to Minecraft to Microsoft for 2.5 billion dollars. That's a lot of moolah. Notch personally owned more than 70 percent of the company, so he ended up doing pretty well for himself.

So, what's next for Minecraft? Time will tell, but with Microsoft behind the wheel, you can bet they are going to make a splash when they figure it out.

And what's next for Notch? Well, your guess is as good as mine, but one thing is for sure: If you follow him on social media, he'll be the first to let you know.

Markus Persson is still very active on Twitter today. He shares indie game news, talks about his current projects, and interacts with fans. Well, not all of them—he has 2.2 million Twitter followers— but he does his best.

MAJOR ACHIEVEMENT UNLOCKED

This isn't going to come as a big shocker, but gamers are passionate about their favorite games. And when you really fall in love with a game, you play that game a LOT. And when you play the game a lot, you can get really good at that game. So good that you need a little something extra to make it *really* challenging.

It's happened to the best of us. We get caught up in something, then for some strange reason this little voice ticks in our mind and we think something like, "Hey, I bet if I spent the next four hundred hours straight without food or bathroom breaks, I could build the entire city of Los Angeles in Minecraft."

It's happened to me, although it wasn't Minecraft that inspired me to go nuts for a crazy video game goal.

For me it was a very cool, pretty difficult, and not very well-known Nintendo DS game called Henry Hatsworth in the Puzzling Adventure. I had a few friends who had worked on the game, and one of them, a fantastic artist and designer, Loel Phelps, challenged me to beat the entire game without upgrading the character once. I thought it was impossible, but he promised me he had done it himself, so I put in a couple hundred hours, and one great and wonderful day, I achieved my goal. I was so proud. And if you knew how hard this was you'd probably stand up right where you are and give me a standing ovation.

Here are a few other amazing gaming feats that show just how much gamers love games, and how much they love challenging themselves to do the (near) impossible.

- Three guys used eighteen million Minecraft blocks to build a massive Game Boy. And as if that weren't amazing enough, they then used Minecraft to build a stop-motion video of Super Mario Land on the screen of the Game Boy. They posted a video on YouTube, and you really must go see it. https://www.youtube.com/watch?t=32&v=4cEn3-t_dWE

- One player beat Elder Scrolls V: Skyrim with his bare hands. That means that this guy beat up giants by serving nothing but knuckle sandwiches.

- Noor the Pacifist, a World of Warcraft player, refused to kill a single other player in the game, and yet he was still able to reach the highest level possible, level eighty. It took him over two years to reach his goal.

- In October 2010, dedicated gamer and grandpa John Bates of Wisconsin played his way into the *Guinness Book of World Records* by playing 2,850 perfect games of Wii Sports bowling. But that didn't end his run of perfect games. Less than a year later, at the age of eighty-five, he was up to 8,550 perfect games and counting. Don't tell Mr. Bates that games are just for kids.

Uncharted 2: Among Thieves © Naughty Dog/Sony Computer Entertainment, Inc.

You know, I've always wanted to be a hero. I've played hundreds of games over the years.

I've grown to three times my height and smashed fire-chucking half-turtle dudes. I've sprinted through dark hallways, blasting muscle-bound gym rats with leather motorcycle vests and pig snouts with my BGF. I've even planted acres of crops on Facebook—heck, if you're on my friends list I've probably even bugged you for a bag of nails so I could finish building my barn.

So what is it about being Nathan Drake, the star of the Uncharted series? He's not all that special.

Drake is thirty-five. His hair kind of stands out like he just woke up from a nap in the back of his 1994 Dodge Aspen. His shirt looks like he found it on the bottom of the laundry pile, and he's kind of a library nerd. I mean, he's always searching for treasures left behind by famous dead guys, like his great-great-great-grandfather, Sir Francis Drake. I think I read about that guy in my middle school World History class.

Maybe that's it. Maybe it is *because* he's normal, yet still pretty awesome at the same time.

Okay, he's not really that normal. The dude can climb

Nathan Drake climbing a building in Uncharted 2: Among Thieves © Naughty Dog/ Sony Computer Entertainment, Inc.

anything. If you haven't had a chance to check out the games, at least fire up YouTube and check out how Drake climbs up a cliff face. If you ask me, he's probably more related to Tarzan than Sir Francis Drake.

But aside from having the climbing skills of a spider monkey, Drake is pretty much your average guy, put in a pretty bad spot. And the team at Naughty Dog didn't do that by mistake. Creative director and video game legend Amy Hennig crafted Drake every inch of the way. She didn't want him to be one of those typical tough-as-nails video game characters that solves all of his problems with superior firepower. She wanted Nathan Drake to be smart and resourceful—a fancy way of saying he was the kind of guy who could always get out of a jam.

He's the kind of guy I want to be. Smart, funny, not worried if I'm wearing a clean shirt or if my hair is straight, and willing to do just about anything to find TREASURE! Lots and lots of amazing, ancient, valuable treasure.

When Naughty Dog set out to create their new franchise, they knew that they had to pull out all the stops. The studio had already made a name for itself creating hit games like Ratchet & Clank and Jak and Daxter. The games were HUGE fan favorites, and their attention to detail and ability to tell a heck of a good story made them very popular with Sony as well.

But the times, they were a-changing, and under the influence of Sony and following the success of the gritty, realistic shooters on the Xbox 360, Naughty Dog decided it was time for a change. No more over-the-top, humorous fantasy games with far-out characters and guns that turned baddies into chickens. Yeah, that's a real thing in Ratchet & Clank: Going Commando.

There would be no changing your enemies into farm animals in the new game. And while the team was initially interested in something far more fantastical, Sony convinced them that the timing was right, and the hardware of the PS3 was tough enough, to try something realistic.

It was a scary, even dangerous challenge. Like I said, up until that point, Naughty Dog had built an impressive following with their cartoony, over-the-top games. The switch to make realistic humans and environments wasn't only very difficult, it could have backfired with fans.

However, when you're good, you're good. And Naughty Dog isn't just good, they're GREAT!

They assembled a team of supergenius engineers, artists, and writers, and got working on blowing game players' minds in a hurry.

The game was ready to show off at E3 (Electronic Entertainment Expo) in 2006, and while it was a long way from being done at the time, it already looked incredible. Fans expecting a new Jak and Daxter were convinced that their favorite developer was not going to let them down.

Well, not really in a hurry. All told, there were people working on the first Uncharted, Drake's Fortune, for more than three years. The bulk of the team spent two years on the game, and the stories of the amount of overtime (usually called *crunch time* in the game industry) are legendary.

The game was set in an area that looked so similar to Tomb Raider that people nicknamed the first showing of Uncharted "Dude Raider." By the time the game shipped, enough had changed that the comparisons were forgotten, although if you squint you can still see why the nickname stuck.

When Uncharted: Drake's Fortune shipped in November of 2007, it was smaller, and perhaps more simple than some had hoped, but there was no doubt it was a Naughty Dog game. The visuals were trendsetting. Naughty Dog had raised the bar for realistic characters and environments. The cut scenes told a story that would make Indiana Jones smile, and the music was nothing shy of what you would hear for a blockbuster movie. But with Naughty Dog doing what they do best, the game play and controls were perfect. The game combined creative storytelling, high-paced action, and hand-to-hand combat with some of the best platforming the PS3 had seen to date. Remember that comment about Drake being an unreal climber? Well, that played a HUGE part in making it such a stellar platformer.

Uncharted: Drake's Fortune © Naughty Dog/Sony Computer Entertainment, Inc.

The Uncharted team drank more than thirty thousand cans of soda during the production of Uncharted 2: Among Thieves. Yeah, they kept count. It's the kind of thing game developers do.

Uncharted went on to be a huge success, and Naughty Dog followed up their introduction of Nathan Drake with what most gamers consider to be the best game on PS3, Uncharted 2: Among Thieves. The opening scene is certainly one that goes down in the Video Game Hall of Fame.

Starting off a game by dangling from the back of a train that has rolled off its tracks above a thousand-foot drop in the snowy Himalayan cliffs is something that gamers will always remember. I know I will. And the game only got better and more intense after that.

It's interesting, because this book has pointed out hundreds of new innovations over the decades of gaming, but every once in a while a game comes along that is amazing and important, but that can't really be called innovative. That's the thing about innovation—it's new, so it's easy to spot when it comes along. But it isn't always as easy to spot when a game, or a franchise of games, for that matter, just does everything right. It takes all the innovations from games that have come before, and it *perfects* those innovations to a point where the game can only be called one thing: a masterpiece.

Okay, some might argue that I'm overstating how great this game is, but I'm not alone by any means. Lots of people agree that Uncharted 2 is the best game ever on PS3, and while these features might not be new and innovative, here's a list of things that Uncharted 2 did right that makes it stand the test of time.

- **A PARKOUR-STYLE CLIMBING SYSTEM.** This isn't easy with just a DualShock 3 Controller. A lot of other games had tried it in the past, with varying degrees of success, but navigating Nathan Drake up the face of a five-hundred-foot cliff, or up the side of a castle ruin, felt totally intuitive.

- **CINEMATIC TUTORIALS.** Okay, this one was pretty innovative, and totally unforgettable. In the opening scene of Uncharted 2, you find yourself hanging off the edge of a cliff, dangling from a train that has crashed. The next thing you know, you are learning Uncharted's climbing system. A square will flash on-screen, and you'll see what might look like a handhold. You tap the square and Drake jumps up to grab the handhold. This continues as you learn more about Drake's controls in the most tense situation possible.

Rumors from some pretty darn good sources, including Paramount Studios, claim that an Uncharted movie is in the works. Not sure who will play Nathan Drake at the moment, but Nathan Fillion, the star of *Castle* and *Firefly*, has said openly he's a fan of the series and would love to play the part. It helps that he not only shares Drake's first name, but he looks like he could be his twin.

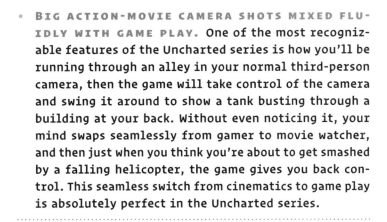

- **BIG ACTION-MOVIE CAMERA SHOTS MIXED FLU-IDLY WITH GAME PLAY.** One of the most recognizable features of the Uncharted series is how you'll be running through an alley in your normal third-person camera, then the game will take control of the camera and swing it around to show a tank busting through a building at your back. Without even noticing it, your mind swaps seamlessly from gamer to movie watcher, and then just when you think you're about to get smashed by a falling helicopter, the game gives you back control. This seamless switch from cinematics to game play is absolutely perfect in the Uncharted series.

- **CO-OP CAMPAIGN MODE.** While it is the single-player game that is most popular in the Uncharted series, Naughty Dog did not leave us hanging with multiplayer and co-op mode. In Uncharted 2 you pair up with a friend, both of you sharing the same screen, and try to hold your ground as wave after wave of enemies flood the area. It's one of the most compelling and addictive co-op experiences of its kind.

- **DESTRUCTIBLE ENVIRONMENTS.** Once again, this was available in games before Uncharted, but Naughty Dog took it to whole new heights. Before, you might have seen windows break, bullet holes on walls, even chunks of concrete falling off buildings, but in Uncharted 2, there is a point where a helicopter fires rockets into a building you are in, and the entire building collapses around you. The camera tilts and sways, and you feel like you're holding on for dear life as it comes crashing down in a pile of rubble and dust. It really is an epic moment.

There's no doubt that Naughty Dog defined *epic* with the Uncharted series. Its influence was felt in Naughty Dog's PS4 masterpiece The Last of Us, and you can count on them blowing more minds down the line.

Nolan North, the voice actor who played Nathan Drake in all three Uncharted games, wrote a book called *Drake's Journal: Inside the Making of Uncharted 3.* Not very many copies were printed, and if you have one it is worth a pretty penny. Collectors eat this kind of stuff up!

One of the hardest-to-find Easter eggs in the Uncharted series was in Uncharted 3. After duking it out in a bar fight early in the game, you can walk over to the bar and chill for a minute before heading out to look for more trouble. There's a small stack of newspapers there, and the headline reads, "Scientists are still struggling to understand deadly fungus." In itself it doesn't sound too horrible, but if you've played The Last of Us, you know that it is pretty bad news. This puts Nathan Drake in the same universe as David and Ellie, and it's not a friendly world. The Last of Us centers around a fungus that killed off more than 60 percent of the planet. It makes you wonder if Drake is going to make an appearance in a future Last of Us game, and if he does, will he be a man or a mushroom?

In the end, Nathan Drake always discovers his fortune, dodges about a bazillion bad-guy bullets, saves the day, and gets the girl. All while sporting a nasty shirt, messy hair, and a chin full of whiskers.

The helicopter scene from Uncharted 2: Among Thieves © Naughty Dog/Sony Computer Entertainment, Inc.

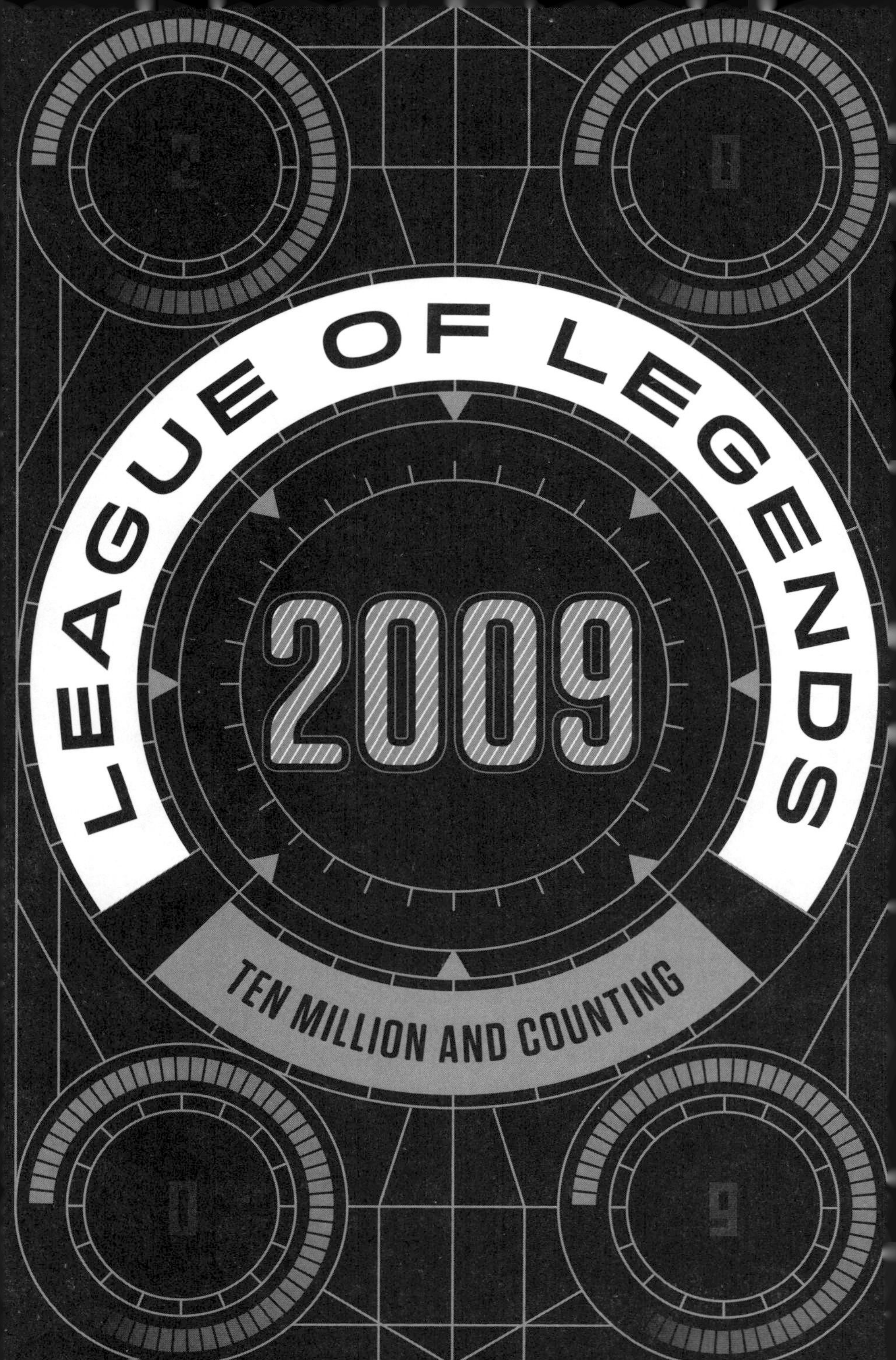

LEAGUE OF LEGENDS
2009
TEN MILLION AND COUNTING

League of Legends © Riot Games

Twenty thousand screaming fans wearing "We're #1" foam fingers are shouting your name.

The crowd goes wild as you and your teammates walk like kings into the arena. They announce your name, and it rumbles from speakers bigger than a house, and echoes off the concrete walls of the Staples Center in Los Angeles, California.

Your opponents enter to a chorus of "Booooo!" They are the enemy. You are the hero. And there is ten million dollars on the line.

An announcer wearing an ESPN jacket stuffs a microphone in your face and asks you your strategy. You look him dead in the eye and say:

"My strategy is to win. I like to keep it simple."

The crowd goes berserk! The camera guy gives you a thumbs-up. You are going to be an international hero in less than two hours.

You slip on your headset as cameras zoom in on your face. You don't even break a sweat as you log on to the server. You have nothing to be nervous about. You've practiced days, months, YEARS for this very moment.

Is this a dream?

Well, kind of.

But is it possible?

Oh heck yes, it is. In fact, there are a lot of gamers living this dream right now, and we owe it all to a bunch of brave modders and a small start-up company called Riot Games. And while millions upon millions of players play the game in the quiet of their own homes, you can't talk about League of Legends, or just plain League to its fans, without talking about big stadiums, crazed fans, huge prizes, and trophies.

Yeah, that's right. You can get a TROPHY for playing League. Granted, the trophy weighs seventy pounds and probably takes the full champion team to lift the thing, but it is still an awesome reward.

But to tell a story like this, it's important to go back and talk about how we got here. Let's go all the way back to 1999.

Okay, I want you to try to remember a few names. Aeon64, Eul, Pendragon, Guinsoo, and IceFrog. No, these aren't characters in a new fighting game—these are the names of the designers responsible for creating a genre—a genre so new we haven't even settled on a name for it yet. Some call it MOBA (multiplayer online battle arena), some call it ARTS (action real-time strategy), but for the sake of this book, we're going to stick with DotA (Defense of the Ancients: Allstars).

It gets a bit crazy, but I'll do my best to keep this simple.

Remember, it's 1999, when a real-time strategy war game by Blizzard called StarCraft was stealing people's free time all over the Internet. The game is shown at a forty-degree angle from a bird's-eye perspective so that you can see lots of troops and multiple armies. The faster you can advance your army's tech and build troops, the better your chances of winning the game. But, in order to build all those troops, you need to gather a ton of resources. In its heart, StarCraft begins and ends with resource gathering.

Aeon64 had another idea. He loved nearly everything about the RTS game, but he just wanted to get to the battling part faster. He wanted a version of StarCraft that was more efficient, more to the point, so he started modifying the game to fit his vision. He removed the resource gathering and granted the player a team of powerful units. This player could control those units as a group, or play with a team of real players over the LAN. There were AI, or artificial intelligence, units that joined in as you battled along, and the goal was simple: destroy the other team's base before they destroyed yours.

This mod was pretty good, and had its fans, but as often happens in the modding community, another guy came along to add more improvements. Eul played a lot of Aeon64's mod, Aeon of Strife, but he thought the game would work better if it were built in Blizzard's new game, World of Warcraft III: Reign of Chaos.

By now, Blizzard was not only aware of the modding community, but they embraced it by including the Warcraft III World Editor along with the game. Eul took full advantage of the new editor and got to work. He published his first modded map in 2002, calling it Defense of the Ancients, or DotA for short.

Eul improved on what Aeon64 had created, and with the advances in technology, the game looked AND played much better.

Over the next year, hundreds of copycat DotA mods were built. Then in 2003, Blizzard released a new expansion pack for Warcraft III called The Frozen Throne. Little did they know at the time that things were about to get crazy.

Along came a modder named Guinsoo. He had a reputation for building quality mods, and he took the best features from Aeon's and Eul's mods and wrapped them into a tidy package. He called his mod DotA: Allstars, and before you knew it, under Guinsoo's direction everyone was playing it. Guinsoo had vision, and he was packed with talent. He balanced all the heroes in the game and added team vs. team competitive play. This was a HUGE step forward. Until this point, all the mods had been a single team playing against AI opponents, but now you could play against other people. He also added the ability to level up, or upgrade your hero. Both of these additions still play a massive part in the DotA world today.

Before long, there were twelve developers, or modders, helping Guinsoo with his mod. Which was GREAT, because updates happened frequently. To put that in perspective, Guinsoo had organized a "studio" of modders the size of a lot of small developers who were all working from their homes around the world. Guinsoo was directing them, selling them on his vision for DotA: Allstars, and they were all working for FREE! Yeah, not a penny changed hands.

But it was still a mod inside someone else's game, and while it was gaining in popularity, Guinsoo's hands were tied. He wasn't able to do what he wanted with the game. There was no online matchmaking (the ability to pair up teams with similar skill sets or tournament matches), no unique art (yeah, everything had to be assembled from existing Blizzard art assets), and no tutorial (no easy way to introduce newbies to the game).

And the game was hard. Really hard, for new users. But that didn't stop gamers from figuring it out. Hundreds of thousands of people were playing the DotA: Allstars mod.

Eventually, Blizzard made such a huge update that Guinsoo would have had to rethink everything in DotA: Allstars, so he figured it was as good a time as any to step aside, leaving the modding scene entirely. But it didn't take long for a new king of the DotA: Allstars modding community to hop up. IceFrog, a modder with a long history in the space, took over the reins and made an impact almost immediately.

IceFrog had a knack for the complicated balancing of characters, making it so each hero had an advantage, while still keeping the playing field level. Fans loved IceFrog's additions.

Under IceFrog's watch, DotA: Allstars really hit the jackpot. The game was social, competitive, fast, and super-rewarding. It was addicting, and not only were gamers taking note, so were the big companies, and all the legal trouble that often comes along with them.

The mod was now too big to ignore. And by 2008, so was the modding community. Not only were gamers flocking to a modified version of Warcraft III, other games like Half-Life 2 were seeing similar stories pop up. The

Half-Life 2 mod Counter-Strike was also on fire, gaining not only fans but the attention of massive game development studios.

Then, in 2009, a brand-new studio, Riot Games, released their game League of Legends. It was stand-alone, beautiful, and a bit friendlier than the DotA games. But that wasn't all. Riot also had a designer that was already well known in the modding community up their sleeve: a guy by the name of Steve "Guinsoo" Feak. That's right. When Guinsoo handed over DotA: Allstars to IceFrog, he did so because he had landed a job with Riot Games—a job where his only requirement was to help them build the game he had been working on for years and had always wanted to build.

Crazy, right?

Soon, people around the world were forming teams and challenging each other online. It took a few years, but once people started looking at the game as a real competition, a sport if you will, the buzz behind League of Legends grew fast.

When Riot Games started organizing tournaments, they knew how to set up the servers. They knew the tech behind pumping the monitors of their players to huge Jumbotron-sized screens. They knew how to handle the thousands of screaming fans. They even knew how to build that ridiculously huge, seventy-pound trophy I mentioned earlier. And that trophy has become the most coveted item in video game eSports. It's called the Summoner's Cup, and it is still the goal of the thousands of professional gamers who play League of Legends full-time.

To put it in perspective, in 2013, thirty-two million people around the world tuned in to the Staples Center in Los Angeles to watch a South Korean team win the Summoner's Cup, along with a grand prize of one million dollars. That's an audience larger than the one that tuned in to the last game of the NBA finals that year.

The original plans Riot had for League of Legends did not include professional leagues and televised tournaments. They just wanted to make the game that they desired to play themselves. A MOBA, a massive online battle arena

League of Legends is the second most profitable game for competitive players in eSports history, with nearly $20 million awarded in prize money since the game's release. That's more than the original Counter-Strike and StarCraft combined!

game that focused on great user experience, the best graphics in the genre, and an easy-to-learn, difficult-to-master journey that would keep players playing for years. Well, they achieved all that in the first two years, and in 2011, when they hosted their first tournament in Sweden, several hundred thousand people logged in online to watch the games on the new streaming service Twitch.tv. Everyone at Riot was shocked.

Since that date, the game has continued to expand. New champions are added every month, and the best gamers in the world grab them right away. Not just so they can learn to play with the new champions, but because they want to know how to BEAT the new champion.

League of Legends is probably best described as a fast-paced, intense competitive online game that blends the speed of an RTS (real-time strategy game) with RPG (role-playing game) elements. Two teams of powerful heroes, each with totally unique designs and play styles, battle head-to-head across multiple battlefields and game modes.

Players are allowed to change or customize their characters as they level up, choosing not only how the character looks, but how the character plays. And Riot Games is great at expanding its roster of champions to choose from, as well as keeping things balanced so the game always feels fair.

Its visual style is stunning. Highly colored, lush environments are a nice backdrop to unique characters that fit every taste a gamer could imagine. And the effects are simply beautiful. They feel powerful and look devastating.

Gamers play on PCs, working their magic on a keyboard and mouse as they swing exotic weapons in a virtual forest filled with traps, turrets, and torches.

The standard game pits two teams of five players each against each other. Each team has one goal: destroy your opponent's nexus, a bright blue-and-purple structure that glows like a neon fountain. And there is nothing quite as satisfying as gathering a group of friends, building a team, and choosing a strategy to defeat another club with a string of powerful moves that knock them out of the game.

While it's typically advisable to stay in school, one of League of Legends' most iconic players, George "HotshotGG" Georgallidis, dropped out of college to pursue a professional career in League of Legends. Youth is a huge factor in rapid reflexes and reaction speed, so he struck while the iron was hot, and it served him well.

The game is fun to play (even if you aren't making millions while doing so) and, as it turns out, super-addicting to watch. In fact, fans are paying between fifteen and fifty dollars a seat to watch these tournaments. It sounds like a lot of money, but Riot Games has said that although the tournaments are gaining in popularity, they are actually a big money loser for the company. However, making money on the tournaments isn't their goal. The tourneys are there to attract more LoL players to the game.

Korean teams are definitely the money winners when it comes to earnings in League of Legends tournaments. As of 2014, Korean players have won a collective total of over 5.5 million dollars. That's more than three times as much money as Americans have won.

Sounds like kind of a bad way to run a business. Lose money on your big gathering of gamers? Well, if that sounds crazy, get this: League of Legends is FREE TO PLAY! That's right. You can get the full version of LoL today for free. Not a penny. In fact, as it stands right now, you could play this superaddicting game for the next five years without spending a nickel.

So how do they stay in business? I mean, you can't keep making new enhancements for a game, let alone give away a million-dollar prize, if you're not making money.

What Riot Games sells to anyone playing the game are enhancements and goodies. Gear, clothing, new spells and effects. And each of these items costs less than ten dollars apiece. This may not seem like the way to become rich, but if you have millions of fans, and the gamers are excited enough about the game, then this plan is actually really smart. And we all know that Riot Games has plenty of gamers. In 2015, there were over sixty-seven MILLION players actively playing each month, and it isn't out of the question for League of Legends to bring in more than $100 million—a MONTH.

What started as a game of field-based capture the flag between friends has turned into the most popular eSport game on the planet and given new hope to young gamers around the world of reaching their dream someday: the dream of playing games for a living.

Oh, one can always dream.

CAN YOU SEE ME NOW?

• • • • • • • • • • • • • • • • •

You've probably watched gaming videos on YouTube. Heck, considering how many viewers celebrity YouTubers like KSI, Sky Does Minecraft, and VanossGaming have, there's a pretty good chance you subscribe to a YouTube gaming channel.

And who can blame you? There's something great about watching another gamer play a game they love and are amazing at, or try out something new and exciting. Heck, it's even fun when they fail, especially if they are cracking jokes.

This idea of recording your game-play session and sharing it with others is generally described with the term *Let's Play*.

Since the invention of YouTube, streaming games has been very popular. There are all kinds of streaming videos: play-throughs, where you might watch up to forty hours of a gamer beating an entire game; speed runs, where you watch expert/pro gamers rushing through games at record speeds; game reviews; and more. But I'll bet you didn't know that the idea of a Let's Play actually started before YouTube was even invented.

It's true. Gamers have been posting images and walk-throughs of difficult games to share with other gamers ever since they could capture images of them using capture cards or screen capture programs on their computers. In fact, it even goes back BEFORE that. Back before they invented the DVD player, a guy named Skip Rogers set up his video camera and recorded tapes of himself playing through classic arcade games to sell to gamers back in the 1980s.

But the website SomethingAwful.com is most often credited as the place where it all began.

Back in 2005, a guy by the name of Michael Sawyer under the user name "slowbeef" took screen captures, a series of single images, of himself playing through a game called The Immortal. He posted the images, along with some humorous and instructional commentary, on the SomethingAwful forums, and within weeks other gamers were following along.

As you can see, gamers had been sharing videos online for years in many different, clunky manners, but YouTube gave them a place to easily store and share all their videos.

Popular Let's Play gamers became celebrities nearly overnight. Millions upon millions of subscribers flocked to celebrity gamer channels to watch them play, fail, and win their way through popular, and not-so-popular, games.

In 2011, a few years after YouTube became the second-biggest search engine in the world, a newcomer to the live-streaming scene arrived. Twitch.tv (which is now owned by Amazon.com) was originally part of a small streaming website called Justin.tv. But things went completely crazy for Twitch when they aligned themselves with League of Legends to become the official broadcast partners of their tournaments in 2013. In fact, it grew so fast that Justin.tv shut down so the company could focus on Twitch, and by October of 2013, Twitch had forty-five million unique visitors to their website in a single month.

Twitch.tv has become a destination for gamers. New games are reviewed there before they are launched. Developers do Let's Plays and provide in-depth commentary about the games. Artists, designers, and engineers are even streaming their workstations so you can watch them work on games years before they even launch.

And then, of course, there is the eSports side of things. Video game competitions streamed live have become such a huge hit that in 2015, Twitch.tv announced they had more than 1.5 million registered broadcasters, which is similar to a YouTube channel, and over 100 million visitors every month.

The live-streaming world is here to stay. In fact, it's possible that someone reading this book right now is going to be the next big Twitch.tv gaming celebrity.

Who knows? Maybe it will be YOU!

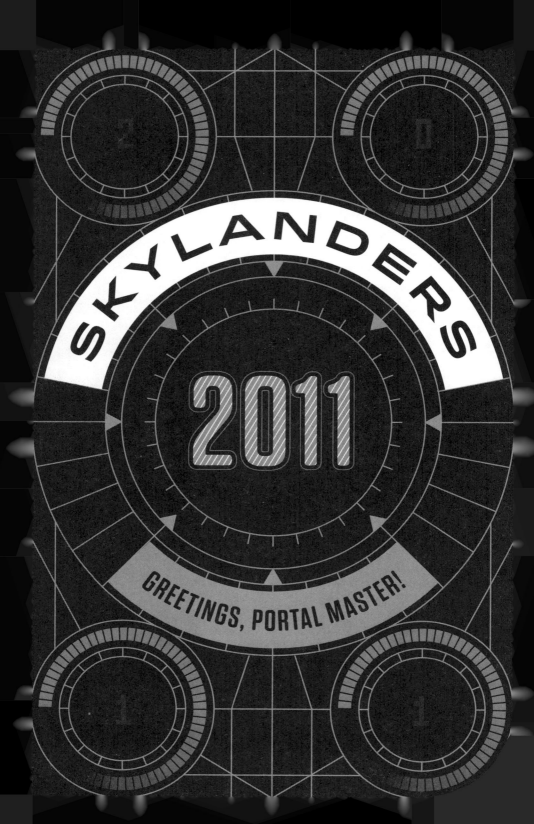

Skylanders: Spyro's Adventure © Activision

All right, it's time to play make-believe.

Let's pretend your favorite uncle Dustin gave you a sixty-dollar gift card for your birthday. Boy, that Uncle Dustin is such a good guy—you should write him a thank-you note. So you have your mom take you to Walmart and you sprint back to the video game area. You know, that place where all the TVs are playing reruns of college football games at the same time. Why are they always playing football games on those TVs? Anyway, you look around for the video games, and you find them, but they look like they are in prison. Yup, locked up in a glass case like they are a bunch of criminals.

Next, you have to find a guy with a key to let you free the game of your choice. And more times than not, the key person is grumpy. But who can blame him? He's probably tired of watching college football reruns on fifty screens at the same time. Let's call him Russ. Yeah, Russ sounds right.

It takes about twenty minutes to get Russ, and then he has to wait there with you while you choose a game, handing you one at a time so you can take a closer look. And if you want to look at a few games, he starts tapping his toe with his arms folded like you're ruining his entire day. You flip over the game to check out the screenshots and read about it, and Russ sighs and rolls his eyes.

All in all, it's a pretty bad shopping experience. Right?

But Activision changed all that by getting their games out from behind the glass wall. If you head down to the game section at your local supermarket now, the shelves are lined with Skylanders, not to mention Nintendo amiibos and Disney Infinity and LEGO Dimension toys. It is awesome, and you get to hold the characters in your hands before you even turn on the game.

Gamers love toys.

Okay, this might not be a scientific fact, but I dare you to prove me wrong. Gamers *love* toys.

And they're not alone—game *developers* love toys, too. I've been in more game development studios than I can count over the years, and it never fails, just about every game developer has a toy on his or her desk. Heck, most of them are surrounded by tiny plastic armies of collectible toys.

And it makes perfect sense, because toys are all about playing and imagination, and if you had only two words to describe how you interact with a game, *play* and *imagination* would be pretty good choices.

So I guess the unavoidable collision of toys and games was destined to happen. In a way, we all should have seen it coming, but it was Fred Ford and Paul Reiche III of Toys For Bob that figured it out first. They gave us Skylanders and changed how gamers and retailers, the stores that sell games, will look at gaming forever.

It's interesting how many times you hear the story of some amazing person, or an incredible new invention, and it starts with something like, "If it weren't for a lot of luck, the lightbulb would never have been invented." Luck is key to great inventions. But all the luck in the world won't help if you're not willing to work at it, and the guys from Toys For Bob totally understood this.

Okay, here's how it all broke down. How Fred Ford and Paul Reiche went from struggling game developers to global gaming pioneers in just a few short decades.

Fred Ford and Paul Reiche started Toys For Bob, a video game studio, almost twenty years before they created Skylanders. For the first ten or so years, the studio focused on

Fred Ford and Paul Reiche are pretty unusual in the game biz. Not only have they managed to keep their company, Toys For Bob, running for nearly a quarter of a century, they have been working together since college. In fact, the two still share an office.

making games based on movies, like *102 Dalmatians* and *Madagascar*. The games they made were always solid, but a funny thing happened in the early 2000s that kind of took the wind out of Toys For Bob's sails. Movie games started to get a bad reputation. Gamers were tired of buying games based on movies they loved, only to be disappointed when the games didn't deliver the experience they expected. This left Toys For Bob in a bad spot, because they had a team ready to make new games and nothing to build.

Fortunately, Activision had already purchased the company before this dip in movie games happened. Activision supported Toys For Bob, but if it wanted to keep the studio open, it needed the studio to make games, so Activision asked Toys For Bob to make something new and exciting.

Now, here's where the luck starts. A year or so before the movie game slump, Toys For Bob had hired a guy named I-Wei, even though, at the time, it didn't make sense. I-Wei wasn't your typical game artist—he was actually a toy maker and concept artist. It was a strange hire at the time, but Ford and Reiche had a good feeling about him, so they rolled the dice and gave him a job.

Turns out, when you let a concept artist and toy designer do his own thing for a while, he makes toys. It still seemed like an odd fit for the game development studio, so they kind of stuffed I-Wei off into a corner with another of their misfit employees, Robert Leyland. Now, Robert Leyland *was* a game programmer, but his real passion was playing with old electronics, and lately he'd been messing around with some computer chips called RFID, which stands for *radio-frequency identification*. Basically, it's a technology that uses tiny computer chips, sometimes smaller than a grain of sand, to identify items and keep track of them. Leyland had been gluing RFID chips on the bottoms of things and seeing how they would work as controllers for the Wii.

Pretty weird stuff, but as luck would have it, seating I-Wei and Leyland next to each other was a stroke of genius. Before they knew it, I-Wei's characters had Leyland's RFID tech stuck to the bottoms of them, and a

Around the time this all happened, Activision merged with another video game publisher, Vivendi. This also ended up being pretty fortunate for Toys For Bob, because Activision let them pick through Vivendi's old gaming franchise to see if there was something that would spark an idea. There was a lot to choose from, but the team kept coming back to a spunky little dragon named Spyro. He had attitude and a good sense of humor, and the little dragon that could became the mascot for the first Skylanders game.

star was born. After a bit of prototyping and a whole lot of hacking and gluing, the first Skylander came to life, and everyone who saw it knew it was destined to be a hit.

Spyro the dragon in his original appearance in Spyro the Dragon
© Sony Computer Entertainment, Inc.

Seeing that the idea had big potential, but also recognizing that the game needed more time to really be a huge hit, Activision CEO Bobby Kotick offered another full year of development to Toys For Bob to get things right.

Now Toys For Bob had everything they could hope for: a cool new technology, a fun group of characters, and the backing and time from Activision to make the game really great.

Over the next year, the game took shape. More characters and toys were designed, a fun exploration platformer game was developed, and the Portal of Power was invented. The Portal of Power was a small base, about the size of a cereal bowl, that plugged into the Wii and "zapped" your Skylander toy into the game. It did it with RFID chips, so when a gamer put his or her Skylander on the Portal of Power base, the base knew exactly which Skylander it was.

Spyro toy on Portal of Power © Activision

Not only that, but the game could also use the Portal of Power to send information BACK to the toy, saving important game information on the toy itself.

It was like magic, because you could level up your character, then pack him over to your friend's house, and all your info would be zapped into his or her game.

Everything was looking great, but there was just one problem—and it was a big one. No matter how they tried to cut costs, Toys For Bob and Activision just couldn't figure out a way to make a profit with their new Skylanders product.

The RFID chips that were required for the game to really be great were just too expensive at the time. Toys For Bob couldn't figure out how to get the chips they wanted in their toys for the right price.

Then something totally out of their control happened. The London Underground, London's subway system, moved away from cash and tickets and toward RFID-based Oyster cards. These cards look like a regular credit card, but they have an RFID chip inside that allows subway travelers to keep track of their account and ride the subway with a simple swipe of their card. The London Underground was now ordering millions of RFID chips, and RFID makers started dropping their prices fast to meet the demand. In less than one year, the technology had a boom. The RFID tech was smarter, and the price dropped to a point where Toys For Bob could put the chip they had always wanted inside their toys. Once again, timing and luck were on their side.

Another part of Skylanders' success has to do with how Activision was working with manufacturers (the people who actually make things like plastic guitars and RFID-filled toys). Activision had learned a lot in the past few years about how to get toys built right, and for the right price. If it weren't for the success of Guitar Hero, Skylanders might have been dead before it ever started.

But once it launched, Skylanders went on to be the MUST-HAVE toy for the holiday season in 2011. In fact, by the time the holidays hit, it was nearly impossible to find some of the toys. Activision and Toys For Bob recognized their game was a phenomenon, and they had the next wave of Skylanders toys already in production. Wave two hit the following spring in March, and the craze for new Skylanders toys only got more insane. They kept rolling out new toys, and gamers kept gobbling them up the moment they hit the shelves.

If you purchased every character in the Skylanders universe at its original price in 2015, it would cost you $4,200 to complete your collection! However, some of the toys you could only get as Con exclusives and for other rare events. Some of those rare Skylander toys can sell for over $1,000 each! Man, I wish I'd kept the special-edition E3 bronze hot dog figure. I think I traded it to a friend of mine for an actual hot dog one day. Rookie mistake!

But perhaps the best thing about Skylanders, and the thing that keeps them fresh, is the fact that not only do they release cool new toys regularly, but with every new game release they find new ways to innovate. They change the way we play and collect games, and the proof of their greatness is in the record books.

- **For the first time, toys were truly brought to life as you zapped Skylanders figures into your game with the RFID chip.**

- Activision shipped toys with a "brain" that allowed gamers to store their characters' information right on the toy. That meant that if you took your set of toys over to your friend's house, you could pick up and play where you'd left off.

- Skylanders reached the two-billion-dollar mark in 2014, just three years after its release, making it the second-fastest game to hit that astronomical amount, right behind Wii Fit.

- Also in 2014, Activision announced that for the first time in history a video game company had the best-selling action figure in the world by a LONG shot.

- And, keeping with a tradition of cool new innovations, Skylanders games have continued to give gamers cool new tech with each game release.

  - Skylanders: Giants introduced LightCore figures. These toys light up when they are placed over the Portal of Power.
  - The Skylanders: Swap Force characters can separate their bodies and legs and mix with other characters to create unique combinations, both in the real world and in-game.
  - In Skylanders: Trap Team, gamers can trap the villains of Skylanders, including the ultimate bad guy, Kaos, and play them to fight the forces of evil.
  - Skylanders: SuperChargers allows players to scan in vehicles and match them up with their collection of Skylanders toys. A card game also comes with SuperChargers and plays on mobile phones, where players can scan in the cards and duel with their friends.

A Skylanders toy is sold every two seconds. That adds up quickly. In fact, in 2015 Skylanders passed the Zelda franchise on the all-time earnings list.

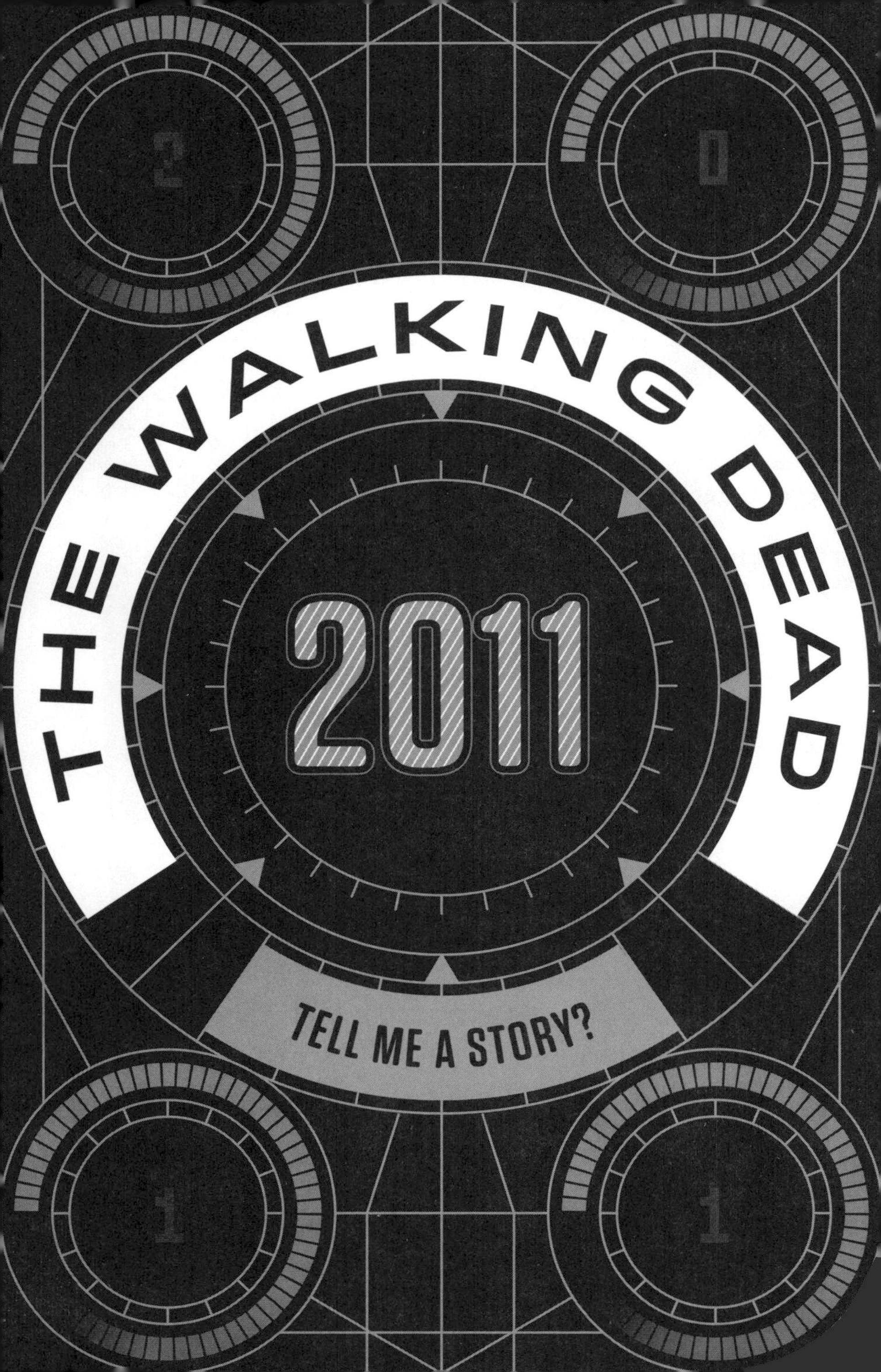
THE WALKING DEAD
2011
TELL ME A STORY?

The Walking Dead © Telltale Games

Lee was a bad man before the walkers came.

He had been doing hard time at the state penitentiary, and now he was on the run. If he got caught, it would probably add another ten years to his sentence. But the way things looked, going back to the pen was the least of his problems.

Zombies. Zombies were a much bigger problem. You know, when he thought about it, being surrounded by a horde of brain-craving walking-dead zombies made all his other problems look pretty darn small.

That is, until he runs across a young girl who needs his help, and Lee is faced with his first real moral choice. The girl, Clementine, wants to stay and wait for her parents, but the area is crawling with zombies, and the house doesn't offer much protection. He knows he can't leave her behind, but he also knows that her parents are never coming back. Lee knows that leaving immediately is probably the safest thing to do, but it's getting dark. Waiting through the night could be dangerous, even deadly, in the unprotected house, but it might be best for Clementine if they wait. Does he run now, taking the risk of running into zombies in the dark, or does he stay the night, hoping that the zombies don't break down their meager defenses and trap them in the house?

What Lee doesn't know is that the decision to stay or leave is nothing compared to the heartbreaking choices he'll have to make down the line. And that is exactly how the genius storytellers at Telltale Games planned it all along.

And these plans started long before zombies surrounded our hero, Lee. Back in 2004, high-paced action thrillers were everywhere. Halo 2, GTA: San Andreas, The Chronicles of Riddick, Ninja Gaiden. They were all great games that made your heart beat in your throat and your fingers twitch. But three guys working at LucasArts decided that they missed the old story-driven games of the past, like Zork or MYST, and they wanted to bring them back. Dan Connors, Kevin Bruner, and Troy Molander left the home of Luke and Vader to start their own studio, Telltale Games.

Telltale started off small, and it took them a few years to really get going. In fact, you have to fast-forward about five years before they started making some noise. During that time the company made games for familiar properties like the TV show *CSI*; *Bone*, a well-loved comic book; and *Tales of Monkey Island*, a popular old LucasArts game. But it wasn't until an original creation starring a large dog and a goofy rabbit hit the scene that Telltale felt any real momentum. The game was called Sam & Max Save the World, and not only did it tell a great story, it also nailed something else that Connors, Bruner, and Molander were really interested in: It felt like a TV show. The game was released in thirty-minute chunks, and each chapter, or episode, left the game on a cliff-hanger. Sometimes literally, as Sam was the type of character to find himself hanging from a cliff from time to time.

While at first people were skeptical of this new episodic approach, by the end of 2010 Telltale was making about ten million dollars a year.

But for Telltale Games, it wasn't all about the money. It was also about opportunity. The success of Sam & Max allowed them to take bigger risks, and it also allowed them to go after one of the hottest properties on TV at the time: *The Walking Dead*.

The Walking Dead (the TV show) was doing very well in 2011. Families were gathered around the TV every Sunday night to watch Carl, a tough sheriff from Georgia, lead his ragtag band of survivors across the South. But rather than follow the plot of the TV show, Telltale Games told an original story set in the same universe with new characters. This allowed them to tell the story they wanted to explore in their own words, while still taking advantage of the TV show's massive popularity.

By this time, the team at Telltale Games had really refined how they made games. They had devised a unique gaming engine, or a system and tool set used by the developers to tell stories. Or, more accurately, it allowed gamers to create their own version of the story the developers were telling by giving them choices and then changing the game based on their actions and decisions.

The action in the game isn't challenging. Just point and click and the adventure continues, but with every choice you get closer and closer to the game, until you feel like you are the guy pulling the trigger.

Here's an example:

You and a group of other survivors are trapped inside a drugstore. The previous owners boarded the place up, but the walls won't be holding for long. However, you've been inside long enough to get to know these people pretty well. You meet Carley, a tough, capable woman who seems kind and smart. You also meet Doug, a guy who obviously has a bit of a crush on Carley, and while he's not the toughest guy in the world, Carley owes him her life for saving her in the past. He also helped you get out of a scrape. He's a pretty good dude with a big heart.

While you're trying to figure out how to escape from the drugstore without being turned into a mumbling brain addict, the horde crashes through the door and puts both Carley and Doug in trouble. SERIOUS trouble.

You have a gun, but only enough ammo and time to save one of them. Also, you have to think quickly because you only have ten seconds before it's too late and they both get gobbled up.

1. Save Carley. She's a survivor and can possibly be helpful down the line. Especially with the young girl you found in the suburbs, Clementine.

Carley in The Walking Dead © Telltale Games

2. Save Doug. You kind of owe him already, and you know he's strong and willing to do whatever it takes to survive.

Doug in The Walking Dead © Telltale Games

3. Save neither, and leave them behind as a distraction while you and the others make your escape.

So, you can see how making any one of these choices could take you down a whole new story path. Whomever you choose to save will be part of your story going forward, and the other, well, they'll be zombie chow.

And whatever you choose, what starts off as a couple of simple choices can end up being a tangled knot of story options down the line. The more choices a game developer allows the player to make, the more story options they have to create. If they're not careful, it can get out of hand. Developers often find themselves either needing to limit the choices to keep things simple, or discover that they'll never finish making the game because of the amount of outcomes. It can be a regular mess, but the developers at Telltale Games handled it perfectly.

In 2010, Telltale shipped six games, each receiving higher ratings and reviews than the last. Their engine was running hot, and the crew had the story-writing thing down. They released a new Sam & Max adventure; Hector: Badge of Carnage; Nelson Tethers: Puzzle Agent; CSI: Fatal Conspiracy; and Poker Night at the Inventory. But the game that really stood out was the episodic Back to the Future: The Game.

Much like Sam & Max and *The Walking Dead* TV show itself, the game was released in episodes they called seasons. The writing was fantastic, and every decision you made along the way shaped Lee into the kind of person YOU wanted to become. I don't care how much of a macho tough guy you are, it was hard not to get a tear in your eye and a lump in your throat at the end of season one. The last few choices you make are nearly impossible, making it, in my opinion, the best example of dealing with a zombie apocalypse out there. Better than the books. Better than the comics. Even better than the TV show.

The whole experience was, and still is, incredible, and it showed up on every possible platform. It sold over a million copies in the first twenty days, topping the Xbox Live, PlayStation Network, and Steam charts.

Eventually, it made its way to the iOS and Android platforms as well.

And this wasn't the end for Telltale Games: Things were just starting to take off. The Walking Dead episodes kept rolling out, and the reviews were still very strong. Then they took their talents and traditions to a new series, A Wolf Among Us, based on the *Fables* comic books, and once again their games just keep getting better and better.

In all this time, Telltale Games has never changed the station. They haven't tried their hands at a shooter or a platformer. Connors, Bruner, and Molander started their company with a vision and a dream, and they have kept their eyes on the goal ever since.

There's no doubt in my mind that things will only end one way for Telltale Games . . .

Happily ever after.

Blowing Against the Wind

Not every game in this book is an adrenaline rush.

Not every game will get your blood pumping, make your palms sweaty, drive your feet to pound with the rhythm of the music. Some games ask you to slow down, ponder, and create your own pace.

Sound fun? Well, Jonathan Blow thinks they are fun, and the indie games guru who brought us Braid (2008) and The Witness (2016) is a master at making games to prove his point.

His first gig in the industry was actually as a software engineer, where he ported DOOM and DOOM 2 from PC to generic TV-specific gaming systems you might find in a hotel. And while the work was challenging, he craved the creative outlet of designing his own games. But at the time, mainstream gaming companies weren't looking for slow-paced puzzle platformers. So Blow took things into his own hands, literally, and started work on Braid on his own.

Over the years, Blow had made tons of small game prototypes and indie projects, but nothing really stood out as special to him —until Braid. The game was inspired by an e-mail discussion about rewinding time, and after monkeying around with the concept for a while, Blow fell in love with it. He believed in it so much that he mortgaged his house to fund the development of the project.

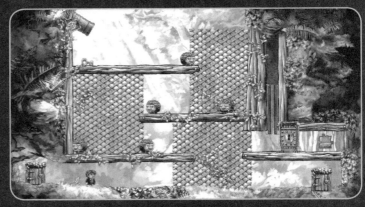

Braid © Number None, Inc.

Blow is a brilliant programmer, artist, and game designer, and he used all his skills to make a truly innovative game. The first time you play Braid, it seems simple: an elegant puzzler with clever ideas about time and some kind of odd story about a princess. But the more you play, the more complicated it gets. Simple jump-here, grab-that tasks turn into mind-bending puzzles where you have to warp the flow of time in unnatural ways. Then, just when you think you have it all figured out, Blow turns the rules upside down in the last level, creating a "my world is crumbling" feeling that must be experienced to truly appreciate it.

The game was a hit with gamers and got amazing reviews. And, better yet, it sold well enough that Blow could set his own pace when developing his next game, which, it turns out, was exactly what he needed.

Jonathan Blow jumped right into creating a new game called The Witness. It was originally scheduled to be released way back in 2009 on the Xbox 360, but then Blow looked at the technology and realized his vision was more complicated than the current console systems could handle. He had a big decision in front of him.

He chose to wait.

And plan.

And rework the puzzles in the game to make it even more compelling.

And that, at its core, is what The Witness is. A massive puzzle game, but also so much more than that. I don't want to go off the deep end here with descriptions, because I really think the game should be played. In a way, The Witness is as much about learning a new language of symbols or way of thinking as it is about solving puzzles. Which is just about the most indie-gamer sentence ever created.

The Witness © Thekla, Inc.

Jonathan Blow's contributions to the gaming world shouldn't be underestimated. He always goes at his own pace. Blow's independent masterpieces change the way we think about time, about language, and about problem solving. His games turn the world on its head and ask gamers to look at things from different directions. Give them a shot. I know you will be glad you took the time.

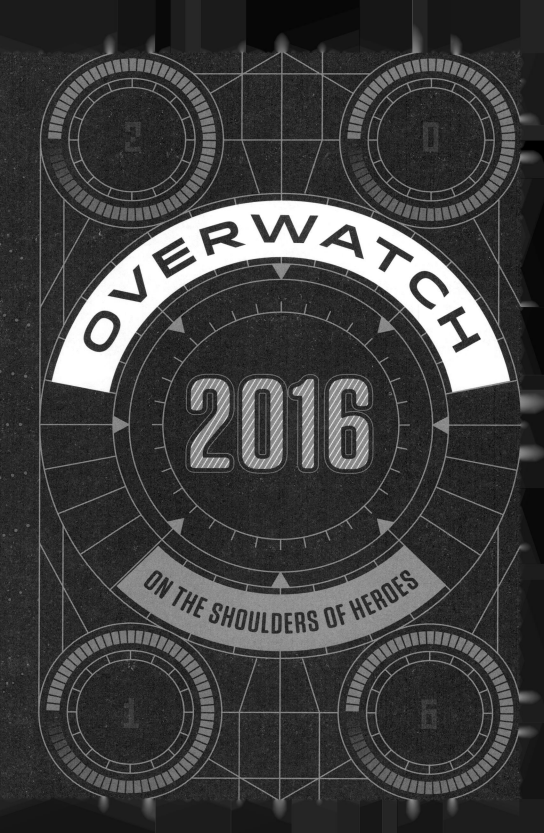

Overwatch © Blizzard Entertainment

Abraham Lincoln once said, "The best way to predict the future is to create it." And if any game developer understands this, it's Blizzard.

Activision's Blizzard is one of the largest, most-talked-about video game companies on the planet. For years they have dominated the MMO and strategy gaming genres with World of Warcraft and StarCraft, and with the addition of Overwatch in 2016, they have taken a big bite out of the shooter RPG genre as well.

Blizzard didn't start off as a gaming juggernaut. It actually started off pretty small with classic games like The Lost Vikings and Rock n' Roll Racing. But even back then, when it was a newbie developer, its commitment to quality art, unique characters, and addicting game play makes it easy to believe it is the same company that brought us the world's largest MMO.

The story of how they grew from those humble beginnings into the media juggernaut they are today is one of the most covered game developer stories out there. They

The name of their company, Blizzard Entertainment, has made a lot of people speculate that the game developer was going to break into the television or movie industries. Well, they were right. In June 2016, Blizzard debuted their first major motion picture based on the World of Warcraft franchise, called simply *Warcraft*. Keep your eyes peeled; this will not be Blizzard Entertainment's last movie.

launched games on just about every console you can think of, from the NES in 1992 to the Xbox One in 2016. They have truly grown up with the gaming industry—pioneers that have helped shape the direction for decades.

By 2010, Blizzard was cranking on all cylinders. A new version of StarCraft was doing well. Diablo III was eating up gamers' time as they cruised through the underworld. BlizzCon, Blizzard's very own convention, was growing in popularity, and, of course, it looked like there was no end in sight for World of Warcraft, their massive MMO. Gamers gathered online to speculate what Blizzard would do next, but the team at Blizzard was way ahead of them.

We build our future on the successes of the past, but only when we learn from its failures.

Three people in particular, creative director Chris Metzen, senior game designer Michael Chu, and game director Jeff Kaplan, had been playing around in the ashes of a newly canceled project called Titan. Blizzard had been working on Titan for years, and while it ended up on the cutting room floor, there was a lot of good inspiration left behind. The three designers brainstormed about what would come next, and a spark of an idea got them all thinking in the same direction. It really started off from a simple wish. Kaplan wanted to try his hand at making a shooter. He was a big fan of the genre, and he'd dreamed of making a story-driven shooter for years.

Metzen thought that Kaplan's idea fit right along with *his* dream of making a game set in a superhero universe. Not a superhero game per se, but one that would rival the amazing and inspiring universes created by comic book giant Marvel.

And Chu, well, he was most interested in building a diverse set of unique characters, each with their own complete backstory and specialized skills that actually showed up as unique game mechanics.

They started with what all games need: a problem, a conflict. A FIGHT! Metzen and Chu dreamed up the Omnic Crisis, a world-toppling robotic uprising. Then they started telling each other the story of how this massive

Overwatch is a game for everyone—men, women, children—and they reflected this in their diverse character lineup. No matter who you are in real life, there's a character that represents you. Even if you are a giant hog or a glasses-wearing gorilla.

crisis would be resolved, and from that came the Overwatch heroes.

The story moved along, although they didn't really have an ending or a middle for it. In fact, they just kind of made it up as they went along. Sometimes it was driven by mechanics—for example, they might say "Hey, we need a long-range-sniper-type character." And then next thing you know, Widowmaker was born. They'd play with her backstory (often playing other shooters for reference to find out what was the gold-standard long-range-sniper experience), then they'd let her influence the game's story going forward. And then they'd design the next character.

Widowmaker from Overwatch © Blizzard Entertainment

An art director, Bill Petras, was added to the team, and the stories Metzen and Chu had been creating *really* came to life. Before long, the powers that be at Blizzard were falling in love with the game, and since Blizzard was an ENTERTAINMENT company as well as a game company, they made a movie-style trailer to announce Overwatch to the world.

The original Overwatch trailer stars two brothers, one about thirteen and the other only about nine. They are visiting the Overwatch Museum, watching a historical video about how the Overwatch crew defeated the Omnic Crisis. The younger brother can't contain his joy as he jumps around, pretending to be his favorite Overwatch character, when he notices the Gauntlet—a powerful relic item, a glove that was worn by Doomfist, a notorious butt-kicker.

From the Overwatch trailer © Blizzard Entertainment

While they are checking out the Gauntlet, all heck breaks loose as Overwatch characters drop through the glass ceiling of the museum. We meet Tracer, a genetically modified British athlete who can actually jump through time in small spaces. We meet Widowmaker, a lethal sharpshooter with a bad attitude. Winston, a silverback ape wearing glasses and armor, comes to the rescue, pounding his hands on the floor, showing his wit and muscle as he does battle with Reaper, a cloaked and dangerous man who can shift into a vaporous cloud of smoke. And we learn that after the Omnic Crisis, there was a divide in the Overwatch. Bad guys, good guys, and perhaps a few stuck in the middle.

The boys are caught in the middle of the battle, hiding behind whatever cover they can find to stay safe. And sorry to spoil things if you've not seen it yet, but the trailer ends with the line, "The world could always use another hero," giving the young boys, and every gamer who watched the short movie, goose bumps, because who doesn't want to be a hero?

The quality of the trailer is nothing less than you'd expect from a hit blockbuster animated movie from Pixar or Disney, and it doesn't just appeal to hard-core gamers. It appeals to EVERYONE.

When the trailer was created, Metzen didn't have a plan for the Gauntlet. In fact, he didn't even have an idea that there was going to be a character named Doomfist until after the trailer had released.

At the time, Blizzard didn't even have a launch date planned for Overwatch. They just knew that gamers would love it, and felt that the game would release when it was ready. I mean, they had a few core ideas, but they didn't really have a complete concept of where to go with the game. In a way, when the trailer released, they were just getting going. Just starting off their new project.

Which brings up a good point. An important one, actually. How do you start a new project? Maybe you start with an idea, a story perhaps, or a fun mechanic that you think might be fun or unique. And sure, there are plenty of games that began that way, especially in the early days of game development. But what happens next?

Well, often a wise game developer will look at the games that have come before. Just look at what we have covered in this book. Remember, it was 2016. It had been forty-four years since Nolan Bushnell and Al Alcorn packed their coin-op Pong machine into Andy Capp's Tavern. You could fill an entire library with all the video games—the good, the bad, and the ugly—that have launched since then. Brilliant minds, like Miyamoto, Will Wright, Gunpei Yokoi, Kim Swift, John Carmack, Siobhan Reddy, Jonathan Blow, and a thousand others have solved difficult problems and presented them in perfect packages for gamers to reference and play.

What I'm saying is that only a foolish game developer would ignore the heaps and mounds of great games that came before when they are beginning to build a new project. And the team at Blizzard is not composed of fools. In fact, they've mentioned a few of their inspirations in various interviews, but I'm confident that list is only the beginning.

In many ways, Overwatch is totally innovative and unique, but in other ways, the standout hit shooter is the perfect blend of many of the best games that came before. Here is a partial list of possible inspirations, and the lessons that might have been taught:

- **From Space Invaders, they could have learned that shooting and taking cover are equally important—the yin and yang of every shooter.**

- **From Pac-Man, the team might have learned that inspiration can come from everyday objects.**

- **E.T. teaches lessons that Blizzard understands perfectly: Build the right game, because fans will be able to spot quality—or its opposite.**

- **From The Legend of Zelda, the team at Blizzard could have learned that sometimes the most unlikely hero is the most memorable.**

- **John Madden Football could have taught them that realism is interesting, but heightened realism is another form of fantasy gaming, and that is even more compelling than reality.**

- **Sonic the Hedgehog shows that gamers will exceed your expectations. If you build a character so fast you can barely control it, gamers will keep working at the challenge until they perfect it. Never underestimate a gamer.**

- **Street Fighter II taught the world that character diversity, both visually and with gaming mechanics, builds fan loyalty and lets gamers see themselves in the games they love and play.**

- Super Mario Kart could have reminded the team that rubber-banding—keeping the game close for all players—makes everyone feel like they have a chance to win.

- From MYST, the team could have learned that if you build a world worth exploring, and a story worth telling, gamers will explore, then tell their friends all about it.

- DOOM's inspiration is obvious: Shooters are fun, but shooters within live and unpredictable environments are so much better.

- From Gran Turismo, the team might have learned that attention paid to the smallest detail, even if the majority of gamers don't notice, will be appreciated by your most die-hard fans.

- Final Fantasy VII might have inspired them to build a deep lore within the game, then tell that story through movie-quality cinematics. Make the story epic, deliver it in the best possible quality, and gamers line up in droves to play your game.

- Half-Life taught game developers that the entire cast needs to feel alive, and a part of the story. A living world and AI characters that react to a gamer make them feel a connection to the story that can't be delivered in any other way. You, as a gamer, feel responsible for them, and that makes you feel even more powerful.

- Pokémon might have shown the team at Blizzard that a collection is compelling, but building and nurturing your collection is what keeps you coming back for more.

- World of Warcraft obviously taught the team at Blizzard more than this book could contain, but one of the biggest takeaways was that you need to plan game play for each of the gamer play types: the Explorer, the Achiever, the Socializer, and the Destroyer.

- **Halo 2 showed Blizzard that gamers love playing together as a community. All for one, and one for all.**

- **Guitar Hero isn't just a music game; it teaches us that the best games sell a fantasy. In Guitar Hero it's the fantasy of being a rock star, and in Overwatch it's the fantasy of becoming a hero.**

- **Wii Sports showed game developers that EVERYONE loves to play games, but you have to invite them in and show them how to win.**

- **Portal could have inspired the team by showing them that unique mechanics are not just important, they are engaging.**

- **League of Legends might have shown Blizzard that making a game fair and competitive, then giving gamers a stage to perform on, is a recipe for fame and success. Not just for the game developer, but for the gamer, too!**

And this is just the tip of the iceberg. Playing a masterpiece like Overwatch reminds us of so many games that have come before. Team Fortress, Rocket League, Mass Effect, The Last of Us, and I'm sure you also have a long list that you could add.

So here's my last challenge for you, gamer. Next time you play a new game (and if you haven't had a chance, Overwatch is a good one to check out), make a list of all the features that make that game great. The innovations, the things that make your eyes light up, the mechanics, the story, the art, the music, the lighting, the mood. Write them down, and then see how they shape the direction of games going forward. And don't forget to look back from time to time at your long list of gaming's greatest moments and see how they all built each other up.

I'm confident that if you do this, you'll see whispers and echoes of the games of the past, games that belong in the Video Game Hall of Awesome, giving you little nods that remind you that the future stands on the shoulders of heroes from the past.

If you can remember all the way back to the beginning of this book, we talked about two things: (1) how fast things change in the game industry, and (2) how the games that came before shape the games of today and tomorrow.

And after looking more deeply into these great games, I think you'd have to agree that both these things are true. But what comes next? What is that next game that's just out of reach, and better yet, who's going to design it?

Things change so fast in the game industry that it can be hard to keep up with what is current, let alone guess what the future holds. But guessing or dreaming about what is next is exactly where innovation comes from. Dreamers are the doers in the game industry, and if you aren't willing to make a crazy jump into the unknown, well, then you are just going to repeat the past.

So, with that in mind, here are a few predictions of what I hope we'll be playing next.

Oculus Rift © Oculus VR, LLC

Virtual Reality Will Be a Reality.

Okay, I'm a bit biased here, but virtual reality was already in the news way back in 2015, and it is so promising that I know it will play a HUGE part in video games' future. The Oculus Rift was the first to lead the charge here, and with solid funding and passionate creatives, it is going to be great for years to come. It works by slipping on a headset that has two monitors inside, one for each eye. It has high-quality stereo headphones and 360-degree head tracking. When you move your head to look around, the game responds, and you feel like you are in the game, not just playing it.

The tech is really cool, but I think it's just scratching the surface. It will be a massive move forward for the game industry. By the year 2020, there's a good chance there will be fifty million or more VR devices out there, and with that many, you know game companies will get in line and make some great new games.

But that's not where VR will end. VR will replace TV in a lot of homes, or at least be a major player in the personal movie-watching arena. Netflix is already showing interest in this area, and can you imagine watching a nature documentary in full 360, where you are plopped down in the middle of the jungle? Or sitting in the cockpit of a Formula One car being driven by the best driver in the world? How about watching reruns of *The Big Bang Theory* and sitting on the couch right next to Sheldon while the show goes on? It would be pretty amazing, and there's nothing keeping this from happening. The tech is already there.

Games Will Be Part of Education.

This is also already happening now, but it is going to be an even bigger part of education going forward. Teachers are struggling to compete for children's attention when students have access to critical-thinking, fast-decision-making games at home. Scientists and educators

Facebook purchased Oculus Rift in 2014 for two billion dollars. I'm not sure how fun it will be to see your Facebook feed in true 3D, but I'm sure owner Mark Zuckerberg has bigger plans.

have taken note, and they are starting to see the massive benefits in learning through play.

In 2014, Electronic Arts opened their doors to Glass-Lab in Redwood Shores, California. EA helped rework their city-building simulation game SimCity to teach children about the impact of environmental change, community-based decision making, and economics.

While developing this special version, EA and Glass-Lab realized that games already "grade" gamers. We call it a score in games, but it is no different from getting a grade on a test.

And don't forget that the entire country of Sweden is already using Minecraft in schools. The teachers of today already understand the benefits of using games, as we talked about in the Minecraft chapter. Just imagine how fast this will spread, since the teachers of tomorrow grew up PLAYING Minecraft as kids.

Learning while having fun is something that educators want. I know you might not believe it all the time, but teachers want students to enjoy learning, and they know that games will get them there.

No, really. They do. Well, all except Miss Trunchbull, but that's another story altogether.

Points, Points, and More Points

I love the word *ubiquitous*. It is pronounced *you-bick-quit-us*, and saying it makes you sound really smart. Especially if you know what it means. *Ubiquitous* means "found everywhere." As in, video games in the future will be ubiquitous. And I do mean UBIQUITOUS!

Right now just over one-third of the world population has access to the Internet. And while you might see cell phones in every pocket in your middle school, most people across the globe can't even think about owning a gaming device. They are just too expensive.

But that is changing. And so is our opinion of what makes a game.

With the drop in price for inexpensive computers,

we are on the edge of a massive revolution. We now have things like conductive ink, which can literally be printed out on a piece of paper or plastic. This new and ultrathin invention will allow us to print a computer on something as small as a postage stamp. And it is cheap. Really cheap, like pennies cheap. Crazy—right?

So, what will this mean? This means that when you are eating your bowl of Fruity Toasty O's in the morning, you'll actually be able to play a game on the back of your cereal box. It won't be Call of Duty: Fruity Toasty O's edition, but something simple like an interactive word search or a drawing game might certainly be on the cardboard horizon.

This is pretty cool, but imagine taking these small, cheap devices and putting them everywhere. Let the life games begin.

Brush your teeth. The toothbrush counts how many strokes you've made. It will tell you how hard you're pressing, which teeth are getting missed, and if you skipped a night. But you brushed your teeth this morning, so TEN POINTS.

You used MintyMouth Mouthwash, and you just reached the halfway point on your bottle. Great job! Ten points, plus an achievement unlock for hitting 50 percent in two weeks. Twenty points from MintyMouth Corporation.

You pour out a bowl of cereal and it tells you you've added exactly 160 calories to your bowl. You choose skim milk and rack up another 80 calories. Ten points for making a healthy breakfast choice, then you rinse out your bowl and put it in the dishwasher. The new LG dishwasher flips you ten life points for helping out Mom.

You skip the bus and ride your bike to school. Thirty points.

You run extra hard in PE. Thirty points.

You turn in your math assignment in class one day early. Ten points plus a ten-point bonus from the teacher.

And so on, and so forth. Everything you do adds these magical life points to your account. But what do you do with them?

Well, this could get crazy. Big-name companies would

love this because they can send you discounts and freebies of their products for your points. There are a lot of possibilities out there, but let's just pretend your mom lets you cash them in for free time. In one day, you might earn six hundred points, and maybe she'll give you one minute for every ten points. So, one hour of uninterrupted Play-Station 6 time to squash zombies in COD 10. Who knows?

But the *point* (see what I did there?) I'm trying to make is that ubiquitous gaming means that you will be able to turn the everyday, boring things you do now into games. And that doing this will earn you real-life rewards. Even if it is only fewer cavities at your next dentist visit.

Back to the Future

One thing is for sure: If we learn anything from looking at the history of games, it is that there are themes that keep coming up again and again. Wii Sports is just Pong plus better graphics and new tech. The Walking Dead, MYST, and Zork all have the same DNA. Activision's Pitfall! for the Atari 2600 is the great-grandfather of Sony's Uncharted. And so on.

We return to these great games because they are—well, because they are GREAT. They are fun and entertaining, and new technology only makes the experience better.

What we'll see in the future is going to be similar to what we see now, only it will be WAY more immersive. The experiences will make us feel more and more like we are part of the games we play.

We'll have more action. Better stories. Less bulky and awkward controllers. And some people today are even predicting that we won't have consoles in the future. Many have claimed boldly that the PS4 and the Xbox One are the last consoles we'll ever see. I say, hooey!

Video game streaming services similar to Netflix and Amazon will arrive on the scene, but when it comes down to it, gamers like games. We like to hold a controller, and we like yelling at the TV. We like going to old-school arcades and blowing away wave after wave of "invaders."

We like chasing bright-colored ghosts, and jumping on angry mushrooms, and jamming on plastic guitars.

I guess the most exciting thing for me about the future of games is that today's gamers—that means you, gamer—are going to school to become the game developers of tomorrow. They are playing and learning from great games made today. They are studying the history of games, and making their own games in their spare time. These young gaming fans are smart, funny, and full of love for the games they play. And someday, when I'm old and gray, my grandkids will bring me a copy of their newest game, and they will beat me so bad I'll feel like an old man. A happy old man who is still playing amazing games made by brilliant young minds. Curious young minds like yours.

And then I'll walk my grandkids to my basement. I'll lead them into a room that smells an awful lot like hand-cut french fries and fake-strawberry Italian ice. I'll give them each a few quarters, then hobble over to my vintage Space Invaders arcade machine. And I'll show them that I still know a thing or two about the games that shaped me. The games that shaped us all.

ACKNOWLEDGMENTS

This is a book more than two decades in the making.

When I started in the video games industry in 1995, I had no idea what a journey I was embarking upon. I've worked with hundreds, probably thousands of game developers who have inspired me, challenged me, made me laugh, and yes, some of them have even made me cry. Literally. There is no way I could list all the bright and powerful men and women who have played a part in this adventure of mine, but I would be crazy not to mention a few. Thank you to Jon Dean, Jason Barnes, Scott Nagy, Aaron Walker, Joe Vance, Kari St. John, Farrell Edwards, Joe Bourrie, Loel Phelps, Alan Copeland, Matt Copeland, Vance Cook, John Turk, Bryan Brandenburg, Mark Mongie, Joe Hoffman, Nathan Walpole, Brenda Hawkins, Ryan Burnsides, Chip Lange, Donald Yatomi, Kelly Mondragon, Laura Warner, Dan Matkowsky, Chance Thomas, Tracy Hickman, Curtis Hickman, and Ken Bretschneider.

And then there are those who transcend being a colleague and move into the role of mentor and friend. Michael John played that part for me. Thanks, MJ. You're solid gold.

This book is infinitely better because Christine Brownwell gave up hours upon hours of her valuable time to read, critique, correct, and instruct me along the way. Her unique viewpoint on the history of the game industry broadened my own in ways that will affect and improve me forever.

Thanks to my constant writing group. Okay, constant is a stretch, but knowing that you are all typing words late into the night with me gives me strength. I really do love and admire each of you greatly. Jamie Ford, Aprilynne Pike, Kristan Hoffman, Margaret Dilloway, Ben Brooks, and Natalia Sylvester, how does Wednesday at noon PST sound?

A million thanks to my wife, Jodi, the first non-gamer to read my book. When she was hooked, I knew I was on the right track. Thanks, Jodi, for helping me understand that *Game On!* is more than just a book about video games, it's a book about people.

A special thanks needs to go to my little gamers, Tanner (Destiny), Davis (Monster Hunter 4), Malorie (League of Legends), and Annie (Mario Kart). I love you all more than you can imagine, and yes, you all cheat when we play Smash Bros. I know it!

Game On! would not be here without my agent, Gemma Cooper, and a passionate editor, Holly West. I don't know how long Holly and Gemma started concocting this concept before they got me involved, but I do know that the two of them saw the vision first. Thanks for believing in the book, and for believing in me.

But most of all, I have to mention a young man from Arizona who pored over every word in this book in its roughest form. His comments, ideas, and passion for games were what kept me fueled throughout this entire process. Ian Tenney, I'm glad that we have become friends, and I can't wait to see what you do down the line to shape the future of games. I'll be watching!

FOR FURTHER INFORMATION

Hey, gamer. The following is a list of some of the sources and sites I used while putting this book together. It isn't a complete list, by any means, for a few reasons. First, I've read thousands of articles, watched hundreds of YouTube videos, and listened to hours of podcasts over the years. In one way or another, all those sources have fed into the information of this book, and it's simply not possible to list them all. But most important, part of the fun about researching more about video games is the process of digging around, and I hope you will do some of that on your own.

That being said, here are some of the sources that helped me fact-check and build the story of *Game On! Video Game History from Pong and Pac-Man to Mario, Minecraft, and More*. I've arranged them by chapter, where applicable, and all these articles, blogs, and videos contain fun and interesting details if you want to dig a little deeper.

OVERALL

Video Games: The Movie

The Official Price Guide to Classic Video Games: Consoles, Arcade Games, Handheld Games by David Ellis

Extra Lives: Why Video Games Matter by Tom Bissell

"Best Selling Game Franchises"
http://vgsales.wikia.com/wiki/
Best_selling_game_franchises

"Gaming Records," Guinness World Records
http://www.guinnessworldrecords
.com/explore-records/gamers

"The 10 Longest Games Ever"
http://www.nowgamer.com/the-10-
longest-games-ever/

"Memorable Quotes from Video Game History"
http://venturebeat.com/
community/2013/01/15/
memorable-quotes-from-
video-game-history/

"The 6 Most Absurdly Difficult Video Game Puzzles"
http://www.cracked.com/article
_19974_the-6-most-absurdly-
difficult-video-game-puzzles_
p2.html

"27 Mind-Blowing True Backstories of Famous Video Games"
http://www.cracked.com/
photoplasty_1260_27-mind-
blowing-true-backstories-
famous-video-games/

"20 Unseen Consequences of Video Game Universes"

http://www.cracked.com/
photoplasty_1194_20-unseen-
consequences-video-game-
universes/

"The 5 Most Baffling Celebrity Appearances in Video Games"
http://www.cracked.com/blog/
the-5-most-baffling-celebrity-
appearances-in-video-games/

"15 Famous Actors Who Voiced Video Game Characters"
http://mentalfloss.com/
article/53687/15-famous-
actors-who-voiced-video-game-
characters

"18 Best Indie Games of the Decade (So Far)"
http://whatculture.com/gaming/18-
best-indie-games-of-the-decade-
so-far

"16 Mind-Blowing Facts You Didn't Know About Xbox"
http://whatculture.com/gallery/16-
mind-blowing-facts-you-didnt-
know-about-xbox/2

"The Year 1993 from the People History"
http://www.thepeoplehistory
.com/1993.html

PONG

"Video Game History"
http://www.ralphbaer.com/
video_game_history.htm

"Pong for Your Home TV: Part 1"
http://www.atarimuseum.com/
videogames/dedicated/homepong
.html

"Welcome to Pong-Story"
http://www.pong-story.com/intro
.htm

SPACE INVADERS

"Space Invaders"
http://www.arcade-museum.com/
game_detail.php?game_id=9662

"Replay: The Evolution of Video Game Music"
http://www.npr.org/templates/
story/story.php?storyId=89612882

"The 50 Greatest Video Game Records"
http://www.gamesradar.com/the-50-
greatest-gaming-world-records/

"History of Space Invaders"
http://www.classicgaming.cc/
classics/space-invaders/history

PAC-MAN

"Pac-Man: A Visual History"
http://pacman.com/en/pac-man-
history

"Pac-Man: History"
http://www.classicgaming.cc/
classics/pacman/history.php

"The History of Pac-Man"
http://www.todayifoundout.com/
index.php/2013/08/the-history-of-
pac-man/

"Q&A: Pac-Man Creator Reflects on 30 Years of Dot-Eating"
http://www.wired.com/2010/05/
pac-man-30-years/

ZORK

"The History of Zork"
http://www.gamasutra.com/view/feature/1499/the_history_of_zork.php?print=1

"Eaten by a Grue: A Brief History of Zork"
http://mentalfloss.com/article/29885/eaten-grue-brief-history-zork

"The History of Zork"
https://web.archive.org/web/20060427000213/http://www.csd.uwo.ca/Infocom/Articles/NZT/zorkhist.html

"Zork, the Great Underground Empire"
http://archive.org/stream/byte-magazine-1981-02/1981_02_BYTE_06-02_The_Computer_and_Voice_Synthesis#page/n263/mode/2up

DONKEY KONG

"The Secret History of Donkey Kong"
http://www.gamasutra.com/view/feature/134790/the_secret_history_of_donkey_kong.php

"How Donkey Kong and Mario Changed the World"
http://time.com/3901489/donkey-kong-anniversary/

"10 Little-Known Facts About Donkey Kong"
http://mentalfloss.com/uk/games/27395/10-little-known-facts-about-donkey-kong

"Nintendo Seeks to Trademark 'On Like Donkey Kong'"
http://edition.cnn.com/2010/TECH/gaming.gadgets/11/10/on.like.donkey.kong/index.html?hpt=T2

E.T.

"The True Story of the Worst Video Game in History"
http://www.engadget.com/2014/05/01/true-story-et-atari/

"Retail Revenue of the U.S. Video Game Industry from March 2014 to March 2016 (in Billion U.S. Dollars)"
http://www.statista.com/statistics/201093/revenue-of-the-us-video-game-industry/

"Complete Atari 2600 Game Library"
http://www.listal.com/list/complete-atari-2600-game-library

"G4 Icons Episode #32: The Video Game Crash"
https://www.youtube.com/watch?v=RuHbRPoOEEA

"From Landfill to Smithsonian Collections: 'E.T. the Extra-Terrestrial' Atari 2600 Game"
http://americanhistory.si.edu/blog/landfill-smithsonian-collections-et-extra-terrestrial-atari-2600-game

MARIO

"Mario's Many Fathers"
http://www.wsj.com/articles/SB10001424053111904006104576502744235853146

"IGN Presents: The History of Super Mario Bros."
http://www.ign.com/articles/2010/09/14/ign-presents-the-history-of-super-mario-bros

"11 Origins of 11 Super Mario Characters' Names"
http://www.11points.com/Games/11_Origins_of_11_Super_Mario_Characters%27_Names

"History of Mario"
http://www.themushroomkingdom.net/mario_history.shtml

"Super Mario Bros.—The Game That Saved Video Games"
http://classicgames.about.com/od/consoleandhandheldgames/p/Super-Mario-Bros-The-Game-That-Saved-Video-Games.htm

"Nintendo's Shigeru Miyamoto Expresses Desire to Design 'More Advanced Games'"
http://www.techtimes.com/articles/14412/20140902/nintendos-shigeru-miyamoto-expresses-desire-to-design-more-advanced-games.htm

ZELDA

"IGN Presents the History of the Legend of Zelda"
http://www.ign.com/articles/2012/07/06/ign-presents-the-history-of-the-legend-of-zelda

"In the Game: Nintendo's Shigeru Miyamoto"
http://web.archive.org/web/20071220062126/http://www.amazon.com/gp/feature.html?docId=117177

Interview: Superplay Magazine with Shigeru Miyamoto
https://web.archive.org/web/20120208160357/http://www.miyamotoshrine.com/theman/interviews/230403.shtml

MADDEN

"The Franchise: The Inside Story of How 'Madden NFL' Became a Video Game Dynasty"
http://espn.go.com/espn/eticket/story?page=100805/madden

"In a First, Madden NFL Accurately Predicts Score for Super Bowl XLIX"
http://www.latimes.com/sports/nfl/la-sp-madden-super-bowl-20150203-story.html

"Game Changers: How Videogames Trained a Generation of Athletes"
http://www.wired.com/2010/01/ff_gamechanger/all/

"Museum of the Moving Image Looks Back on 25 Years of Madden"
http://www.polygon.com/2014/1/8/5287758/madden-nfl-25-years-exhibit-museum-of-the-moving-image

"Madden: How the Franchise Became King of the Gaming Gridiron"
http://www.denofgeek.us/games/madden-15/168481/madden-how-the-franchise-became-king-of-the-gaming-gridiron

TETRIS

"The Complicated History of 'Tetris,' Which Celebrates Its 30th Anniversary Today"
http://www.businessinsider.com/tetris-history-2014-6

"Tetris History: The Soviet Mind Game"
http://www.watchmojo.com/video/id/10998/

"History of Tetris"
http://inventors.about.com/od/tstartinventions/a/Tetris.htm

"Tetris: Fun in the Cold War?"
http://americanhistory.si.edu/blog/2014/09/tetris-fun-in-the-cold-war.html

SONIC

"Confirmed: Michael Jackson Composed the Music for Sonic the Hedgehog 3"
https://techcrunch.com/2009/12/03/confirmed-the-music-for-sonic-the-hedgehog-3/

"Mr. Needlemouse"
http://info.sonicretro.org/Mr._Needlemouse

"25 Things You May Not Know About Sonic the Hedgehog"
http://arcadesushi.com/things-you-may-not-know-about-sonic-the-hedgehog/?utm_source=zergnet.com&utm_medium=referral&utm_campaign=zergnet_59576

"22 Things You Didn't Know About Sonic the Hedgehog"
http://www.gamesradar.com/22-things-you-probably-didnt-know-about-sonic-hedgehog/

"Video Game Sales Wiki: Sonic"
http://vgsales.wikia.com/wiki/Sonic

"'Sonic the Hedgehog': By the Numbers"
http://content.usatoday.com/communities/gamehunters/post/2011/06/sonic-the-hedgehog-by-the-numbers/1#.VTG9UvnF_mc

"Sonic News Network: Doctor Ovi Kintobor"
http://sonic.wikia.com/wiki/Doctor_Ovi_Kintobor

STREET FIGHTER

"Street Fighter II: An Oral History"
http://www.polygon.com/a/street-fighter-2-oral-history

"IGN Presents the History of Street Fighter"
http://www.ign.com/articles/2009/02/16/ign-presents-the-history-of-street-fighter

MORTAL KOMBAT

"The History of Mortal Kombat"
http://www.ign.com/
articles/2011/05/05/the-
history-of-mortal-kombat

"Box Office Mojo: Mortal Kombat"
http://www.boxofficemojo.com/
movies/?id=mortalkombat.htm

"The History of Mortal Kombat"
http://web.archive.org/
web/20021207203601/http://
gamespot.com/gamespot/features/
video/hist_mortalk/p2.html

"The Original Mortal Kombat Cast:
Still Kicking Ass Two Decades Later"
http://kotaku.com/the-original-
mortal-kombat-cast-still-kicking-
ass-two-1599017196

"Ed Boon Talks Freddy Krueger in
Mortal Kombat, Secret Origins of
DLC Characters"
http://blog.us.playstation
.com/2011/07/22/ed-boon-talks-
freddy-krueger-in-mortal-kombat-
secret-origins-of-dlc-characters/

"Inappropriate Content: A Brief
History of Videogame Ratings and
the ESRB"
http://www.escapistmagazine
.com/articles/view/video-games/
columns/the-needles/1300-
Inappropriate-Content-A-Brief-
History-of-Videogame-Raings-and-t

"Geek Trivia: What Was the First
Video Game to Receive a 'Mature'
Rating?"
http://www.howtogeek.com/trivia/
what-was-the-first-video-game-to-
receive-a-mature-rating/

MARIO KART

"The Complete History of Mario
Kart"
http://venturebeat.com/2014/05/28/
the-complete-history-of-mario-
kart/

"A Brief History of Mario Kart"
http://techraptor.net/content/
brief-history-mario-kart

MYST

"Hulu Lands 'Myst' Drama from
Legendary TV & Matt Tolmach Based
on Video Game"
http://deadline.com/2015/05/
myst-tv-series-video-game-
hulu-legendary-matt-tomach-
1201421271/

"9 Things You Didn't Know About
Myst"
http://www.buzzfeed.com/joseph-
bernstein/9-things-you-didnt-
know-about-myst#.htxVP5b5N

DOOM

"Doom Marine's Name"
http://web.archive.org/
web/20140203112006/
http://rome.ro/smf/index.php/
topic,1521.msg31827.html

"Masters of Doom"
http://en.wikipedia.org/wiki/
Masters_of_Doom

"10 Most Important Video Games of
All Time, As Judged by 2 Designers,
2 Academics, and 1 Lowly Blogger"
http://web.archive.org/web/
20140422035847/
http://www.joystiq
.com/2007/03/12/10-most-
important-video-games-of-all-
time-as-judged-by-2-design/

"Doom Press Release"
http://web.archive.org/
web/20120825053443/
http://www.rome.ro/lee_killough/
history/doompr3.shtml

"See the Original Sketch and Model
That Inspired Doom's Doomguy"
http://www.gameinformer.com/b/
news/archive/2014/12/13/see-the-
original-sketch-and-model-that-
inspired-doom-39-s-doomguy.aspx

Interview Between Doomworld and
John Carmack
http://web.archive.org/
web/20131028050052/
http://www.doomworld.com:80/
interviews/int7.shtml

"Doom Easter Egg"
http://doom.wikia.com/wiki/
Easter_egg

TOMB RAIDER

"The Redemption of Lara Croft"
http://uk.ign.com/articles/
2011/11/04/the-redemption-of-
lara-croft

"Eidos Montreal Co-Developing Rise
of the Tomb Raider with Crystal
Dynamics"
http://www.gamercenteronline
.net/2015/06/23/eidos-montreal-
co-developing-rise-of-the-tomb-
raider-with-crystal-dynamics/

"History of Tomb Raider: Blowing
the Dust Off 17 Years of Lara Croft"
http://www.digitaltrends.com/
gaming/the-history-of-tomb-
raider/

GRAN TURISMO

"History of Gran Turismo Series"
http://www.game.co.uk/webapp/wcs/
stores/servlet/ArticleView?
articleId=89670&catalogId=10201&
langId=&storeId=10151

FINAL FANTASY

"Sony PlayStation vs Nintendo 64:
Gaming's Greatest Rivalries"
http://www.digitalspy.com/
gaming/news/a443707/sony-
playstation-vs-nintendo-64-
gamings-greatest-rivalries
.html#~pbzQUIJkkL63Gz

"Top 100 RPGs of All Time"
http://www.ign.com/top/rpgs/1

"IGN Presents: The History of Final
Fantasy VII"
http://www.ign.com/articles/
2008/05/01/ign-presents-the-
history-of-final-fantasy-vii

HALF-LIFE

"The Gamasutra Quantum Leap
Awards; First-Person Shooters"

http://www.gamasutra.com/view/
feature/1832/the_gamasutra_
quantum_leap_awards_.php

"The Half-Life Saga Story Guide"
http://members.shaw.ca/
halflifestory/

DDR

"A Case History of the Success of
Dance Dance Revolution in the
United States"
http://web.stanford.edu/group/
htgg/sts145papers/dliu_2002_1.pdf

"Dance Dance Revolution
Revolution"
http://vgc.gameology.org/content/
dance-dance-revolution-revolution

POKÉMON

"Total Sales for Mainline Pokémon
Games Surpass 200 Million"
http://nintendoeverything.com/
total-sales-for-mainline-pokemon-
games-surpass-200-million/

"History of Pokémon"
http://bulbapedia.bulbagarden.net/
wiki/History_of_Pok%C3%A9mon

THE SIMS

"A Visual History of the Sims"
http://www.ign.com/
articles/2014/09/04/a-visual-
history-of-the-sims

"From Ant to City and Beyond: A
History of All Things Sim"
http://mentalfloss.com/
article/48610/ant-city-and-beyond-
history-all-things-sim

"History of Sims Games"
http://www.sims-hr.com/history-
sims-games-facts-sims-games.html

"The History of the Sims"
http://www.eurogamer.net/articles/
the-history-of-the-sims-article

GTA

"IGN Presents the History of Grand
Theft Auto"
http://www.ign.com/articles/
2013/05/06/ign-presents-the-
history-of-grand-theft-auto-2

"The History of Grand Theft Auto
(Documentary)"
https://www.youtube.com/
watch?v=6xhY9LSGbNk

"The Complete History of Grand
Theft Auto"
http://www.gamesradar.com/the-
complete-history-of-grand-theft-
auto/

WoW

"8 Interesting Facts You Might Not
Know About World of Warcraft"
http://www.mmorpg.com/blogs/
Fatality001133/042013/24991_8-
Interesting-Facts-You-Might-Not-
Know-About-World-of-Warcraft

"Number of World of Warcraft
Subscribers from 1st Quarter 2005
to 3rd Quarter 2015 (in Millions)"

http://www.statista.com/statistics/276601/number-of-world-of-warcraft-subscribers-by-quarter/

"World of Warcraft Subscription Numbers Are on the Up" http://www.polygon.com/2014/10/15/6981137/world-of-warcraft-subscription-numbers-blizzard-draenor

"Hackers Create Robots, er, 'Helpers,' to Automate Play in World of Warcraft" http://venturebeat.com/2009/08/03/hackers-create-robots-er-helpers-to-automate-play-in-world-of-warcraft/

"World of Warcraft Politician Wins State Senate Race" http://www.dailydot.com/news/world-of-warcraft-lachowicz-win/

"USA President Barack Obama Plays WoW, No Joke!" https://burningwowgen.wordpress.com/2008/12/03/usa-president-barack-obama-plays-wow-no-joke/

"7 Celebrities that Play WoW" http://allwomenstalk.com/7-celebrities-that-play-wow

"14 Pop Culture References in World of Warcraft" http://mentalfloss.com/article/17748/14-pop-culture-references-world-warcraft

HALO 2

"IGN Presents: The History of Halo" http://www.ign.com/articles/2012/07/11/ign-presents-the-history-of-halo-2

"Halo's Story Got You Confused? This Chart *Might* Help." http://kotaku.com/5959105/halos-story-got-you-confused-this-chart-might-help

"Vista Halo 2 Plans Details" http://news.softpedia.com/news/Vista-Halo-2-Plans-Details-42033.shtml

"Halo 2 Tops Live Most-Played List" http://www.eurogamer.net/articles/news210206xboxlivetopten

GUITAR HERO

"The Beats to Beat: A History of Guitar Hero" http://historycooperative.org/the-beats-to-beat-a-history-of-guitar-hero/

"The Life and Death of Guitar Hero" http://www.ign.com/articles/2011/02/11/the-life-and-death-of-guitar-hero

Wii SPORTS

"Wii Sports" http://nintendo.wikia.com/wiki/Wii_Sports

"Top Selling Software Sales Units" https://www.nintendo.co.jp/ir/en/sales/software/wii.html

PORTAL

"The Unseen History of Portal" https://www.youtube.com/watch?v=iRAw9q2F4II

"The Never-Before-Seen History of Portal" https://www.vg247.com/2016/02/22/the-never-before-seen-history-of-portal/

LITTLE BIG PLANET

"Media Molecule's Marvelous Time Machine" http://www.mediamolecule.com/about/history#startofthe universeasweknowit

"LittleBigPlanet Story" http://littlebigplanet.wikia.com/wiki/LittleBigPlanet_Story

FARMVILLE

"A Brief History of Farmville" https://www.adweek.com/social-times/farmville-history/313411

"FarmVille Coming to the iPhone in Late June" https://techcrunch.com/2010/06/07/zyngas-farmville-comes-to-the-iphone-in-june/

ANGRY BIRDS

"The Origins of Angry Birds" http://www.pcworld.com/article/206831/the_origins_of_angry_birds.html

"Angry Birds: The Story Behind iPhone's Gaming Phenomenon" http://www.telegraph.co.uk/technology/video-games/8303173/Angry-Birds-the-story-behind-iPhones-gaming-phenomenon.html

MINECRAFT

"Minecraft Game" https://minecraft.net/

"The Amazingly Unlikely Story of How Minecraft Was Born" http://www.wired.com/2013/11/minecraft-book/

"How Minecraft Became One of the Biggest Video Games in History" http://articles.latimes.com/2013/sep/03/business/la-fi-tn-how-minecraft-video-games-20130822

UNCHARTED

"The Official History of Uncharted: Part 1/3—Uncharted: Drake's Fortune" http://community.us.playstation.com/t5/UNCHARTED-Drake-s-Fortune/The-Official-History-of-Uncharted-Part-1-3-Uncharted-Drake-s/td-p/36859541

"Uncharted: The Nathan Drake Collection Is a Great History Lesson" http://www.destructoid.com/uncharted-the-nathan-drake-collection-is-a-great-history-lesson-315656.phtml

LEAGUE OF LEGENDS

"League of Legends: A Brief History of MOBA Domination" http://blog.games.com/2013/01/15/league-of-legends-history/

"How Riot Games Started and Grew League of Legends" https://www.cleverism.com/how-riot-games-started-and-grew-league-of-legends/

SKYLANDERS

"History of Skylanders!!!" https://www.youtube.com/watch?v=rcSfsHMEXeg

"How Skylanders Became a Giant" http://www.telegraph.co.uk/technology/video-games/video-game-news/9613766/How-Skylanders-became-a-giant.html

"Toys for Bob and the Story Behind Skylanders" http://www.polygon.com/2014/4/16/5614716/skylanders-story-toys-for-bob-skylanders-swap-force

WALKING DEAD

"The Walking Dead: Michonne Coming from Telltale Games this Fall" http://www.polygon.com/2015/6/15/8782869/the-walking-dead-michonne-mini-series

"Telltale's The Walking Dead—Robert Kirkman Interview" http://www.ign.com/videos/2016/04/25/telltales-the-walking-dead-robert-kirkman-interview

OVERWATCH

"The Making of Overwatch: How the Failure of Titan Gave Rise to Blizzard's Next Big Thing" http://www.ign.com/videos/2016/04/25/the-making-of-overwatch-how-the-failure-of-titan-gave-rise-to-blizzards-next-big-thing

"Blizzcon 2014: Blizzard on the Making of Overwatch" http://www.ign.com/articles/2014/11/08/blizzcon-2014-blizzard-on-the-making-of-overwatch

"How Blizzard Is Making Up Overwatch's Story as It Goes" http://www.pcgamer.com/overwatch-story-chris-metzen-interview/